THE ARDEN SHAKESPEARE

GENERAL EDITORS:
RICHARD PROUDFOOT, ANN THOMPSON and DAVID SCOTT KASTAN

AS YOU LIKE IT

THE ARDEN SHAKESPEARE

* Third Series

THE ARDEN EDITION OF THE WORKS OF WILLIAM SHAKESPEARE

AS YOU LIKE IT

Edited by
AGNES LATHAM

LONDON and NEW YORK

The general editors of the Arden Shakespeare have been

First Series
W. J. Craig (1899–1906) and R. H. Case (1909–41)

Second Series
Una Ellis-Fermor (1946–58), Harold F. Brooks (1952–82),
Harold Jenkins (1958–82) and Brian Morris (1975–82)

Third Series
Richard Proudfoot, Ann Thompson and David Scott Kastan

This edition of *As You Like It*, by Agnes Latham,
first published in 1975 by
Methuen & Co. Ltd
Reprinted four times
Reprinted 1987

Reprinted 1989, 1991, 1993, 1994, 1996
by Routledge
11 New Fetter Lane, London EC4P 4EE
29 West 35th Street, New York, NY 10001

Editorial matter © 1975 Methuen & Co. Ltd

ISBN (hardbound) 0 416 17830 8
ISBN (paperback) 0 415 02681 4

Printed in England by Clays Ltd, St Ives plc

CONTENTS

Acknowledgements

My thanks are due to the Keeper of Manuscripts in the National Library of Scotland for the correct reference to Adv. MS 5.2.14; to Roger Lowman and J. H. Wallis for helpful correspondence; to Mrs P. A. Burnett for permission to quote from her Oxford B.Litt. thesis, which is an annotated critical edition of Lodge's *Rosalynde*; to colleagues and friends; and to the general editors for advice and support, in particular to Professor Harold Brooks for much patient instruction and many stimulating suggestions, even more than have been acknowledged in particular places. I am indebted to Judy Karasik of Princeton University and to Russell Jackson for correcting errors in the first printing.

INTRODUCTION

I. TEXT

i *A 'staying entry'*

The only source for the text of *As You Like It* is the Folio of 1623. On 4 August 1600 four plays were entered in the Stationers' Register 'to be staied'. They were

As you lyke it / a booke
Henry the Ffift / a booke
Euery man in his humour / a booke
The Commedie of muche A doo about nothing. a booke.

A staying entry is generally supposed to have been provoked by a threat of piracy. The Chamberlain's Company were unable to prevent an unauthorized publication of *Henry V*. They countered with a better text of their own, entered on 14 August to Thomas Pavyer. *Every Man in his Humour* was entered the same day to Cuthbert Burby and Walter Burre. On 23 August *Much Ado About Nothing* was entered to Andrew Wyse and William Aspley. *As You Like It* did not appear in quarto, and thereby rated an entry to Blount and Jaggard, on 8 November 1623, with the rest of the plays 'not formerly entred to other men', before it was published in the Folio.

The attitude of theatrical companies to publication in the sixteenth century has not been satisfactorily established. The brisk trade in legitimately published plays makes it plain that they had no consistent objection to their books becoming public. They certainly disliked having a play in circulation in a pirated text, for they took trouble to replace bad quartos. They may have been particularly jealous of a play that was drawing large crowds, as *Henry V* and *Every Man in his Humour* undoubtedly were. There is little evidence of any sort as to the popularity of *As You Like It*. It can be reduced to a conjectured revival in 1603, for which first-hand documentary proof is wanting. In August 1865, William Cory, Assistant Master at Eton, made a tantalizing entry in his private journal.[1] He was resident at the time at Wilton, the seat of the Pembrokes, coaching the son of the house in Greek. He noted a conversation with Lady Herbert, about the historical associations of the place and the family papers. She told him of a letter of 1603, from the then Lady Pembroke to her son, the third earl, asking him to bring James I from Salisbury to see a performance of *As You Like It* at Wilton House and adding, 'We have the man Shakespeare with us'. An ulterior motive on Lady Pembroke's part was to influence the king in favour of Sir Walter Ralegh, charged with treason. The court was at Salisbury to avoid the plague in London. Cory does not claim to have seen the letter, and it has not since come to light, at Wilton or anywhere else. Lady Herbert's story is corroborated by the Chamber Accounts of December 1603, which record a payment to John Heminge, on behalf of the Chamberlain's Company, for coming to Wilton 'and there presenting before His Maiestie an playe'.[2] Unhappily the play is not named.

Since *As You Like It* has pleased audiences for the last 200 years and more, it seems probable that it proved effective on the stage for which it was originally designed, but the theory that it never came out in quarto because it was a closely guarded box-office success cannot be substantiated. The opposite may even be the truth, that Shakespeare for once failed to gauge the public taste and that *As You Like It* proved less delightful than *Much Ado*. Doubtless the appearance of the second quarto of *Henry V* was in direct consequence of the pirated first. The reason why *Much Ado* and *Every Man in his Humour* came out in quarto and *As You Like It* did not is still to seek. A 'staying entry' was not a promise of publication. It was an assertion of copyright.

ii *The copy*

The Folio text can be described as good, in so far as it is clear and orderly and presents few problems. Nobody has ever suggested that it derives directly from Shakespeare's own draft or foul papers. It preserves very few typical Shakespearian spellings. The punctuation is profuse and rather insensitive. Stage directions are brief imperatives. Speech headings are clear. Everything seems to point to a transcript by a playhouse scribe. The purpose of this was normally to serve as a prompt book, while the author's

1 *Extracts from the Letters and Journals of William Cory*, ed. F. W. Cornish (1897), p. 168.
2 P. Cunningham, *The Revels Accounts* (1842).

foul papers were kept in reserve, in case of loss or injury. So long as a play was in their repertory a company would not surrender the prompt book. Apart from any other consideration, it carried the allowance of the Master of the Revels. If the staying entry of 1600 went along with plans for publication while the play was still holding the stage, a scribe would have been set to prepare a second fair copy, specifically for the press. Such a copy would have been perfectly acceptable to the Folio editors of 1623. If nothing of the kind was available they would, unless the company had no further interest in the play, by then over ten years old, have had one made from the original prompt book.

As You Like It derives from a very neat manuscript. It is carefully divided into acts and scenes, with a meticulousness not always observed in prompt copy. After an initial uncertainty, speech headings are remarkably consistent. The banished Duke, whom the author forgot to name, is distinguished as Duke Senior. There are costume notes, 'Enter Rosalind for Ganymede', 'Enter Duke Senior and lords, like outlaws'. The full text of the songs is included. A careful analysis of entrances does not support the idea that they reflect to any marked degree the prompter's alleged tendency to signal them early. Because of the way the Folio was printed, there is some confusion about the lineation of the prose, which is sometimes set as verse, but this has nothing to do with the manuscript copy, which seems to have been notable for clarity and order.

As You Like It, therefore, may be said to derive from good prompt copy, transcribed for the press. The transcript may have been made about 1600, when the play was new and was holding the stage, or much later, for the First Folio in 1623.

iii *Acts and scenes*

In the matter of act and scene divisions, *As You Like It* is thorough and dependable, and a modern editor may accept them as they stand. As is usual in Shakespearian texts, localities are not given in the stage directions. It is tempting to try and make some distinction between the forest, where the Duke hunts and lionesses couch, and the cleared land, where Corin keeps sheep, Audrey fetches up her goats, and Rosalind and Celia live 'like fringe upon a petticoat'. Doubtless the whole neighbourhood was known locally as 'the Forest'. Shakespeare would be familiar with such usage with reference to the Warwickshire Arden, by his day barely forested at all. There is not, however, sufficient indication in the text for an editor to be precise about locations. It is a decision which the scenic stage forces on a producer. We hear of the Duke's 'abandoned cave' and Orlando leads Oliver to his 'cave', but these scenes are always off-stage. So is 'the rank of osiers by the murmuring stream' and the 'cottage fenced about with olive trees'. *As You Like It* may well have been played without so much as a property tree, although these were available on public stages. At the end of IV. i Rosalind has to go off to find 'a shadow'. Orlando can hang his verses on one of the pillars that support the 'heavens'.

iv *Stage directions, entrances and exits*

The stage directions are very few and are expressed in the briefest imperatives, e.g., at I. ii. 138, 'Flourish'; at I. ii. 200, 'Wrestle'; at I. ii. 203, 'Shout'; at IV. iii. 40, 'Read'; at II. v. 35, 'Song. Altogether here'; at IV. ii. 10, 'Musick. Song'; and at v. iv. 107, 'Still Music'. These look like prompt copy and nothing else.

The direction 'Enter Rosalind for Ganymede, Celia for Aliena' reminds us that Rosalind is now in doublet and hose and Celia in homespun. Greg thinks it is Shakespeare's.[1] He quotes similar directions, involving the distinctive use of 'for', from *Mer. V.*, IV. i. 160 and *LLL*, v. iii. 365 and 592. It has been suggested that 'Clown alias Touchstone' indicates that Touchstone also had changed his name and was in disguise.[2] He wore motley in the forest, as Jaques witnesses when he reports that he has met a 'motley fool'. Felver thinks he may have worn motley as a disguise, in place of the Duke's livery.[3] Kökeritz sees a pun on 'harden' in 'Now am I in Arden' and supposes he wore 'an overall of this coarse material'.[4] With or without motley, he must have been instantly recognizable by anyone familiar with the usurper's court, a line of thought that the play does not invite us to follow to its logical conclusion.

Two if not three further directions indicate costume. They are 'Enter Duke Senior, Amiens, and two or three lords like foresters' at II. i, and 'Enter Jaques and lords, foresters' at IV. ii. These also probably reflect Shakespeare's original draft. The 'two or

1 W. W. Greg, *The Shakespeare First Folio* (1955), p. 293.

2 K. Muir, *Shakespeare's Sources*, I (1957), p. 57 note, 'Touchstone. The name the Clown assumes when he leaves for Arden'.

3 C. S. Felver, *Robert Armin, Shakespeare's Fool. A Biographical Essay*. (Kent State University Series No. 5, 1961.)

4 H. Kökeritz, *Shakespeare's Pronunciation* (1953), p. 91, 'Touchstone in Arden', *Modern Language Quarterly*, VII (1945), pp. 61–3.

three lords' would settle down in performance to something more definite.

If it can be seen that some entrances are marked well in advance of the actual moment when an actor is required to step on to the stage, it is generally accepted that they derive from prompt copy. The early signal was a means whereby the prompter could check that an actor was ready to take his cue. There are, however, other considerations governing stage entrances. One is the practice of the printer or scribe, who may not care to interrupt another character's speech, particularly a prose speech, to note an entrance. Verse has natural breaks at the line ends. Another is the time it took for an actor, entering upstage, to make his way down to the front. There appears to be either a real or a conventional time lapse during which persons on stage may make remarks about a newcomer which he is not supposed to hear. This is presumably a consequence of the very long distance between the entrance doors at the back and the unlocalized front stage, where *As You Like It*, with its predominantly outdoor setting, is played.[1] After Adam's 'Yonder comes my master, your brother', Orlando says 'Go apart Adam, and thou shalt hear how he will shake me up' (i. i. 26–8). Celia caps Rosalind's 'Look, here comes the Duke' by her short and significant 'With his eyes full of anger' (i. iii. 35–6). Touchstone's comment upon William is of this nature:

Aud. Here comes the man you mean.   *Enter William.*
Touch. It is meat and drink to me to see a clown. By my troth, we
     that have good wits have much to answer for: we shall be
     flouting: we cannot hold.
Will. Good ev'n, Audrey. (v. i. 9–13).

Greg thinks the direction to enter here is premature and the mark of prompt copy,[2] but it follows with perfect propriety on Audrey's announcement. Le Beau's entrance, at i. ii. 248, in the midst of Orlando's soliloquy, which was presumably delivered downstage, gives him time to draw level before he speaks. It would be awkward for Orlando to fall silent while Le Beau purposefully

---

1 See R. Hosley, 'The playhouses and the stage', in *A New Companion to Shakespeare Studies*, eds. K. Muir and S. Schoenbaum (1971). The stage of the Fortune theatre, as specified in the builder's contracts (1599), was 43 feet wide by 27 feet 6 inches. The effect of these dimensions, which Hosley thinks were average for a public theatre, can be studied today at Harrow School, which has such a stage. cf. Appendix A.

2 W. W. Greg, op. cit., p. 294.

advances. He is therefore given two lines of verse while Le Beau comes up.

A notable instance where an entrance must follow an announcement, but where it is some considerable time before the newcomer is allowed to open his mouth, is Touchstone's appearance at I. ii. 45. Celia cannot be expected to say 'hath not Fortune sent in this fool to cut off the argument' upon a stage where no fool is visible. Yet she and Rosalind continue their conversation for some eight or nine lines and Touchstone has to wait their pleasure. It is his first entrance, and the audience may have taken time to greet a favoured actor, possibly Armin making his début at the Globe. J. P. Kemble has Touchstone singing off-stage at 'fall into the fire' and marks his entrance at 'cut off the argument'.[1] Later in the same scene, at l. 86, the girls treat Le Beau in a similar way, exchanging witticisms at his expense, though not at such length and presumably not in his hearing. Again Greg sees prompt copy, though Le Beau's entrance is placed appropriately after Celia's 'Here comes Monsieur Le Beau'. It is arguable at what point Touchstone and Audrey enter in v. iv, but it seems likely that the audience has them in view when, or very shortly after, Jaques says 'Here comes a pair of very strange beasts, which in all tongues are called fools' (ll. 36–8).

Rosalind's refusal to speak to Orlando at IV. i. 25 is inherent in the dramatic situation. She ignores him deliberately and holds Jaques in conversation. In the circumstances it is impossible to be sure whether he enters, as in F, after l. 24 and waits his opportunity to speak, or whether he greets Rosalind as soon as he steps on to the stage, which would require an entrance after l. 27. What is certain is that for six lines after Jaques has addressed him Rosalind pointedly fails to acknowledge his presence. A conceivably premature direction to enter is given to Rosalind at v. ii. 12, but even so she is not held longer on the stage with nothing to say than others have been.

In *As You Like It* twenty-three mid-scene entrances are announced, generally with some form of the conventional 'But who comes here?' In thirteen instances the direction to enter precedes the announcement and in ten it follows it. Often the distinction seems to be without significance. The rule that entrances are either announced, or entirely expectable, is adhered to very closely, with the possible exception of the last scene. Here there is

---

1 *As You Like It*, Acting Copy (1815).

a good deal of coming and going without greetings or explanations. Whereas Orlando, interrupting the Duke's banquet, had
his formal 'Who comes here?', Jaques de Boys enters at v. iv. 149
without attention being focused on him by any kind of comment.
Hymen is preceded by mysterious music. No one can announce
him since he is a totally unexpected apparition.

Exits do not concern the prompter in the same way as entrances. An actor can be trusted to get himself off the stage when
he is no longer required. *As You Like It* overlooks a number of
exits. They propound no great problem, with the exception of the
right placing of the Duke's departure at the end of the play, which
F places at v. iv. 197. We must, however, suppose that the Duke
stays for the dancing he has himself initiated. It is Jaques who will
see no dancing and who leaves at l. 195.

In order to keep the direction to enter as close as possible to the
stage announcement of an entrance, without interrupting any
speaker on the stage, this edition as a general rule places it
immediately after not before the announcement. Dyce followed a
very similar plan. An exception is made when an entrance has the
effect of changing the mode of speech employed by a character on
stage from prose to verse, e.g., at II. iv. 17.

v *Punctuation and variant readings*

The punctuation of *As You Like It* must derive ultimately from
the author's manuscript, probably by way of a professional copyist.
It would take its final form in the printing house in 1623. The
editors were not likely to tamper with their manuscript copy
much, if at all. A great deal of the rationalizing of spelling and
punctuation which occurred in the late sixteenth and early
seventeenth centuries was the work of the printers. Punctuation is
careful on the whole and even rather fussy. Commas accompany
and, *but*, *when* and *that*, with monotonous regularity. Sometimes a
rhythmical pause in a line is marked by a comma which logic does
not demand. Sometimes the natural pause at a line-end has
satisfied the scribe or printer, who has not used a point at all.
Parentheses are sometimes marked only at the beginning or only
at the end. In any case the system of punctuation is not that of a
modern text. Not only are the points different, e.g., colons where
we should have full stops, or question marks instead of exclama-
tions, but the whole system is directed very much towards
marking rhythm and stress than towards indicating the logical
structure of a sentence. Because the text is in fact a sixteenth-

century text, there seems to be good reason to retain some of what, whether authorial or no, is a sixteenth-century system. The scribe cannot have known Shakespeare's mind and was probably not very careful to preserve such indications of it as were carried by his foul papers, but he did have these papers before him and he had an ear tuned to the speech of the period—perhaps, if he was a playhouse scribe, rather particularly to stage speech. The rhythmic character of the Folio pointing can be a valuable corrective to modern speakers, who naturally tend to fall into modern patterns of rhythm and stress, especially when they are confronted with what they think is meant to be naturalistic prose.

As a rule, a point in this edition reproduces a point of some sort in the Folio, though they may not be identical. In the case of a parenthesis one of the points may be implied by the presence of the other, and may not actually appear in the Folio. The plethora of commas is abated a little. The Folio occasionally uses round brackets for no very obvious reason. This edition may replace them by commas, or by dashes, which the Folio text of *As You Like It* never employs. Full stops are not used as freely as they would be in a modern text, since the longer sentences are often carefully interwoven, and colons and semi-colons come nearer to retaining the unity and interdependence of the original.

Actors will treat the text as seems best to them. It is their privilege. The Arden edition is not specifically an acting edition and must maintain a neutrality. It may be that on the Elizabethan stage the player taking the part of Rosalind introduced a pretty hesitation at I. iii. 121 and said 'And therefore look you call me—Ganymede!' or at IV. i. 99–101: 'And the foolish chroniclers of that age found it was—Hero of Sestos!' There is nothing in the Folio text to recommend these interpretations. The text shows no interest in indicating pauses of this kind, or in setting incomplete or broken sentences. It seems proper to mark a break at I. ii. 109, 112 and 114, and at IV. i. 122, but not, as many editors do, at III. ii. 35 and III. v. 83.

For the text of *As You Like It*, the First Folio is the sole authority; and this distinguishes it completely from F2, F3 and F4 and indeed from all later editions. They are derived from Shakespeare's autograph manuscript (which we do not possess) only through the First Folio itself. That edition records all the evidence we have of what stood in the manuscript; it derives from it in a direct line of descent, along which we cannot get any nearer to the lost original. Where later editions, including the later Folios, differ from it, they do so not by access to new evidence, but by errors of the printing house, and by attempts, some clearly mistaken, some probably successful, to correct apparent errors in the text as they know it. These attempts are editorial guesswork guided, as editorial practice improves, more and more by scholarly knowledge. F2, F3 and F4, which as derivative editions are not to be classed in any way with the First Folio, are edited texts 'corrected' so far as the intelligence and knowledge of those who produced them allow. Except that they have no named editors, they are thus on a par with the editions by Rowe and his successors. In accordance with Arden practice, all edited texts are here treated in the same way.

The textual apparatus indicates deviations from the Folio readings. It does not extend to punctuation except in particular instances, where it enters into a textual argument or concerns interpretation of the sense, as for example at II. vii. 151 or at III. ii. 155. The first editor to make an emendation is noted, but not the frequency with which it has been adopted. The acceptance of the primacy of the First Folio has made it unnecessary to pay great attention to the readings of Folios 2 to 4, or to the personal guesswork of eighteenth- and nineteenth-century editors. Some of these readings however are almost as familiar as the Folio text, and for historical reasons are worth preserving, even though there is not much support for them in modern scholarship. A reader accustomed to 'tune his merry note' at II. v. 3 and 'Loves to lie in the sun' at l. 36, where F reads turn and live, may reasonably want to know where the readings, rejected in this edition, came from. He may also want to know whether an emendation that seems to him desirable has been conjectured by others before him. An unusually large number of conjectural emendations shows where the Folio reading has proved unacceptable to a large number of editors.

The text of *As You Like It* occupies pp. 185 to 207 (sigs. Q3 to S2) in the Folio. It is preceded by *The Merchant of Venice* and followed by *The Taming of the Shrew*. According to Charlton Hinman it was set by compositors B, C and D, not more than two of them working on it at one time.[1] It is the last appearance of D on the Folio. B, who set 12½ pages, was working singlehanded towards the end. C set 7½ and D set 3½.[2] Some sheets were

---

1 *The Printing and Proof-Reading of the First Folio of Shakespeare* (1963), II, pp. 436, 442 and 447.

2 B set Q2, Q4, Q6ᵛ, R1–R3ᵛ, R6ᵛ, S1, S1ᵛ, S2 (a final half page). C set Q3, Q3ᵛ, Q5ᵛa, R4–R6. D set Q4ᵛ, Q5, Q5ᵛb, Q6.

corrected during printing. Speech headings were righted at v. i. 20, where uncorrected sheets read *Orl.* for *Clo.*, and at l. 21 in the same scene, where uncorrected sheets read *Clo.* for *Will.* They are obvious errors and would not have required reference to copy. Other errors are typographical and are not noted in this edition.

vi *Verse and prose*

The sections that follow examine the dramatist's use of his medium, a matter in part textual, especially in the distinction between verse and prose, but demanding to be considered also in a wider context.

As You Like It is distinguished by a high proportion of prose, which modulates easily into verse. It can be anything from an alexandrine to a rhyming jingle, a casual chorus or a graceful air.

The blank verse shows considerable metrical freedom. It has puzzled early editors, who demanded more regularity than they found. Some of the lines can be smoothed by a slight rearrangement but there is no reason to suppose that Shakespeare wanted a high polish. Others will adapt, as they stand, to a sympathetic voice. The deadening effect of an unvarying metrical scheme, to which all passions must be fitted, can be observed in the plays of many of Shakespeare's contemporaries. In particular the exchange of question and answer becomes mechanical. It is worth noting how Shakespeare exploits the tendency of English prose to fall into pseudo-pentameters at emotional moments. Orlando's 'Good day and happiness dear Rosalind', in the middle of a prose scene, is a case in point. Jaques instantly detects the giveaway rhythm: 'Nay ... and you talk in blank verse—' (IV. i. 29–30). Rosalind and her creator are equally aware of what she is doing when, in another prose scene, she cries 'O ominous! he comes to kill my heart!' (III. ii. 242).

There are times when it is difficult for an editor to decide whether verse or prose is intended and the distinction may not be profound. The Folio does not set out the contribution of a new speaker to an incomplete verse line at a distance from the margin. All speeches start level with one another, a custom which Steevens was the first to abandon in his edition of 1793. It is therefore hard to be sure whether half lines in early editions are to be thought of as prose or verse. In this edition doubtful places are discussed in footnotes. When lines that might be set as verse occur among prose speakers, in a predominantly prose scene, it is assumed that verse is not intended. It is a mistake to think that a line which it is possible to speak as verse must necessarily be spoken so, or that it is not good prose. A prose speaker has a choice of a variety of rhythms.

The abrupt modulations have caused some understandable confusion in the printing house. A further cause of faulty lineation is a technical procedure known as 'casting off'. If two or more compositors were setting type simultaneously, they had to divide their copy beforehand as best they could. Blank verse on the whole was amenable, prose less so, though Hinman says there should not have been much difficulty, except with copy untidily made up. In *As You Like It*, however, the rapid alternation of verse and prose is baffling in itself. A workman who found he had too little to fill his sheet was inclined to spread out prose as though it were verse, in order to use more space.[1] This has happened at II. vi, on page 192, column 2, of the Folio. It was set by compositor B. All three compositors who worked on this play at some time or other set prose as verse. If B does it more often, it is because he did most of the work.

When verse is spoken in *As You Like It* it is often no more than a rapid rhythmic *façon de parler*. The prose tends to be more vigorous, more highly stylized and more obviously artificial. It has point, gaiety, imagination, formal patterns and rounded cadences. Examples proliferate, especially where Rosalind is the speaker.

Verse is considered proper for high and grave matters. Duke Frederick banishes Rosalind and dismisses Orlando in verse, whereas when he watches the wrestling he speaks prose. Duke Senior uses verse to sweeten the uses of adversity. He is very much a verse speaker. Jaques is temperamentally opposed to verse and mocks it, but his natural gravity and his character as courtier, scholar and moralist ensure that he often speaks it. Orlando comforts Adam in prose. When he approaches the Duke's company with his sword drawn he is tense and wary, all his powers concentrated, and he speaks verse, to which the Duke replies in kind. Silvius and Phebe, as pastoral lovers, are born verse speakers and draw Rosalind, a born prose speaker, into their idiom, so that to Phebe she talks in verse. Left to herself she prefers prose. It is a prose of her own and helps to establish her own special kind of reality. She is natural, spontaneous and unaffected, destructive of all assumed poses. Her most poignant confessions are made in prose. 'O coz, coz, coz, my pretty little coz, that thou didst know

1 C. Hinman, 'Cast-off copy for the First Folio of Shakespeare', *Shakespeare Quarterly*, VI (1955), pp. 259–73.

how many fathoms deep I am in love!' Touchstone lives entirely in
a prose world. He never speaks blank verse, although he can produce extempore doggerel with ease.

It is tempting to call the prose of *As You Like It* euphuistic
because there is no more comprehensive epithet to describe its
intricate rhetorical patterning. It is a variety of Renaissance prose
of which euphuism is strictly a subdivision. Euphuism, even in the
sixteenth century, became a byword for extreme preciosity.
Shakespeare did not adopt Lyly's airs in an effort to be up-to-
date. By the end of the century they were faded. Nor did he
ridicule them. He parodied Lyly once only, with devastating
effect, in 1 *Henry IV*, II. iv. 387 ff., but he learnt from him lessons
he never forgot and when he imitates as distinct from parodying
him the flattery is sincere. By the time he came to write *As You
Like It* he was a master and his prose was his own. It is surprising,
when his source book is so very euphuistic, that he shows so few
traces of its drier, more intellectual and more formal manner. The
first scene has something of it, as the two brothers wrestle in
words. Duke Senior has a trace of Lyly's sententiousness and even
of his similes. The toad with a precious jewel in his head and
sermons in stones are very Lylyan.[1] But the Duke cannot repro-
duce Lyly's prose because he is not a prose speaker. His bent for
set similes is a point of characterization. He is a trifle old-
fashioned, with a beard of formal cut.

For the most part the effect of the prose in this play is one of
informality, of people talking rather than of actors declaiming.
Touchstone's cleverness is dedicated to the service of nonsense.
Rosalind's high spirits jet like a fountain. It seems effortless, not
least when it slips, accidentally as it were, into ritual litanies. How
can the lovers help parodying one another when they are all in a
similar plight?

> And so am I for Phebe. And I for Ganymede.
> And I for Rosalind. And I for no woman.

This prose is functional. It is a way of intensifying the comedy
of disguises and misapprehensions. Phebe thinks she can have
Rosalind. We know she can't. Orlando thinks he can't have her.
We know she is already his. Rosalind declares that she loves no

---

1 The toad and his jewel actually occur in *Euphues* (I, p. 335) and in *Euphues
and His England* (II, p. 99). Stones such as flint and diamond were common in
proverb lore, but Lyly carried his references much further, e.g. to 'the stone
Sandastra', 'the stone Topason', 'Emeraud', 'a true Saphire', 'Anthracitis',
'amber' (ibid., pp. 61, 62, 82, 138).

woman, but we know she is in love. The intrinsic delightfulness of these ironic situations is carried by and carries the formal statements and receives at the end a satisfying formal solution in the Masque of Hymen. The play has already begun to turn into a ballet before Hymen comes in.

vii The masque

The Masque of Hymen has been no better received than the rest of Shakespeare's masques, Jupiter on his eagle and the chanting ancestors in *Cymbeline*, the wedding masque in *The Tempest*, and Queen Katharine's vision of angels in *Henry VIII*, which have not in the past been popular with editors and are often suspected of being by another hand than Shakespeare's. 'The foolery of masques', says Capell, 'was predominant: and the torrent of fashion bore down Shakespeare' (*Notes*, i, p. 69). Grant White doubts that Hymen's part is by Shakespeare, especially the song. 'There is', says Dover Wilson, 'no dramatic necessity for this masque-business; the appearance of Hymen is completely unexpected, seeing that what we have been led to anticipate is a magician (5.2.58–68; 5.4.31–4). Hymen's words, whether spoken or sung, do not seem to us in the least Shakespearian; and they might all be omitted without loss to the context.' He agrees with Capell that the popularity of masques as a court entertainment under James I accounts for what he takes to be an interpolation, and compares the rhyming couplets 'in their obscurity and tortuousness' with similar couplets in *Measure for Measure*, which he considers to be of similarly doubtful authenticity.[1]

It is generally agreed that the masques in the late plays of Shakespeare are related to the masque form in the seventeenth century. But even early plays show a tendency to some kind of formalism at the conclusion. Not obviously a masque, yet serving a similar purpose, is the scene at the end of *A Midsummer Night's Dream*, in which the fairies bless the sleeping house, and Puck falls into rhymed couplets, with 'Now the hungry lion roars'. An extremely slight but telling instance of more than human power being called upon to achieve a comedy dénouement is the sudden appearance of the Abbess at the end of *The Comedy of Errors*. A riot of marrying and giving in marriage is the usual end of a Shakespearian comedy. What is important from the point of view of the

1 On these couplets see J. W. Lever's note in the New Arden *Meas.*, at III. ii. 254. He accepts them as 'a sententious finale to an act full of surprises . . . a much-needed point of rest'.

masque ending is the tendency to present this with a certain formality, to give it a sacramental or symbolic value. It is notable that Wilson Knight, whose reading of Shakespeare's plays is largely in terms of symbolism, is an ardent defender of the authenticity of the masques.

The unique character of the masque, as a literary form, lies in its power to show human life momentarily as an ideal tableau, which dissolves when the compliment to the guest of honour is spoken and the masquers leave the stage for the dance floor, entering ordinary life again. Thus the Lady, in *Comus*, changes from the champion of virtue, putting by the magic cup, to Lady Alice Egerton presented to her parents. This is an effect that a stage play cannot hope wholly to achieve, since in a play the actors must remain actors. They cannot mingle with the audience and reveal themselves as creatures of like kind. If at the end they abandon their roles, they are still professionals, in undress.

On the stage a masque has the function of a play-within-a-play. Its heightened illusion makes the rest of the play seem momentarily more real. The emphasis on reality is particularly important at the end, when Shakespeare is anxious to clarify the relation of his fable to life as it is lived. It is, as in the masque, a two-way traffic. We must see that the fiction, though it is only a fiction, has something to do with fact, and at the same time see that fact can be illuminated by the fiction. The happy ending is more than superficial entertainment, more than wishful thinking; it is a vision of an inward truth. It is implicit in the epithet 'romantic' applied to Shakespeare, and it is present in its most concentrated shape in the four plays that are specifically called 'romances'. The nearer the story comes to fairy tale, the deeper the intuitive truth it conveys. At the moment when the masque formalizes it we become aware of two things simultaneously, that life *is* and *is not* like that.

The effect can be best tested in performance, which is as it should be, for a masque is very emphatically something to be seen, not something to be read. The 'still music', the mysterious appearance of the robed and crowned Hymen, presenting Rosalind to her father and her lover, provide a serene and solemn moment, after which everyone can join in the ordinary rejoicing that accompanies an ordinary wedding. As for the magician-uncle, who is present as a minor plot device in the source book, he paves the way for a promised resolution which it seems only magic can achieve, just as Paulina, in *The Winter's Tale*, affects to call Hermione's statue to life by a 'spell', while protesting it is 'lawful' and that she is not 'assisted / By wicked powers' (v. iii. 105 and 90–1). The appearance of Hymen, even if he is demonstrably an attendant lord or a singing-boy, provided with a torch and a wreath, is a kind of magic and an appropriate one, in that he is no major god from a machine, no intrusive pagan deity, and not to be thought of by modern readers as any sort of pantomime fairy activating a mechanical happy ending. He is merely a 'presenter', a familiar personification, who must have presided over innumerable homemade wedding masques within the period. His business is to make manifest a daily mystery, in which unity and harmony bring happiness and increase.

Readers who reject Shakespearian masques are probably unsympathetic to the masque form as such. They see it as something frivolous, idle and unreal. When it is allied, as it often is, with Shakespearian doggerel, it becomes doubly distasteful, because they don't like doggerel either. Shakespeare did. He habitually uses it, or something very like it, especially in the form of four-stress couplets, when he is handling the preterhuman, the fairies in *A Midsummer Night's Dream*, the witches in *Macbeth*. Couplets are the language of prophecy and of gnomic statement when the Duke uses them in *Measure for Measure*. They explicate the contents of the caskets in *The Merchant of Venice*. A high polish would be inappropriate in lines addressed to an unsophisticated level of understanding. They are heavily stressed and the rhymes fall heavily. At times they are riddling and oracular, compressed to the point of obscurity. Nothing could be further from natural speech. That is their purpose. They range from Puck's jingles, to which nobody has ever objected as unworthy of Shakespeare, to the clear inhuman bell notes of *The Phoenix and the Turtle*. Hymen's lines fall somewhere between. They are a conjuration. They put a spell on the assembled company, establish the atmosphere of reconciliation in which the play ends, and call up Rosalind in her true shape.

> Then is there mirth in heaven,
> When earthly things made even
> Atone together.

viii *Songs*

There are more songs in *As You Like It* than in any other play by Shakespeare. Many of them are provided by Amiens, who is a person in the play and not an anonymous singing-boy brought in for a special occasion. 'Blow, blow, thou winter wind' and Hymen's choral song are used to fill the time while characters on the stage recount adventures already known to the audience. 'What shall he have that killed the deer?' passes the time between Orlando's promise to return to Rosalind 'at two o'clock' and his failure to keep that promise. 'Under the greenwood tree' gives Jaques a chance to display himself in person, after the long account of him at second hand, at II. i. 25 ff. 'It was a lover and his lass' suggests a time lapse before Rosalind's revelations, promised at v. ii. 113 for 'to-morrow'. This is a play to which it was particularly important to impart a feeling of time passing and life going on, of the world wagging, rather than of violent happenings.

The songs evoke a carefree mood and conjure up a woodland on a bare stage. They also dwell very forcefully upon the cares from which the singers have freed themselves, twice repeating the theme of the banished Duke's introductory speech. Rough weather is a welcome relief from the insincerity and treachery of court life. It is true that we have not actually seen much feigned friendship or ingratitude. It is the songs that establish it as a theme in the play. Neither have we seen much of the flattery and false values that the Duke complains of. Jaques has to turn to the sequestered stag to illustrate the way that 'misery doth part the flux of company'. The Duke himself is loyally attended. These reported evils pervade the play like a light haze. Even 'It was a lover and his lass' has a hint of sadness, 'How that a life was but a flower'. The personal estrangement of brothers would not have been by itself adequate to carry the full pastoral statement.

'What shall he have that killed the deer?' can be related to very ancient rituals, and perhaps some primitive wood-magic hangs about the scene, but this is little stressed. Mostly it provides a cheerful choral interlude, with a broad joke at the expense of the cuckold's horns. Jaques shows himself the reverse of a spoilsport and quite forgets the slaughtered deer, openly falling in with the mood of masculine jollity as, despite his affectation of perversity, he falls in with the whole scheme of life in Arden.

Apart from their function in the play, two reasons have been suggested for the frequency with which songs appear. One is that they were an answer to the challenge of the children's companies, which were naturally well supplied with singing voices, and were released from inhibition in 1599.[1] Another is that Shakespeare, having a good adult singer at his disposal when Robert Armin joined the company, wrote the part of Amiens for him (see below, p. liv).

1 R. Noble, *Shakespeare's Use of Song* (1923), p. 72.

The music to which the songs were originally sung has not survived, though plenty has been supplied since, much of it undistinguished. Dr Arne composed his well-known settings of 'Under the greenwood tree' and 'Blow, blow, thou winter wind' for a performance at Drury Lane in 1740. The former has been set to a tune from Playford's *English Dancing Master*.[1] 'What shall he have that killed the deer?' was set by John Hilton, Jr, organist of St Margaret's, Westminster (b. 1599, d. 1657). It appeared in *Catch that Catch can* in 1652. The tune is reprinted by Knight. Hilton turned it into a round for four basses, each of whom has a couplet to sing. In consequence, he omits altogether the disputed line 'Then sing him home, the rest shall bear this burden', thereby encouraging editors to omit it from their text. Despite the late date, Peter Seng thinks Hilton's catch may have been based on the original tune.[2]

'It was a lover and his lass' is the only song for which there is a contemporary setting. It cannot have been the one used on the stage since it is for a single voice. It appears in Thomas Morley's *First Book of Ayres*, published in 1600 and made, the composer says, 'this vacation time'. A manuscript copy of words and music, very close to Morley, is in the National Library of Scotland, Adv. MS 5.2.14, f.18, dated 1639. Halliwell (1856) gives a facsimile. Morley's songbook has survived in a single copy, now in the Folger Library. It was transcribed and edited in 1932 by E. H. Fellowes, revised in 1958 by R. Thurston Dart. David Green edited a facsimile in 1970. Fellowes believed that Shakespeare took both words and music from Morley's book, but he did not consider the effect such a theory must have on the dating of the play.[3] Noble thinks Morley was of too high a standing as a musician to be given a commission by the players.[4] Morley lived in Bishopsgate between 1596 and 1601, and musician and playwright could have been personally acquainted.[5] There is considerable force in a contention, reported but not accepted by Sir Frederick Bridge, that the two boy singers rendered the song in canon, 'both in a tune like two gipsies on a horse'.[6] Noble (p. 75) takes the simile to mean that they sing in unison, overlooking the proverbial fact that when two ride a horse, one must

1 J. M. Gibbon, *Melody and the Lyric from Chaucer to the Cavaliers* (1930).
2 *The Vocal Songs in the Plays of Shakespeare* (1967).
3 Op. cit. (above) and *TLS*, 5 January 1933.
4 *TLS*, 12 January 1933.
5 J. Hunter, *Illustrations of the Life of Shakespeare* (1845).
6 *Shakespearian Music in the Plays and Early Operas* (1923), p. 20.

ride behind. Roger Lowman, in private correspondence, has pointed out that the text not only specifies two boys, but supplies speaking parts for both of them. Once it is accepted that the boys sing unaccompanied in canon there can be no question of Touchstone's joining in. He is established as a non-singer, leaving it open for Armin to double the part with that of Amiens. See below, p. liv. Had Morley originally composed a canzonet, rather a speciality of his, it would have cost him no great pains to adapt it for his book of airs. Fellowes has arranged the air as a two-part canzonet, published by Stainer and Bell.

II. DATE

i The date of the play is fixed by the fact that it does not appear in the list Meres gives in *Palladis Tamia*, in 1598, and it does appear in the Stationers' Register in August 1600. A play that provoked a 'blocking entry' is not likely to have been an old play. A further pointer towards a date shortly after 1598 is the popularity of two Robin Hood plays, *The Downfall of Robert Earl of Huntingdon*, by Anthony Munday, and *The Death of Robert Earl of Huntingdon* by Munday and Chettle, which in 1598 were drawing audiences for the Admiral's Men at the Rose. Fleay[1] was the first to suggest that *As You Like It* might be the Globe's attempt to meet a taste for forest outlaws. The rival plays have a strong romantic–historical bent, wanting in *As You Like It*, which does not pretend to anything that can be called history. There was also at this time a revival of interest in the pastoral plays of John Lyly and their like, which provided suitable material for the reconstituted boys' companies. R. B. Sharpe suggests that Shakespeare designed his pastoral comedy in the hope of attracting to the Globe Theatre the kind of refined and courtly persons who frequented the private theatres, where such plays were shown.[2] He dates it 1600. J. H. Walter propounds a theory that *As You Like It* was not written for public performance but was designed to grace the private marriage of Southampton to Elizabeth Vernon in 1598. This would give point to the wedding masque and would explain why Meres had never heard of the play. Walter joins Sharpe in relating the themes of melancholy, exile and friends' ingratitude to the banishment of the Earl of Essex from the court. The pastoral was notoriously a veil for personal allusions. These however are highly speculative contentions.

1 *Life of Shakespeare* (1886), p. 208. See also A. H. Thorndike, 'The relation of *As You Like It* to Robin Hood plays', *JEGP*, IV (1902), pp. 59–69.
2 *The Real War of the Theatres* (1935).

The figure of the satirical Jaques and the discussion of the ethics of satire suit the year 1599, which saw in June an act for the suppression of satirical writing and the burning of the pamphlets of Nashe and Harvey. The whole conception of Jaques is *fin de siècle*. The part of Touchstone, the first of Shakespeare's 'allowed fools' or jesters, is thought to have been written for Robert Armin, who joined the company in 1599 and specialized in such roles.

Though publication dates are of qualified value in a century in which works circulated in manuscript, it is worth noting a number of allusions in the play which may be related to books published in or around 1598, notably Lyly's *The Woman in the Moon* (1597), Marlowe's *Hero and Leander* (1598) and Yonge's translation of Montemayor's *Diana*, in the same year. Shakespeare had already borrowed from Montemayor when, c. 1593, he wrote *The Two Gentlemen of Verona*, and from *Hero and Leander* c. 1594, when he wrote *A Midsummer Night's Dream*. He seems at all times to have read widely and variously. There was a new edition of Lodge's *Rosalynde*, the major source book, in 1598, and of Greene's *Orlando Furioso*, a possible influence on one scene, in 1599.

Allusions to the events of the late nineties are tenuous. *NCS* relates the two references to Ireland, the practice of rhyming to death (III. i. 173–5) and the howling of Irish wolves (v. ii. 110–11), to Tyrone's rebellion in 1598. Johnson suggests that 'the little wit that fools have was silenced' (I. ii. 82–3) refers to the burning of satirical books in June 1599. Jaques's 'All the world's a stage' would be particularly timely if it were spoken on the stage of the Globe, newly opened in 1599, with the motto *Totus Mundus Agit Histrionem*. A striking coincidence, if it is not something more, is the report in a letter of March 1599 that the Duc de Joyeuse 'is once more become humerous' and has rejoined the Capuchin order, thus paralleling the behaviour of Shakespeare's humorous Duke at the end of the play.[1] No one year more than another fits Rosalind's remarks about 'pretty oaths that are not dangerous' and the perils of practising magic.

Against the evidence which points to 1599 must be set certain indications of a much earlier date, for which Dover Wilson argued strongly when he first edited the play in 1926. He did not doubt that *As You Like It*, as we know it, was performed in 1599, but believed it to be a rewriting of an earlier play, which he assigned to 1593. Since the nature, extent and purpose of the revision are unknown it is equally difficult to prove or disprove

1 *Letters of John Chamberlain*, ed. N. F. McClure (1939).

alleged traces of it. Before critics ceased to see Shakespeare as a revamper of other men's plays, Furness had toyed with the idea that Lodge's story had been dramatized before. He was particularly struck by an apparent inconsistency in Touchstone's character, by what he took for weaknesses in the last scene, and by the mystery of the 'staying entry'.

Dover Wilson's argument raises some points which even without it would call for clarification. It depends on an apparent confusion between verse and prose in the play, which is both typographical and rhythmical, and leaves many broken lines which he finds suggestive of cuts and rearrangements; on the contradictory time scheme; on the confusion at i. ii. 262 as to which girl is the taller; on the confusion as to which Duke is 'old Frederick'; and on links with events and publications of 1592.

ii 'Verse fossils'

The rhythmical and formal character of the prose in this play and the ease with which it slips into verse and out again are discussed above, pp. xviii–xxi. Dover Wilson, prompted by A. W. Pollard, observed what he calls 'verse fossils', suggesting that passages now in prose were at one time in blank verse. He may have been encouraged by Walker's attempts to rearrange some of the prose passages in the play. The objections raised by E. K. Chambers, who points out that the rhythmical effects commented on tend to occur whenever Shakespeare writes prose, shook him a little.[1] In a postscript to a later edition (1947) he allowed that he would 'reconsider some of the arguments' but he did not wholly abandon the theory. His procedure can be illustrated from i. ii. 174–82. Shakespeare's version is a carefully considered and elaborately constructed prose scheme. What emerges from Dover Wilson's 'innocent faking' is very indifferent verse.

But let your fair eyes and gentle wishes go with me to my trial; wherein if I be foiled, there is but one shamed that was never gracious; if killed, but one dead that is willing to be so. I shall do my friends no wrong, for I have none to lament me; the world no injury, for in it I have nothing; only in the world I fill up a place which may be better supplied when I have made it empty.

---

1 *William Shakespeare* (1930), I, pp. 233–4.

go with me to my trial:
Wherein if I be foiled, there is but one shamed . .
My friends no wrong, for I have none to *mourn* me,
The world no injury, for in it I have nothing:
Only *i'th* world *do* I fill up a place . . .
Better supplied when I have made it empty.

The fact that 'verse fossils' proliferate in certain passages and are almost entirely wanting in others may be referred to the kind of prose Shakespeare was writing. Some kinds fall more easily into verse rhythms than others do. The typographical peculiarities of the Folio are best related to faulty casting off (see p. xix), about which there was no information available when Dover Wilson first edited the play.

iii *The time scheme*

The time scheme of *As You Like It* has long engaged critics. It is typical of what has come to be called 'dramatic time'. The time references serve the need of the moment and audiences are rarely disposed to question their consistency. In the first scene Oliver asks for 'the new news at the new court' and Charles tells him that the Duke and his loyal followers have been banished and have taken to the Forest of Arden, implying that this is a fairly recent occurrence. In the second scene Rosalind's grief is still raw. Yet at I. iii. 63, when Duke Frederick tells Celia that he spared Rosalind for her sake, she retorts 'I did not then entreat to have her stay . . . I was too young that time to value her', suggesting a considerable time lapse. This impression is reinforced at II. i. 2, when the banished Duke speaks of the effects of 'old custom' and indicates that he is familiar with winter in the Forest. The discrepancy in the first scene is adequately explained by the pressing need to inform the audience of something of which Oliver does not really need to be informed. The opening of *As You Like It* is devoted to placing a whole rather complicated state of affairs squarely before the spectators with a minimum of fuss. Orlando tells Adam what he already knows, Charles tells Oliver what he already knows, and nobody tells anybody how the ducal brothers came to fall out and what weakness in the elder permitted the younger to prevail.

iv *The relative height of Rosalind and Celia*

The reading *taller*, apparently applied to Celia at I. ii. 262, is discussed in the footnotes to the text. Dover Wilson thinks the original parts were played by a tall fair boy as Celia and a small dark one as Rosalind, not so impossible a casting as it may at first sound, and that by 1599 the acting personnel had altered and the parts were reversed. A pert pageboy could be smaller than his mistress, and in Lodge's story Rosalynde was page to Alinda. In Shakespeare's play they are brother and sister, and one imagines Rosalind the elder, though it is worth remembering that in Milton's *Comus* both brothers were in fact younger than Lady Alice Egerton, towards whom they play a protective role in the masque. Colouring cannot have mattered very much, even on a daylight stage, but relative heights are past concealment. More than one of Shakespeare's comedies make play with a contrast in stature between the heroines, notably *A Midsummer Night's Dream*, where the dark girl is the smaller. See also *Much Ado*, I. i. 116: 'Leonato's short daughter'.

v *'Old Frederick'*

In the Folio, at I. ii. 77, Rosalind claims 'old Frederick' as her father and grows warm in his defence against Touchstone's irreverent epithet. Dover Wilson will not have the speech re-assigned to Celia, contending that Shakespeare had originally used Frederick as the name of the banished Duke and had forgotten this when he came to revise. The usurper is twice referred to as Frederick, by Orlando at I. ii. 223, when he is declaring that he would rather be the youngest son of Sir Rowland than 'heir to Frederick' (i.e. to the reigning Duke, who alone has any advantage to bestow) and again at v. iv. 153. A mistake in speech headings is not at all uncommon. (See above, p. xviii.)

Those who would rather not give the line to Celia argue that Touchstone dare not speak of the reigning Duke as 'old Frederick', that Frederick was in any case the younger brother and the new Duke, and that Rosalind, who loved her father and grieved at his banishment, would be quicker to resent a disrespectful epithet than Celia, with a father who needed no protection and who was far from lovable. This places Touchstone in an unsympathetic light. It might be safer to taunt a man in exile but it would be more like Touchstone to skirmish with authority. Whoever answers him takes him peremptorily to task, very much the mistress of the household, and this is surely Celia not Rosalind. The forsworn knight, no admirable figure, can then be relegated to the usurper's retinue. He is spoken of in the present tense, the Duke 'loves' him. A follower of the banished Duke might well rate the past. The joke about him is feeble. It was pilloried by

Bernard Shaw.[1] Furness uses it as evidence that the 'roynish' clown of the first act is a different person from the later Touchstone and a survival from an 'old play'. Its tedious insipidity perhaps means no more than that Shakespeare's play, like many other people's plays, is slow to warm up. Touchstone has his good moments, even in the first act.

vi *Early printed sources*

Arguments from printed material stress the early date of the major source book. Lodge's *Rosalynde* appeared in 1590, and again in 1592, 1596 and 1598. It has great wit and charm, and in whatever year Shakespeare first read it, he was unlikely to forget it. There are, however, enough verbal reminiscences to suggest that he had read or reread it at a time close to the writing of the play.

Greene's *Orlando Furioso* was played probably in 1591, the year in which Harington published his translation of Ariosto's *Orlando*. The first scene of the second act bears a curious resemblance to Shakespeare's II. i. The hero in both plays is called Orlando. Both Orlandos address heavenly bodies, as sympathetic goddesses. Shakespeare's Orlando invokes the moon as Diana, and Greene's Orlando invokes the planet Venus: 'Faire pride of morne, sweete beautie of the Eeuen / Looke on Orlando languishing in love' (II. i. 558). Shakespeare's Orlando hangs verses on trees in praise of Rosalind. Greene's Orlando finds the trees already hung with 'roundelayes', which are the work of a rival, hoping to arouse his jealousy. Rosalind accuses Orlando of abusing young plants (III. ii. 351) and Jaques prays him to 'mar no more trees with writing love-songs in their barks' (ll. 255–6). Greene's Orlando inquires 'Who wronged happy Nature so / To spoyle these trees with this Angelica?' Lodge's shepherds, and Rosader (Orlando) with them, make long inscriptions in bark, for which no one rebukes them, but they hang no papers on trees. Rosader carries his in his bosom.

The parallels are less striking when they are seen as poetical commonplaces. Such is the reference by Greene's Orlando to Zephyrus blowing his lady's 'dignities alongst Ardenia woods' (II. i. 588–9). The woods of the Ardennes were a well-known pastoral region which is why Lodge set his story there. (See I. i. 114 note.) The lover's address to the moon was especially favoured by the sonneteers, and Orlando's rhyming lines are only one quatrain short of a sonnet. The carving of verses on trees was frequent

1 *Dramatic Opinions and Essays* (1913), II, p. 119.

in pastoral romance. Lodge's heroines, as soon as they come upon such inscriptions, instantly and rightly conjecture that there are shepherds in the neighbourhood. Both Shakespeare and Greene owe the name Orlando to Ariosto. Shakespeare used it to pair with Oliver, and it may have helped him to the idea that Rosalind should undertake to cure Orlando of what she sees fit to call love-madness.

Dover Wilson claims that both scenes take place by night,[1] and that Shakespeare's scene, ending in daylight, is evidence of hasty revision. Since Greene's Orlando hails Venus in the same line as both morning and evening star, he can hardly be particularizing a time of day. Nor is Orlando, unless we take his poetical fury quite literally and suppose he would not address the moon unless the moon were in the sky. Alternatively we may suppose that he comes in reciting a sonnet. He does not seem to have very much idea where he is or what he is doing. There is no denying that this sensible and normally level-headed young man is nearer, in this scene than in any other, to 'a mad humour of loving'. The stage must be vacant for a moment after he rushes off, before Corin and Touchstone come in.

A striking verbal echo of a work published in 1593 is Touchstone's joke, which comes hard on the heels of the reminiscence of Greene and Ariosto, about Rosalind 'infecting' herself with 'the very false gallop of verses', further described as 'the right butter-women's rank to market' (III. ii. 111 and 95–6).

In *Strange Newes* Nashe writes

I would trot a false gallop through the rest of his ragged Verses, but that if I should retort his rime dogrell aright, I must make my verses (as he doth his) run hobling like a Brewers Cart vpon the stones, and obserue no length in their feete; which were *absurdum per absurdius*, to infect my vaine with his imitation.

Malone noted 'false gallop' as a borrowing, Furness added 'infect', and Dover Wilson has plausibly argued an 'unconscious trans-mutation of a brewer's cart rumbling upon the stones into a row of butter-women ambling to market'. *Strange Newes*, published in 1592, was presumably still available in 1599 though not tied in any particular way to that year, till in June it went on the official bonfire as a satirical book. If there were premonitory rumours of

1 John Gilbert represents it thus in his illustrations to Staunton's edition of 1859. The scenic potentiality of the Globe did not include a darkened or a moonlit stage.

this event, readers may have felt them to be a recommendation to read Nashe. He is a mine of Elizabethan colloquialisms and lively language, and it is possible to find parallels, not necessarily borrowings, throughout Shakespeare's plays.

vii *The death of Marlowe*

An event which may link *As You Like It* with 1593 is the death of Marlowe, stabbed in a house in Deptford on 30 May, during a dispute about the bill, or as the depositions have it, 'le recknynge'. On 14 May 1925, O. W. F. Lodge wrote to the *TLS*, calling attention to Touchstone's observation, at III. iii. 9–12, that

> When a man's verses cannot be understood, nor a man's good wit seconded by the forward child, understanding, it strikes a man more dead than a great reckoning in a little room.

In these words, Lodge conjectured, lies a concealed reference to the little room at Deptford where Marlowe was struck dead, together with an echo of a famous line in *The Jew of Malta*, conjecturally dated 1589–90 and frequently played. It was entered in SR in 1594, but the first extant edition is 1633. The Jew describes the jewels over which he is discovered gloating as 'infinite riches in a little room' (I. i. 37). In 1592 the death of Marlowe was news. By 1599 it was less likely that an audience would pick up the reference or care particularly to be reminded of the event.[1] Marlowe was undoubtedly in Shakespeare's mind when he wrote *As You Like It*. He gave Phebe a quotation from *Hero and Leander*, attributing it to a 'dead shepherd' (III. v. 81–2). If the play is to be put back to 1592 it must be assumed, as it reasonably may be in view of his borrowings in *A Midsummer Night's Dream*, that he saw Marlowe's poem in manuscript. It was not printed till 1598. At IV. i. 95–101 he burlesques the story of Hero and Leander, and T. W. Baldwin suspects one of the phrases used, 'though Hero had turned nun', to be a reminiscence of Marlowe's description of Hero as 'Venus Nun' (I, l. 45).[2]

Many commentators have been impressed by this evidence, even when they continue to date the play 1599, but nobody explains why Shakespeare should think Marlowe's death by violence was material for a stage jester. It seems preferable to

---

1 J. Bakeless, *Christopher Marlowe* (1942), I, pp. 143ff. gives a list of references in print between 1593 and 1601.

2 *William Shakespeare's Five-Act Structure* (1947), p. 645.

suppose that the verbal associations, if any, were unconscious on Shakespeare's part and that he did not expect the audience to participate. It is, moreover, highly unlikely that the word *reckoning* = bill, in common use among Elizabethans, would have the same associations for them as it has for the literary world of the twentieth century. The modern reader, to whom the documents in the case have been made available in a way they were not in the 1590s, may be familiar with the word in no other context than the legal jargon of the Deptford depositions.[1] It would be easier to argue that Touchstone's remark needs no additional source of interest if it could be shown in itself and in its context to have some point and meaning. Why should the plight of an exiled sophisticate denied an appreciative audience, Touchstone among the goats and Ovid among the Goths, be associated with any kind of a *great reckoning* in any kind of a *little room*? Neither a bill to be paid, Warburton's interpretation, nor a sum to be worked, Hunter's, seem particularly appropriate. The solution, especially when Touchstone is the speaker, may lie in a hitherto unsuspected bawdy significance, an intellectual paralleled with a physical insufficiency.

A curious addition to the verbal reminiscences in *As You Like It* has been supplied by J. H. Walter. He notes the following parallels in Chapman's poem, *Ovids Banquet of Sense*, published in 1595.

> He saw th'extraction of the fayrest Dames
> The fayre of Beauty, as whole Countries come
> And shew their riches in a little Roome.   St.29.

This recalls both Orlando's prolonged and commonplace conceit, at III. ii. 138–49, in which, following Pliny, he represents Rosalind as made of the distilled excellences of other beauties, and Marlowe's 'riches in a little room', with its possible echo in *As You Like It*. A third, less impressive echo may be discussed in

> Now Ovid's muse as in her tropic shined
> And he, struck dead, was heaven-born become.   St.57

Here we have both 'Ovid's muse', on which Touchstone ruminates, and 'struck dead', a key phrase in the supposed allusion to Marlowe. The case for an earlier version of the play seems insufficient to overset a date of composition probably early in 1599, and a first performance in the autumn of that year.

1 See L. Hotson, *The Death of Marlowe* (1925).

III. SOURCES

i *Lodge's* Rosalynde

Shakespeare's major source for *As You Like It*, identified by Capell and Farmer in the same year, 1767, is a prose romance by Thomas Lodge.[1] The title page reads *Rosalynde. Euphues Golden Legacie. Found after his death in his Cell at Silexedra. Bequeathed to Philautus sonnes, nursed-up with their Father in England.* It was written during a voyage to the Canaries, in 1586–7, 'hatched in the storms of the ocean, and feathered in the surges of many perilous seas'.[2] The author does not at first seem to have considered publication. It appeared in print in 1590, possibly at the instigation of Robert Greene, at whose hand it seems to have undergone some revision.[3] There were nine editions during the next fifty years, testifying to the inherent attractiveness of the work and to the vogue for pastoral in the early seventeenth century. The only editions other than the first which might have contributed to *As You Like It* were in 1592, 1596 and 1598.

Lodge was one of the original euphuists, owing his style less to Lyly than to a common original. A group of young men who studied at Oxford under John Rainoldes in the 1570s all tried to make their mark at much the same time with the epigrammatic, witty, elaborately balanced style they had learned in the lecture hall. What they heard in Latin, they reproduced in English.[4] Lyly was the most successful and the style in which he wrote *Euphues* and *Euphues and his England* and which he later adapted for the stage in a series of prose comedies, became known as euphuism.[5] Lodge used the name of Lyly's hero to recommend his book to a similar audience, but *Rosalynde*, apart from the style and a determination to be edifying, has little to do with *Euphues*. An epilogue sums up the many morals of the piece, which are to be traced in the way the three sons of Sir John of Bordeaux either succeed or fail in living up to their father's precepts.

1 Reprinted in full in the Furness Variorum (1870), by G. Bullough in *Narrative and Dramatic Sources of Shakespeare*, II (1958), and by W. W. Greg, *The Shakespeare Classics* (1907). An unpublished B. Litt. thesis (Oxford, 1968), by Paula Burnett, offers an annotated critical edition.

2 Burnett, op. cit., p. xxiii.

3 Burnett, op. cit., pp. iv and clx. The idea was first put forward by H. C. Hart, *Notes and Queries* (17 March 1906).

4 W. Ringler, 'The immediate source of euphuism', *PMLA*, LIII (1938), pp. 678–86.

5 For an example of Lyly's prose see Intro., p. lxiv. A sustained specimen of Lodge's prose may be found at pp. lix–lx.

For the ill-treatment of the youngest son by the eldest, Lodge was indebted to a Middle English poem, *The Tale of Gamelyn*. The fortunes of the girls, Rosalynde and Alinda, seem to be his own invention, together with the subplot of the shepherds, Montanus, Phoebe and Corydon. Mrs Burnett finds the story 'an amalgam of narrative elements from *Gamelyn*, Sidney and Greene, with some hints from Lyly, all ingeniously adapted to form a homogeneous whole' (op. cit., p. iv). According to C. J. Sisson (*Thomas Lodge and Other Elizabethans* (1933) p. 157) Lodge needed to look no further than his own family for an instance of a quarrel between brothers about an inheritance. Thomas was the dispossessed brother, in a situation 'almost ludicrously parallel' to his story. No characters comparable with Jaques, Touchstone, William and Audrey appear in it.

Lodge's romance is a very polished piece of work, which exploits the vogues of euphuism and of pastoralism. It is laced with a succession of facile lyrics in the mid-Elizabethan style. Rosalynde's madrigal, 'Love in my bosom like a bee', has become a favourite with anthologists. The prose, sufficiently fluent to permit some rapid narrative and some lively conversation, settles periodically into those long self-communings, 'meditations', 'passions' and 'complaints', to which it is particularly suited, and which have no real parallel in Shakespeare's play. Shakespeare owes his plot to Lodge but not a great deal else. He may also have consulted *The Tale of Gamelyn*, which Zachary Grey, in *Critical Notes on Shakespeare* (1754), I, p. 156, proposed as his source, in ignorance of the large debt to Lodge. It appeared in several manuscripts of *The Canterbury Tales*, in one of which Lodge must have read it, but it is not Chaucer's, and was not included in the black-letter editions. It can be consulted today in Skeat's edition of 1884. In one or two places it can be argued that Shakespeare was closer to *Gamelyn* than to Lodge's story.[1] They are not points of great importance and the parallels could be fortuitous. The general impression of indebtedness, however, which may come of reading the *Tale*, is not necessarily reducible to a series of quotable passages. There seems little doubt that it is to *Gamelyn*, either at first or second hand, that Orlando owes his essential Englishness.

In Lodge's story the good Sir John of Bordeaux gives much sage counsel on his deathbed to his three sons, Saladyne, Fernandyne

---

[1] See W. G. Stone, *New Shakespeare Society's Transactions*, II (1882), p. 277 (reprinted as an appendix to Greg's *Rosalynde*) and W. W. Lloyd, *Critical Essays*, in Singer's *Works of Shakespeare*, III (1856).

and Rosader,[1] warning them against the follies of love, advising them of fraternal duty, and dividing his land in proportion to their merits. This means that Rosader, the youngest, is the best endowed. Saladyne considers whether or not to observe his father's will, finally concluding in himself, '"What, man, thy father is dead, and he can neither help thy fortunes, nor measure thy actions; therefore bury his words with his carcase, and be wise for thyself"'. He decides that his youngest brother shall 'know little, so shall he not be able to execute much'. The second brother, because he 'hath no mind but on Aristotle', is encouraged to bury himself in otherworldly pursuits at the university. Shakespeare does not perpetuate these rational motivations.

Rosader bears his lot patiently,

till on a day, walking in the garden by himself, he began to consider how he was the son of Sir John of Bordeaux, a knight renowmed for many victories, and a gentleman famosed for his virtues; how, contrary to the testament of his father, he was not only kept from his land and entreated as a servant, but smothered in such secret slavery, as he might not attain to any honorable actions.

Saladyne's attempt to recall him to his 'wonted reverence' leads Rosader to set about his brother's men to some purpose with a garden rake. There is a false reconciliation, after which Saladyne urges Rosader, for the honour of the family name, to match himself with a powerful wrestler, who is challenging all comers at the sports. He has already bribed the wrestler to do the young man all the harm he can.

The sports have been arranged by the bad King Torismond to keep his subjects from brooding on the fate of the good King Gerismond, whose throne he has usurped. Despite their twinned names, the two kings are not brothers. Shakespeare has a more symmetrical and more shocking situation, that parallels the bad blood between Oliver and Orlando. An old countryman loses two sons to the wrestler, and unlike Shakespeare's old man, who makes 'pitiful dole', he bears his loss with a stoicism which arouses in Rosader a desire to avenge him. Further inspired by the beauty and kind glances of Rosalynde, the banished king's daughter, Rosader contrives to turn the tables. Everyone is delighted, including Torismond, who shows no resentment on hearing that the young man's father was Sir John of Bordeaux. It is Shakes-

---

1 Accented, like Rosalind, on the first syllable.

peare who makes Sir John a friend of the banished duke, thus forging a link between Orlando and Rosalind. Lodge's Rosalynde is provocative, rashly confident that she can play with love and retreat when she wishes, an idea which is reflected by Shakespeare in the conversation in Act I, scene ii, where Rosalind proposes falling in love as 'a sport', and Celia begs her not to fall in love 'in good earnest'. 'To make Rosader know she affected him, she took from her neck a jewel, and sent it by a page to the young gentleman.' Rosader goes home to find that his brother has locked the doors against him. He breaks them down and makes free with the house to feast his friends, served by Adam Spencer, an old servant of his father. Adam persuades him not to harm his brother, and again they appear to be reconciled.

Meanwhile Torismond banishes Rosalynde, fearing 'some one of the peers will aim at her love, end the marriage, and then in his wife's right attempt the kingdom'. Alinda, having pleaded passionately on her behalf, is banished with her, a brutality which Shakespeare does not impute to the usurper. Rosalynde suggests a suitable disguise. ' "I, thou seest, am of a tall stature, and would very well become the person and apparel of a page; thou shalt be my mistress, and I will play the man so properly, that, trust me, in what company soever I come I will not be discovered." . . . Thus fitted to the purpose, away go these two friends, having now changed their names, Alinda being called Aliena, and Rosalynde Ganymede.'

Seeking for company in a desert place, the girls come upon verses carved by the lovesick Montanus on the trees, and find the shepherd himself engaged in reciting an eclogue with an old man, Corydon. They ask for lodging and Aliena explains that she means to buy a farm and flock, for, says she, ' "I have heard the swains say, that they drunk without suspicion, and slept without care" '.

'Marry, mistress', quoth Corydon, 'if you mean so you came in good time, for my landslord intends to sell both the farm I till, and the flock I keep, and cheap you may have them for ready money: and for a shepherd's life, O mistress, did you but live awhile in their content, you would say the court were rather a place of sorrow than of solace. Here, mistress, shall not fortune thwart you, but in mean misfortunes, as the loss of a few sheep, which, as it breeds no beggary, so it can be no extreme prejudice: the next year may mend all with a fresh increase. Envy stirs not us, we covet not to climb, our desires mount not above our degrees, nor our thoughts above our fortunes. Care cannot harbour in our cottages, nor do homely couches know broken slumbers: as we exceed not in diet, so we have enough to satisfy: and, mistress, I have so much Latin, *Satis est quod sufficit*'. 'By my troth, shepherd', quoth Aliena, 'thou makest me in love with your country life, and therefore send for thy landslord, and I will buy thy farm and thy flocks, and thou shalt still under me be overseer of them both: only for pleasure sake I and my page will serve you, lead the flocks to field, and fold them. Thus will I live quiet, unknown, and contented'.

Saladyne attempts once more to destroy his brother, taking him asleep, binding him to a post in the hall, refusing him food, and declaring him mad. From this situation Adam Spencer rescues him. He tests the friends and kinsfolk whom his brother has invited to dine by pretending to be still chained and he does not break out until he finds his pleas are met with mockery. Saladyne enlists the sheriff of the county, and Rosader and Adam, at last forced to flee, lose their way in a forest. There Rosader nearly expires, in spite of all Adam can do to cheer him. Not until Adam offers to open a vein for him to suck does he play the man and set off to hunt some food. Coming upon Gerismond feasting, he courteously asks for help, is seen to be a gentleman, and is invited to sit and eat.

'Gramercy, sir' quoth Rosader 'but I have a feeble friend that lies hereby famished almost for food, aged and therefore less able to abide the extremity of hunger than myself, and dishonour it were for me to taste one crumb, before I made him partner of my fortunes: therefore I will run and fetch him, and then I will gratefully accept your proffer'.

Gerismond hears Rosader's story, and accepts his service for his father's sake. At the court Torismond seizes the opportunity to annex the revenues of Saladyne and Rosader by banishing the elder brother because he has wronged the younger.

Once they are all in Arden it is easy to contrive meetings. Rosalynde and Alinda encounter Rosader, recognize him and hear his love-plaint. Rosalynde, 'loath to let him pass out of her presence', suggests that he shall show his mettle as poet and lover in an eclogue. '"Seeing thou sayest thou art so deeply in love, let me see how thou canst woo. I will represent Rosalynde, and thou shalt be as thou art, Rosader. See in some amorous eclogue, how if Rosalynde were present, how thou couldst court her; and while we sing of love, Aliena shall tune her pipe and play us melody".' So to Alinda's piping, Rosader and Rosalynde exchange extempore verses, at great length, a situation far too artificial for

Shakespeare's purpose, though as natural as breathing in a pastoral romance. The love-cure is not part of Lodge's story. Lodge has Alinda propose the mock marriage, from which Rosader proceeds to the discovery of his sleeping brother menaced by a lion. The situation evokes a splendid antithetical soliloquy. Shall he take his revenge or shall he live up to his father's precepts? Saladyne fails at first to recognize Rosader and tells the story of his remorse as if to a stranger, which leads to a genuine reconciliation, after which the banished king gladly accepts Saladyne's service. Rosader makes his excuses to the girls for having absented himself and Saladyne joins them just in time to frustrate an attack by outlaws, intent on carrying off Alinda as a present to the lecherous Torismond, unaware that she is his daughter. With this favourable introduction, Alinda and Saladyne fall in love. Alinda meditates upon her paradoxical situation, in thrall to the man to whom she owes her freedom. She doubts whether Saladyne will care for her when he realizes that she is the daughter of the man who banished him. Moreover he is a gentleman and to him she seems to be a shepherdess. Will he stoop to her? No such thoughts cross the mind of Shakespeare's Celia.

Rosalynde can now tease her lovelorn friend, and pay back the mocks she has had to take from her. For Rosalynde, who meant to play at love, is in deeper than she bargained for, and Alinda has not spared her. She utters some sad complaints in private, and is openly outraged when she hears Phoebe pride herself on being love-proof. Phoebe refuses the shepherd on principle.

'Yet, Montanus, I speak not this in pride, but in disdain; not that I scorn thee, but that I hate love; for I count it as great honour to triumph over fancy as over fortune. . . . Wert thou, Montanus, as fair as Paris, as hardy as Hector, as constant as Troilus, as loving as Leander, Phoebe could not love, because she cannot love at all: and therefore if thou pursue me with Phoebus, I must fly with Daphne.'

Rosalynde will not hear this patiently. Coming out of concealment, she reminds the frigid shepherdess of the fate of Narcissus 'passionate and yet unpitied', and proffers the usual arguments against coyness, bidding her 'love while thou art young, least thou be disdained when thou art old'. It becomes immediately obvious that in Ganymede Phoebe has met the fate she challenged.

Since Rosader has been wounded in the battle with the outlaws and is forced to stay at home, Saladyne has the opportunity to court Alinda. He offers her marriage in spite of her antithetical arguments about the difference between what men say and what they do, and the unlikelihood of Venus joining robes and rags together. Then it is Phoebe's turn to be tossed with contrary passions. Montanus visits her sickbed, and having no other messenger available she gives him a letter to Ganymede, to which she annexes a sonnet. 'Poor Montanus saw day at a little hole, and did perceive what passion pinched her, yet, that he might seem dutiful to his mistress in all service, he dissembled the matter, and became a willing messenger of his own martyrdom.' Ganymede, who shows him the letter, tries in vain to persuade him his love is hopeless. It is certainly extravagant, but it has its own nobility. Montanus will not take the revenge which is to hand. He begs Ganymede to be kind to Phoebe since she loves so dearly. Ganymede makes a bargain. Phoebe is to accept Montanus, whose wretchedness she at last understands and pities, if she can with reason be persuaded to refuse Ganymede.

'When reason', quoth she, 'doth quench that love I owe to thee, then will I fancy him; conditionally, that if my love can be suppressed with no reason, as being without reason, Ganymede will only wed himself to Phoebe.' 'I grant it, fair shepherdess', quoth he; 'and to feed thee with the sweetness of hope, this resolve on: I will never marry myself to woman but unto thyself.'

This leaves only Rosader unhappy and Ganymede comforts him.

'Tush, be of good cheer, man', quoth Ganymede: 'I have a friend that is deeply experienced in negromancy and magic; what art can do shall be acted for thine advantage. I will cause him to bring in Rosalynde, if either France or any bordering nation harbour her; and upon that take the faith of a young shepherd.' Aliena smiled to see how Rosader frowned, thinking that Ganymede jested with him.

The gathering for Alinda's wedding gives Lodge the opportunity to describe in some comic detail Corydon 'in his holiday suit'. Phoebe helps to dress Alinda, 'yet her eye was still on Ganymede, who was so neat in a suit of grey, that he seemed Endymion when he won Luna with his looks, or Paris when he played the swain to get the beauty of the nymph Oenone'. Montanus appears 'apparelled all in tawny, to signify that he was forsaken; on his head he wore a garland of willow, his bottle hanged by his side, whereon was painted despair, and on his sheep-hook hung two sonnets, as labels of his loves and fortunes.'

King Gerismond, struck by this extraordinary figure, hears the sonnets, is told of Phoebe's promise, and constitutes himself judge in her case. The stage is set for Ganymede to excuse herself for a moment and to come in again 'having on a gown of green, with kirtle of rich sendal, so quaint, that she seemed Diana triumphing in the forest; upon her head she wore a chaplet of roses, which gave her such grace that she looked like Flora perked in the pride of all her flowers'. Her identity thus disclosed and her story related, her father sanctions her marriage with Rosader, Saladyne is delighted to learn that he too is wedding a king's daughter, Phoebe sees her love is indeed beyond reason, and must accept Montanus. Corydon enlivens the feast with an imitation of Perigot's song in the August eclogue of *The Shepheardes Calender*. At this point Fernandyne, the second brother, brings Gerismond news that 'the twelve peers of France are up in arms to recover thy right'. Gerismond finds horses and armour for all, they join the peers in battle and Torismond is slain, lamented of none but Alinda. Everyone is then given his due reward, including Montanus, made 'lord over all the forest of Arden, Adam Spencer Captain of the King's Guard, and Corydon master of Alinda's flocks'.

This is puppeteering, more than usually clever and more than usually charming. There is gaiety and wit and a strong sense of the comedy of situation. France is a legendary country where 'the twelve peers' rise in defence of the right. When the tale turns pastoral, it assumes the more artificial graces of pastoralism, the extempore eclogues, the shepherd's water-bottle 'painted with despair', and the calm and rather trite assurance that care cannot harbour in cottages. But shepherds can love. 'Experience tells thee', says Alinda, 'that peasants have their passions as well as princes, that swains as they have their labours, so they have their amours, and love lurks as soon about a sheepcote as a palace.' Montanus, indeed, loves to excess. The irrationality of the passion keeps it hovering somewhere between the deplorable and the laughable, yet it can attain heights of self-sacrifice. Shakespeare casts Silvius for a much less heroic part. Lodge's young gentlefolk, on the other hand, mingle a good deal of calculation with their affections. They may wed in defiance of money and rank but they think a good deal about them and are not in the end forced to forgo them.

However he chooses to interpret the story, Shakespeare has first to trim events in order to keep it within dramatic bounds. He omits many of the adventures of Gamelyn and reduces the affairs of Alinda and Saladyne to a sub-plot. From the Gamelyn story he need take no more than a dispossessed younger son, a single quarrel with the elder, the wrestling match and the flight to Arden. The violence of the original tale, with its fighting and roystering, is out of key with the pastoral conclusion. It is acceptable in Lodge's dry and polished narrative. To show it would be another matter, and would prove a distraction to no purpose, since the plot does not require it. There is a positive gain in Orlando arriving in Arden with the image of Rosalind so newly impressed on his heart, and a further gain in that he leaves home too soon to hear that the girls have also packed up and gone. It makes the situation in the forest, where they pass unrecognized, so much the more plausible. In Lodge's story, Gerismond asks both Rosader and Saladyne if they have news of his daughter and they both say that she and her friend have gone no one knows where. The first time Gerismond sees his daughter as Ganymede is at Alinda's wedding and he is instantly struck by the likeness of the supposed boy to the lost girl, a natural touch which Shakespeare also makes use of, when the disclosure is in any case imminent.

Lodge's story might almost as well be called *Alinda* as *Rosalynde*. Alinda takes the lead throughout. Rosalynde masquerades as a boy, but she is a page and always subordinate to her mistress. Traces of Celia's dominant role remain in the play. It is she who plans the escape to Arden, voluntarily exiling herself, and she who buys the house and land. She has spirit and initiative and is no mere confidante. Her courtship is summarily dealt with. The attack by bandits, Saladyne's gallantry and Rosader's wounds, which leave the stage to his brother, are outside Shakespeare's purpose and are omitted. The younger brother's recognition of the elder in the forest, his inward struggle and final victory over the base impulse to leave him to his fate, are relegated to a brief narrative, which seems to be made more fantastic than it need be by the snake with which Shakespeare reinforces the lioness. An adder would be a natural hazard in Arden but this is a thoroughly melodramatic snake, which can hang poised for an appreciable moment over its unconscious victim. As it slides away, Oliver's envy melts, and his wrath goes with the lion. There is, however, no overt hint of any allegorical meaning in the choice of wild beasts, which are the conventional denizens of romantic forests.[1]

1 R. Knowles, in 'Myth and type in *As You Like It*,' *English Literary History*, XXXIII (1966), pp. 11–13, accounts for the choice of beasts by claiming Orlando as a Hercules figure. Harold Brooks sees an archetypal imagery,

xliv AS YOU LIKE IT

Saladyne does not at once recognize his brother and in telling his story as to a stranger he displays a disinterested penitence, which has had time to grow during a spell of imprisonment at the Duke's hands. Thus Lodge offers what, on a rational level, is a very much more convincing picture of the elder brother, a sound reason for Alinda's favouring him, and a protracted courtship.

Shakespeare's omissions make the play compact and manageable. Something is lost in the way of motivation, which is amply made up for by the more natural turn of events. Much that is violent and sensational, distanced by the artificiality of tone and style in Lodge, does not appear at all in *As You Like It*. Duke Frederick does not banish his own daughter. Celia does not vouch for Rosalind's loyalty by declaring she will 'massacre' her with her own hands if she can be proved treacherous. Adam does not offer to open a vein to revive a fainting Orlando. There is no attempt to kidnap Celia. Even so minor a character as Charles the wrestler is not approached with a bribe but convinced that he will be acting rightly if he injures Orlando. Along with violence, Shakespeare dispenses with a good deal of the artifice. Lodge's Arden is inhabited by quaintly dressed shepherds and shepherdesses who exchange verses with Chinese frequency and grace. Touchstone's extemporal rhyming and Jaques's botched 'stanzo' are considerably more realistic. Orlando versifies in the way that many an Elizabethan gentleman did, not very well at the first attempt and better the next, and he is mocked outrageously for his pains. Lodge's hero, immediately on receiving Rosalynde's love-token after the wrestling, 'stepped into a tent, and taking pen and paper wrote this fancy', an impromptu in ten lines. Where he got the schooling his brother denied him neither the play nor the story invites us to inquire.

Though Silvius and Phebe undeniably bring with them a flavour of pastoral artifice, it is not because of what they are in themselves. They are not incredible figures. Girls have teased and young men have languished through the centuries. It is because this is a basic truth about loving that it is important to pastoral, which stresses natural, instinctive behaviour. But literature, ever since Theocritus, has been sophisticating nature, and Silvius and

whereby Shakespeare indicates symbolically a change taking place at a very deep level in Oliver's personality. In Jungian terms 'we have to expose ourselves to the animal impulses of the unconscious—without identifying ourselves with them.' See Jung, *The Integration of the Personality* (1946), p. 153. Lodge, because he is writing a prose narrative, can be more expansive and naturalistic here. Shakespeare uses the method of poetic drama.

Phebe come from a world almost as separate from everyday as if they came from fairyland. This sets them apart from the other people in the play, but the line of demarcation is very delicately drawn. We never see Silvius clothed all in tawny to figure his forlorn state, with sonnets tied to his crook. He is a very distinctive character, none the less, both among the courtiers *en déshabillé* and among the other natives of Arden. Contrasts of this kind are hardly developed at all by Lodge. All Lodge's people tend to speak with the same voice, invoke the same trite mythologies, and one is as likely as another to produce a Latin tag. They are differently situated rather than fundamentally unlike and all they change are their fortunes, not their inner natures. Lodge's range of characters is narrow. Even Le Beau, in Shakespeare, stands out as somebody with an interesting standpoint of his own. Lodge has no Jaques to be a reminder of the corruption of court and city and no Touchstone to vary wit with common sense and nonsense. Touchstone and Jaques, who are extraneous to the plot, are essential to the play. Next to Rosalind, and sometimes before her, they are the characters that an audience values. It is for this reason that critics can disagree about Shakespeare's indebtedness to Lodge, which in respect of plot mechanism is considerable, but in almost everything else non-existent.

In some ways Lodge is more determinedly pastoral than Shakespeare. Rosalynde and Alinda lead out their flocks at dawn and pen them at dusk with exemplary regularity. As well as cottages there are cottage interiors, and gay meals are produced from country larders. The banished king, on the other hand, uses the woods as a refuge and hardly at all as a way of life. Shakespeare evokes the forest as Lodge never does. It is a mysterious asylum, a glorious camp-site, even a source of jokes about horns. His refugees deliberately seek it, whereas Lodge's people come upon it by chance. Lodge gives no real confrontation of town and country and no deep sense of pastoral healing. His responses to the worth of country morals and the absurdity of country manners are combined in the character of Corydon, who is allowed to state the pastoral credo with classic dignity, but is something of a clown when, resplendent in pewter buttons, he makes his awkward bow to Gerismond and offers him 'a fair mazer full of cider'. Rosalynde claims to know a magician, but she appears in her own shape without the solemn magic of the masque setting its seal upon the immense tolerance, the at-one-ness of the play.

Lodge is also more determinedly moral than Shakespeare. His plot does not hinge on a change of heart effected in a woodland sanctuary. It is about the provisions of old Sir John's will and the eldest son's failure to observe them. His story is punctuated by edifying instances of the internal struggles of his characters, but all they are doing is expatiating upon the different situations into which the ingenuity of the plot casts them. They are not expressing their inner selves. Shall I observe my father's wishes or shall I not, asks Saladyne. Can I hope to marry Orlando or can I not, muses Rosalynde. Adam Spencer laments the inconstancy of fortune and arms himself against it. These set pieces have marginal indices, to call the reader's attention to a fine bit of writing. Private meditations and complaints have little part in *As You Like It*, where very few speakers lack a hearer. The character of the hearer modifies our response to what is said. We see persons in relation, contrasted or paralleled not only situationally but in thought, feeling, mood, temperament, character and idiom. This constitutes the play's individuality and is perhaps in part an explanation of its title. It permits people to be themselves. If it teaches anything it teaches a good-humoured acceptance of the seasons' difference, which is comparatively easy, and of people, which is much harder.

ii *Jaques and contemporary satirists*

It is more profitable to trace in Jaques the generic traits of the melancholy man than to suppose him a caricature of a particular person. Towards the end of the sixteenth century a temperamental hypersensitivity and thoughtfulness, often a genuine response to the stresses of an age of transition, was high fashion.[1] It marked one off from the coarse-fibred, mindless crowd. 'Oh, it's your only fine humour, sir, your true melancholy breeds your perfect fine wit, sir . . . Haue you a stoole there, to be melancholy vpon?' (*Every Man in his Humour*, III. i. 89–100). It ranked as a 'humour' because its medical origin was long thought to lie in an excess of melancholy among the four humours of the blood. Only when these were in perfect equilibrium were body and mind in perfect health. 'Melancholy', says Bridget Lyons, 'was classified as a disease, condemned as a vice, or exalted as the condition and symptom of genius. But all these diverse traditions about melancholy expressed, implicitly, the idea of its social importance—it was a physical and psychological condition that expressed an

1 On melancholy see G. B. Harrison's essay in his edition of Breton's *Melancholike Humours* (1929), J. Babb, *The Elizabethan Malady* (1951) and B. G. Lyons, *Voices of Melancholy* (1971).

orientation towards the world and society—and this made it particularly susceptible to literary treatment.'[1] Such undoubtedly is the use Shakespeare makes of the melancholy of Jaques, treasured by its professor, mocked by Orlando and Rosalind, and censured, not too seriously, by the Duke. It is one more attitude to life among the many of which the play is composed. There is never any suggestion that it is a pathological condition, though it is perhaps something more than an affectation. The play does not support the further contention that the name Jaques is associated with 'melancholy dregs and excrement' and that he is antisocial, 'fleeing the companionship even of the forest exiles who have themselves been outcast from society'.[2] He likes to be alone sometimes, and he likes others to miss him and 'to woo his company'. We meet him first, at II. v., as a member of a group, 'merry, hearing of a song'. At II. vii., he is joining in a 'banquet', at IV. ii, he is in robust company, encouraging them to rowdy singing. At III. iii., he joins a wedding ceremony and breaks it up because it is a ramshackle, beggarly business, not sufficiently social and ceremonious. The only social act he objects to is dancing, which bores him. He prefers to talk, if only to a herd of deer (II. i) or listen, if only to a fool's soliloquy (II. vii). He would be much at a loss without society. When he takes himself off at the end of the play it is to converse with the repentant Duke Frederick. He has a kind of sub-acid geniality and a deep curiosity about people.

The melancholy man, says Sir Thomas Overbury is,

a strayer from the drove. . . . His imagination is never idle, it keeps his mind in a continuall motion, as the poise of a clock: he winds up his thoughts often, and as often unwinds them. . . . He'le seldome be found without the shade of some grove, in whose bottome a river dwels. . . . He thinkes businesse, but never does any: he is all contemplation, no action. He hewes and fashions his thoughts, as if he meant them to some purpose; but they prove unprofitable, as a piece of wrought timber to no use.[3]

This is true to the contemplative nature of Jaques and the constant activity of his mind, but Shakespeare does not exert himself to present the thinking as abortive and inhibiting to

---

1 *Voices of Melancholy*, p. 1.

2 Ibid., Intro., pp. 12–13. See also O. J. Campbell, 'Jaques', *The Huntington Library Bulletin*, VIII (October 1935), pp. 71–102.

3 *The Miscellaneous Works of Sir Thomas Overbury*, ed. E. E. Rimbault (1890), pp. 73–4.

action. Neither the Duke nor his retinue are engaged in any major actions in the forest. Were they more perfectly pastoral they would do even less, for they would not even hunt. Contemplation was possible in their circumstances and was esteemed. It is one of the great pastoral values. That Jaques enjoys his melancholy is made abundantly clear. It is not, says Harold Jenkins, 'the fatigue of spirits of the man who has found the world too much for him, but an active principle manifesting itself in tireless and exuberant antics'.[1] We never see him in a mood approaching depression and he is entirely free of the malcontent's sense of personal injury. He never suggests that the world has treated him more unfairly than anyone else. He proposes to 'cleanse' it, but not to pay scores. His banishment seems to have been voluntarily undertaken and he certainly elects to prolong it voluntarily. *Every Man in his Humour* was played by the Chamberlain's Company in 1598. It introduced the 'humorous' character to the stage, the man with a dominant passion carried to the point of absurdity. There is something of this in Jaques, who treats himself and is treated by others as someone who can be depended upon to respond to any situation in a unique and characteristic way.

Scholars who are convinced that Shakespeare drew Jaques from life have come up with the names of three contemporaries. A. H. Gray, seeking a character in a play around the turn of the century to explain a reference in the second *Return from Parnassus*, in which Shakespeare is said to have given 'a purge' to Jonson, selects Jaques as the only possibility.[2] B. H. Newdigate favours Sir John Harington, 'the unlicensed fool of Elizabeth's Court', author of *The Metamorphosis of Ajax*, a book title which puns on jakes meaning a privy.[3] If Jaques is a caricature of anybody it is an affectionate tribute rather than a purge, and there does not seem to be much foundation for the idea that his name stank in Elizabethan nostrils. (See below, p. lxviii.) The claims of John Marston are more impressive, though they do not in the end perhaps amount to more than that satire, like melancholy, was high fashion. In 1925, G. B. Harrison, editing Marston's *Scourge of Villanie* (1598), compared the author's address 'To him that hath perused mee' with the way in which Jaques defends himself at II. vii. 70ff. against the charge, not actually brought by any-

1 '*As You Like It*', *Shakespeare Survey 8* (1955), p. 45.
2 A. H. Gray, *How Shakespeare 'Purged' Ben Jonson* (1928).
3 *TLS*, 3 January 1929.

body in the play, of indulging in personal slander.[1] 'If anyone', says Marston, '(forced with his owne guilt) will turne it home and say *Tis I*, I cannot hinder him. Neyther doe I iniure him.' Apart from this telling version of the proverbial 'If the cap fits, wear it', the rest reads like the common exculpatory Elizabethan epilogue, protecting the writer against the 'constructions' which he feared might be put on his work and which he probably knew he deserved. There is no fresh note for which Shakespeare could be indebted to Marston and nobody else.

In 1934 Theodore Spencer argued from *Proemium in librum tertium* of *The Scourge of Villanie* that Shakespeare may well have had Marston in mind when Jaques declares that given a motley coat he will 'through and through / Cleanse the foul body of the infected world'.[2] What in Jaques is high spirits, in Marston is near-hysteria.

> Faire *Detestation* of foule odious sinne,
> In which our swinish times lye wallowing,
> Be thou my conduct . . .
> O that a Satyres hand had force to pluck
> Some fludgate vp, to purge the world from muck:
> Would God I could turne *Alpheus* river in
> To purge this *Augean* oxstaule from foule sin.[3]

Arnold Davenport, editing Marston's satires, is reminded less of Jaques than of the Duke rebuking him for the 'foul sin' of disgorging on the world 'th' embossed sores and headed evils' which he has contracted through keeping evil company. The Duke, he claims, like Marston, is 'exploring the powerful effects obtainable by the use of grossly physical words in serious contexts'.[4] But would Elizabethans, only too familiar with minor infections, be particularly squeamish about the words which describe them? Davenport sees something of Jaques in an earlier work of Marston, *Certaine Satyres* (1598), in which a character called 'Bruto the trauailer' roams the streets of Westminster with 'a discontented grace', railing at the 'corrupted age' and the scant respect people show for his experience of a wider world.[5] Marston strips his pretensions with the comment that all he ever did was go to

1 *The Scourge of Villanie*, ed. G. B. Harrison (1925).
2 'John Marston', *The Criterion*, XIII (1934), pp. 581–99.
3 *Satires*, ed. A. Davenport (1961), p. 149, ll. 13–20.
4 Ibid., Intro., p. 27.
5 Ibid., Intro., pp. 12–13. See also O. J. Campbell, 'Jaques', *The Huntington Library Bulletin*, VIII (October 1939), pp. 71–102.

Venice, to 'buy a Lute and vse a Curtezan'. He is a lightweight, his nausea an affectation and his experience valueless. This is not Jaques, whom the Duke takes seriously, who never considers himself underrated, and who exchanges easy banter with anyone he meets, showing no resentment when the optimists have the last word. He knows in advance that it will be hard to make the world take his medicine and he plans to shoot his wit under cover of his motley, a strategy beyond the reach of Bruto's limited imagination. There are, however, points of contact. Jaques himself imputes his melancholy to 'the sundry contemplation of my travels' and Rosalind's mocking of the returned traveller, though he may have done nothing to deserve it, is pinned upon him. The Duke reminds him 'thou thyself hast been a libertine'.

Jaques demanding motley is jubilant. When Marston creates satirists for the stage the mirth tends to be sour, the clowning grotesque, and the banter turns to abuse. His are true malcontents. The first and most genial is Feliche in *Antonio and Mellida* (played *c.* 1599), which at v. i. 61–4 carries an apparent reminiscence of *As You Like It*, III. ii. 86ff.

> I'll weep my passion to the senseless trees
> And load most solitary air with plaints.
> For woods, trees, sea or rocky Appenine
> Is not so ruthless as my Rosaline.[1]

There may be no more in this than the coincidence of the lady's name, but it is much in Orlando's vein. When further parallels appear in *The Malcontent* it seems likely that Marston is still the borrower, though E. E. Stoll would like Malevole, in that play, to be the prototype of 'the finished humanly significant Jaques'.[2] The most striking likeness is the way in which Malevole at v. iv. 154ff. dismisses the other persons in the play in rhymed couplets which sum up their deservings as Jaques does at v. iv. 85–91. Both characters are associated with discord in music (*Mal.* I. ii. 1–3, *AYL* II. vii. 5–6) and are free as air to blow on any man (*Mal.* I. iii, 2, *AYL* II. vii. 47–9). For the most part, the two plays and the two characters could hardly be more different. In Marston's sombre world friendship is indeed feigning and loving mere folly. A great deal is said in his play that *As You Like It* takes for granted. It is part of the convention that pastoral sweetness and light are

---

1 Ed. G. K. Hunter (1965), p. 67.

2 'Shakespeare, Marston, and the malcontent type', *Modern Philology*, III (1906), pp. 281–303.

asserted in the face of what is dark and distressing. That is why in its feebler forms the pastoral tends to escapism and sentimentality and its more serious manifestations have a real affinity with satire. *The Malcontent* was not entered in the Stationer's Register till 5 July 1604. It was the property then of the King's Men, though it seems originally to have been written for the Children of the Queen's Revels at Blackfriars and stolen from them. The date of composition has been assigned to 1600 on rather slender evidence. A reference at I. viii. 19 to a freak of nature, said to have been described in a pamphlet 'twelve years since', can be traced to a publication of 1588.¹ Stoll, dating the play 1600, associates it with the entry of *As You Like It* in the Stationers' Register in August 1600. This is a date which T. W. Baldwin would give to Shakespeare's play, in the belief that Armin did not join the company till that year (see p. lii below). The arguments, reinforced by R. B. Sharpe,² who thinks the play reflects the banishment of Essex and was written in the spring or summer of 1600, do not seem adequate to challenge the usual dating of 1599.

iii *Touchstone, Will Kempe and Robert Armin*

Jaques is a type and also a personality. Touchstone never fully develops a character and tends to remain a theatrical convenience, though a very delightful one, to whom a skilled actor can give an illusion of life. He puzzles commentators because his occasional shrewdness and his professional skills, which consist largely in putting up a dazzling façade of pseudo-scholarship, seem to contradict his simplicity. He is ignorant of what marriage is but he knows about Ovid's exile among the Goths. His satire on duelling delights Jaques by its aptness and provokes the Duke to observe that he uses his folly as a stalking-horse and under cover of it shoots his wit. This, however, as James Smith has noted, is 'just what the real Touchstone never does, in spite of what the critics say'.³ His successes are 'the squandering glances of the fool' or as Rosalind puts it, he speaks wiser than he is ware of. It is

1 See *John Webster*, ed. E. E. Stoll (1905), pp. 55–60. A. Caputi, in *John Marston Satirist* (1961), assigns it to 1603. He cannot credit that a Blackfriars play of 1600 would have no reference to the poetomachia then raging. E. K. Chambers, *The Elizabethan Stage* (1923), III, p. 432, does not find Marston associated with the Children of the Revels before 1604.

2 *The Real War of the Theatres* (1935), p. 167.

3 '*As You Like It*', *Scrutiny*, IX (1940), pp. 9–32. It is a pity that the duelling speech, Touchstone's *chef d'œuvre*, can raise little spontaneous laughter these days.

because the audience wants to see him, contrary to all likelihood, score a gold that Shakespeare arranges he shall do so; and the audience wants it because it is a delicious instance of the world turned upside down, of the little man winning. It reassures us that the fool, which in our less confident moments we suspect we are, can put down the wise man. Were he in fact a wise man, only pretending to be a fool, there could be no such reassurance.

His creator's intelligence, not his own, is always putting Touchstone in an advantageous position. In addition, his mastery of the conventions of nonsense, his stock-in-trade, may give an appearance of a cleverness and even of a critical acumen which could make him a real touchstone of values. But his learned allusions, mock logic and fancy words are simply a folk idiom. There is no profundity in them and it is difficult, on investigation, to find him with anything important to say. He does not mock because he encounters anything intrinsically mockable. His business is mocking. He is an allowed fool. Until he came to write *As You Like It* Shakespeare had created fools only dimly aware of their folly, if at all. Dogberry has no idea that he is comical. Touchstone intends to be.

This change in the kind of fooling was at least in part a response to fashion. Audiences were beginning to hold Hamlet's opinion of a clown who interrupted the course of the play and spoke more than was set down for him. In *The Pilgrimage to Parnassus*, a university skit on the world of literature, played at Cambridge in 1599, a clown is literally dragged in by a rope (v. 662–9).[1] For Shakespeare there was a double problem, since in 1599 the company lost their old comedian, who had been with them from their inception, and acquired a new one.

Will Kempe, the leading clown of the Chamberlain's Men, left them some time early in 1599, just as they were moving into the Globe Theatre.[2] His name is printed in the cast of Jonson's *Every Man in his Humour* (1598) and not in the cast of *Every Man out of his Humour* (1599). Thinking of the Globe, he says in his autobiographical *Nine Daies Wonder* (SR 22 April, 1600) 'I haue daunst my selfe out of the world.' He does not say why. He was replaced eventually by Robert Armin, a comedian with different gifts, including a good singing voice.[3] For Armin, Shakespeare

---

1 *The Three Parnassus Plays*, ed. J. B. Leishman (1949).

2 E. K. Chambers, *The Elizabethan Stage* (1923), II, p. 326.

3 On Armin, see T. W. Baldwin, 'Shakespeare's jester', *Modern Language Notes*, XXXIX (1924), pp. 447–55; L. Hotson, *Shakespeare's Motley* (1952), chapter 7; C. S. Felver, 'Robert Armin, Shakespeare's source for Touchstone',

created jester's parts, such as the Fool in *Lear*, Lavache in *All's Well*, Feste in *Twelfth Night*, and Trinculo in *The Tempest*. Armin, however, was quite capable of taking over Kempe's parts, and there is evidence that he played Dogberry in a revival of *Much Ado*. He was brought up to be a goldsmith and describes himself so in his will. He was an educated and intelligent man, who wrote plays and pamphlets. He had acted in his own play, *Two Maids of More-clacke*, before he joined the Chamberlain's Company. A sentence in *The Second Part of Tarlton's Jests* places him 'at the Globe on the Bank side' some time before 4 August, 1600, when the play was entered in SR. In two of his pamphlets, *Quips upon Questions* and *Foole upon Foole*, printed in that year, he describes himself as *Clunnyco de Curtanio Snuffe* (Snuffe the clown of the Curtain). Not until the 1605 edition of *Foole upon Foole* does he appear as *Clonnico del mondo* (clown of the Globe). His biographer, C. S. Felver, assigns the composition of *Quips upon Questions* to 1599, explaining the date clue on the title page, 'clapt vp by a Clown of the towne in this last restraint', as a reference to some special and otherwise unrecorded restraint on the theatres in that year, perhaps in consequence of the war with Spain. T. W. Baldwin, who was the first to assign the pamphlet correctly to Armin, takes it to refer to the usual closing of the theatres for Lent, in this instance Lent 1600. With the principal clown engaged at the Curtain, he cannot see how *As You Like It* could have been played before the summer of 1600, the year in which it is entered in the Stationers' Register, under 4 August.[1] If, however, the company acting at the Curtain were in fact the Chamberlain's Men, Armin can be confidently assigned to them as their clown. E. K. Chambers, using Armin's title pages as part of his evidence, locates them at the Curtain from October 1597 till the autumn of 1599, when it is generally agreed they opened at the Globe.[2] Had Armin's pamphlets been entered in the Stationers' Register, there would be further evidence as to the date of composition, as distinct from that of printing, but they were not.

To the question whether Touchstone was Shakespeare's first attempt at a part to suit Armin, or whether he wrote some or all

Shakespeare Quarterly, VII (1956), pp. 135–7 and 'Robert Armin, Shakespeare's fool. A biographical essay', Kent State University Research Series No. 5 (1961); M. C. Bradbrook, *Shakespeare the Craftsman* (1969), chapter 4, 'The new clown', pp. 49–74.

1 'Shakespeare's jester: the dates of *Much Ado* and *As You Like It*', *Modern Language Notes*, XXXIX (1924), pp. 447–55.

2 E. K. Chambers, *The Elizabethan Stage*, II, pp. 402 and 405.

of it while Kempe was still available, it is impossible to give a
definite answer. Kempe could have played Touchstone. There is
much that suggests his style—the conversation with himself about
horns, for instance, at III. iii. 42–57, which is reminiscent of the self-
colloquies of Launce in *The Two Gentlemen of Verona* and of
Launcelot Gobbo in *The Merchant of Venice*. On the other hand,
Muriel Bradbrook finds his catechisms typical of Armin, notably
the scene with Corin at III. ii. She also notes that Armin's fools
attended on ladies rather than lords, which fits Touchstone.
In *Two Maids of More-clacke* Tutch, the fool, is turned out of service
for fidelity to his young mistress.[1] The early descriptions of Touchstone as 'the clownish fool' and 'the roynish clown' introduce him
as a rather uncouth character, and not at all as a sophisticated
jester, such as Feste is. Rosalind calls him a natural, but Douce
argues that this is merely for the sake of a play on nature and natural
wits.[2] He does not, however, live up to this description. He is undoubtedly a trained court jester with an excellent repertoire. He
never falls back on the clown's trick of 'mistaking his words',
common in Kempe characters and at its best in Dogberry. An
uncertainty on Shakespeare's part as to what actor he was writing
for may go some way towards explaining inconsistencies.

It is surprising that in a play which is filled with songs none is
given to the jester. It is doubtful whether Touchstone sings when
he mocks Martext with a ballad-snatch at III. iii. 90 and he almost
certainly doesn't join the two pages, at v. iii. 14, in what seems to
have been an unaccompanied canzonet for two voices. Felver
thinks that Armin may have doubled the parts of Touchstone and
Amiens, a situation in which it would have been unwise to endow
them both with the same, instantly recognizable singing voice.[3]
Armin had done some spectacular doubling in his own *Two Maids
of More-clacke*, playing a half-wit called Blue John, a jester called
Tutch, Tutch disguised as Blue John, and Tutch as a Welshman.
Doubling was, in any case, something that was expected of a
competent actor. Touchstone's long coat, the livery of the
acknowledged fool, would make changes of costume easy. Amiens
and Touchstone are never on the stage at the same time, except
in the last scene of the play, when Amiens is given an entrance by
name but has nothing to say. It is conceivable that Armin joined
the company as a singer and not, at first, as a clown, in which case

1 Bradbrook, op. cit., pp. 55, 57.
2 F. Douce, *Illustrations of Shakespeare* (1807), I, p. 292.
3 Felver, op. cit., p. 45.

he and Kempe may have played side by side, before Kempe danced himself out of the world. The resemblance between the names Armin and Amiens would not have been obvious in the sixteenth century because of the rolled *r* in Armin.

Touchstone wears the common garment of the fool which, whether he was a court jester or just the weak intellect in the family, was a child's long coat. His immaturity kept him in this for life. It was gathered at the waist and fell in voluminous folds below the knee. There was a certain practicality about the dress, which was made of a coarse woollen material, warm and hard-wearing. An indulgent affection added such things as would please a child, a bauble, bells on the sleeves, a cap with a cockscomb or feather. Wherever he wandered, the fool was known for what he was, mocked, perhaps, but also protected. If he was an allowed fool, kept to entertain a court or noble household, this was his livery. It was imaginatively designed, as can be seen in the portraits of court fools, but it was not, as the stage has so long believed, a short tunic divided in colour down the middle with stockings that reverse the two colours. The particolour of the fool's motley was in the weave of the material, and not in the cut of the coat.[1] Favourite colours for a fool were green and yellow, emblematic of his unripe intellect, and doubtless cheap, fast dyes. It appears from an article by E. W. Ives that Hotson was mistaken in supposing that the colours were mingled in the subtle and unemphatic style of modern tweeds, which require advanced manufacturing techniques.[2] They were arranged in stripes or checks or any other simple pattern that can be produced with yarns of two colours on a hand-loom. Thus a fool's costume, often described as pied, patched, or particoloured, could be very fantastic. It seems likely that Touchstone at court cut a startling figure. In Arden he may have been more sober. He was well enough dressed to be treated as a gentleman, an irony used by Armin in *Fool upon Fool*, when he related how Henry VIII's famous fool was saluted by the poor people, 'taking him for a worthy personage, which pleased him'.[3]

iv *The country clowns*

William and Audrey are true clowns, awkward and ignorant, though indulgently treated by their creator. Geoffrey Bullough

1 L. Hotson, *Shakespeare's Motley* (1952), chapter 1.
2 'Tom Skelton—a seventeenth-century jester', *Shakespeare Survey 13* (1960), pp. 90–105.   3 Hotson, op. cit.

suggests that they may derive from an old play called *The Historie of Sir Clyomon and . . . Clamydes*, which was belatedly published in 1599.[1] In it, a princess, escaping in disguise from an undesired suitor, serves a shepherd called Corin, as his boy, and all the maids fall in love with her. Corin speaks in a broad dialect and the matter of his rambling talk is equally unrefined.

> But tis as world to zee what mery lives we shepheards lead,
> Why were Gentlemen and we get once a thorne, bush over
>   our head,
> We may sleep with our vaces against the zone, and were hogs
> Bath our selves, stretch our legs ant were a cennell of dogs:
> And then at night when maides come to milkin, the games
>   begin,
> But I may zay to you, my nabor *Hodges* maid had a clap,
>   wel let them laugh that win.
> Chave but one daughter, but chould not vor vorty pence
>   she were zo sped.[2]

This is far removed from Shakespeare's serious, decent Corin. Nor is it like William and Audrey. Audrey is an obsessively moral girl. 'I do not know what poetical is. Is it honest in deed and word? Is it a true thing?' It was surely she who insisted on a wedding. William, in terror of his life, still clings desperately to his manners and his forelock. 'God rest you merry, sir.' The town has always tended to see the country as comical. Actually Shakespeare spares his Corin even the mild fun that Lodge extorts from Corydon's awkwardness in fine company. Corin has a natural dignity. The awkwardness is concentrated in William and Audrey. If he had needed precedent for bringing comically bucolic characters into a pastoral, Shakespeare could have found it in the shepherd Dametas and his uncouth wife and daughter in Sidney's *Arcadia*. Indeed he had models in his own Costard and Jaquenetta, who are such a contrast to the elegance of the courtly characters in *Love's Labour's Lost*.

v *Love's Labour's Lost* and *The Two Gentlemen of Verona*

There are a number of parallels between *Love's Labour's Lost* and *As You Like It*.[3] The formal setting-to-partners of the four or five couples, and a plot of conversation rather than action, invite

---

1 *Narrative and Dramatic Sources of Shakespeare* (1958), II, pp. 155–7.

2 B. J. Littleton ed (1968), XV, ll. 1293ff.

3 See J. Dover Wilson, *Shakespeare's Happy Comedies* (1969), pp. 159–60 and G. K. Hunter, *John Lyly* (1962), p. 342.

comparison between the plays. Resemblances include the clever, mocking ladies (one of them called Rosaline), the young men's lyrics and their quadruple love-capers, and the hunting scene in the park. Costard has something of Touchstone in his determined, earthy good sense, and his wooing of Jaquenetta is reminiscent of Touchstone and Audrey, though they are better matched. The incongruity comes when Armado confesses his love for Jaquenetta. Armado's distinctive, quirky character stands out among the rest rather as Jaques's does. His pedantic rhetoric recalls Touchstone. At the end of both plays a scene of festivity is unexpectedly interrupted by news which changes the immediate future of most of the *dramatis personae*. G. K. Hunter claims that the plays have similar themes of affectation versus naturalness. He sums up the differences as a more delicate discrimination, a deeper emotional involvement, and the old formal patterns used differently.

An even earlier play parallels *As You Like It* quite strikingly at two points in the text, as well as repeating the theme of escape to the greenwood. At the beginning of *The Two Gentlemen of Verona* v. iv. 1–6, Valentine meditates on his life as a banished man, recalling (1) Duke Senior's 'uses of adversity' (*AYL* II. i. 1–17); (2) Orlando's description of Arden as 'this desert inaccessible' where the Duke and his company are living 'Under the shade of melancholy boughs' (*AYL* II. vii. 111), and Amiens 'turns' his note 'unto the sweet bird's throat' (*AYL* II. v. 4).

> How use doth breed a habit in a man!
> This shadowy desert, unfrequented woods,
> I better brook than flourishing peopled towns:
> Here I can sit alone, unseen of any,
> And to the nightingale's complaining notes
> Tune my distresses.

A similar situation has called up a similar response in the author, and Harold Brooks has shown that he turned to the same source, Seneca's *Hippolytus*.[1] The other parallel is between the conventional marks to know a lover by, which Speed professes to find in his master at II. i. 17, and which Rosalind fails to find in Orlando at III. ii. 363ff. It is a stock piece of Elizabethan caricature.

vi *Montemayor's* Diana

A major source of Renaissance pastoral romance is the *Diana*

1 See *The Two Gentlemen of Verona*, ed. C. Leech, notes to v. iv.

of the Portuguese, Jorge de Montemayor, published in 1559.[1] Bartholomew Yong completed an English translation from Montemayor's Spanish in May 1583, which was published in 1598. There were two other English translations, one by Thomas Wilson, of which the first book is extant in manuscript, and one by Edward Paston, which has not survived. How Shakespeare came by an English text it is impossible to say, but his knowledge of the work certainly predated 1598. It has been acknowledged as a strong influence on *The Two Gentlemen of Verona* and *A Midsummer Night's Dream*, and probably on *Twelfth Night*, and is traceable in *Macbeth* and *Cymbeline*. Shakespeare had it in mind when Rosalind threatens to 'weep for nothing, like Diana in the fountain'.[2] Diana jilts her constant lover, Syrenus, marries another man with whom she is not happy, and spends much of her time weeping in a pastoral setting of shades and springs. Cervantes, in *The Dogs' Colloquy*, mocks 'the swooning of Sireno and the repentance of Diana', which clearly have no place in a dog's eye view of the world.[3] Cervantes never makes the mistake of seeing the literary pastoral as other than a country of the mind, a place where hyper-refinements of sentiment are possible and even delightful.

Montemayor's characters are not always blind to the comicality of their situation. Selvagia's amused account of a love-tangle in which she is herself involved reminds one strongly of *As You Like It*: 'And it was the strangest thing in the world to heare how *Alanius* sighing saide, Ah my *Ismenia*; and how *Ismenia* saide, Ah my *Montanus*; and how *Montanus* saide, Ah my *Selvagia*; and how *Selvagia* saide, Ah my *Alanius*.'[4] Pastoral lovers are quite capable of laughing, somewhat ruefully, at themselves. G. K. Hunter quotes a similar passage from Sidney's *Arcadia* (Lib. I, chapter 15), though here it is the author who points up the comedy, not one of the actors.[5] J. P. Wickersham Crawford has traced the situation back to the sixth idyll of Moschus.[6] The fact that Silvius and Phebe are displayed in a ridiculous light does not mean that

1 See J. M. Kennedy, *A Critical Edition of Yong's translation of George of Montemayor's 'Diana'* (1968), pp. xliv, xlvii and 1.

2 Paul Reyher, 'Alfred de Vigny, Shakespeare et George de Montemayor' *Revue de l'enseignement des langues vivantes*, XXXVII (1920), pp. 1–4.

3 *Exemplary Stories*, trs. C. A. Jones, Penguin Classics (1972), p. 201.

4 Kennedy, op. cit., p. 42.

5 *John Lyly*, p. 346.

6 'Analogues to the story of Selvagia in Montemayor's *Diana*', *Modern Language Notes* XXIX (1914), pp. 192–4. In the Loeb edition it is Number V: 'Pan loved his neighbour Echo; Echo loved a frisking Satyr; and Satyr, he was head over ears for Lydé' etc.

Shakespeare is satiric. The cross-loves of *A Midsummer Night's Dream*, not easy to think of as a satirical play, are if anything more ridiculous, and significantly both Corin and Puck use the same term to describe them. They are 'fond pageants', the natural comedy of love, the predestinate merry-go-round.

vii *Lyly and the 'love-cure'*

One of the most striking debts that *As You Like It* owes to Lyly is Rosalind's proposed 'love-cure'. This is not a debt he shares with Lodge for it has no parallel in Lodge's story. Rosalind suggests that if Orlando will pretend she is his mistress, she will treat him to such a display of feminine temperament as will give him a permanent distaste for women. It is because this is foreign to her nature that she finds it amusing to threaten Orlando with it, yet there is a grain of truth in it that she values. Orlando must take her for better or worse, and he must, though he does not yet know it, take her as the woman she is, not as the boy she is pretending to be. Mocking at women and at lovers is part of her masculine disguise. Lodge, and possibly Lyly in *Gallathea*,[1] are initially responsible for the situation in which a boy-girl initiates a courtship. On the part of Lodge's Rosalynde it is pure play. It takes the form of a sentimental wooing eclogue, which ends in a 'marriage', in which Aliena says she will play the priest, but in which no such binding words are spoken as Shakespeare's Rosalind extorts from Orlando.

As soon as they had taken their repast, Rosader, giving them thanks for his good cheer, would have been gone; but Ganymede, that was loath to let him pass out of her presence, began thus:

'Nay, forester', quoth he, 'if thy business be not the greater, seeing thou sayest thou art so deeply in love, let me see how thou canst woo: I will represent Rosalynde, and thou shalt be as thou art, Rosader. See in some amorous eclogue, how if Rosalynde were present, how thou couldst court her: and while we sing of love, Aliena shall tune her pipe and play us melody.'

'Content', quoth Rosader, and Aliena, she, to shew her willingness, drew forth a recorder, and began to wind it. Then the loving forester began thus.

The exchange of verses occupies five lengthy stanzas, in which the mock-Rosalynde's coyness is overcome.

When thus they had finished their courting eclogue in such a

1 See p. lxiii below.

familiar clause, Ganymede, as augur of some good fortunes to light upon their affections, began to be thus pleasant:

'How now, forester, have I fitted your turn? Have I not played the woman handsomely, and shewed myself as coy in grants as courteous in desires, and been as full of suspicion as men of flattery? and yet to salve all, jumped I not all up with the sweet union of love? Did not Rosalynde content her Rosader?'

The forester at this smiling, shook his head, and folding his arms made this merry reply:

'Truth, gentle swain, Rosader hath his Rosalynde; but as Ixion had Juno, who, thinking to possess a goddess, only embraced a cloud: in these imaginary fruitions of fancy, I resemble the birds that fed themselves with Zeuxis' painted grapes; but they grew so lean with pecking at shadows, that they were glad, with Aesop's cock, to scrape for a barley cornel. So fareth it with me, who to feed myself with the hope of my mistress's favours, sooth myself in thy suits, and only in conceit reap a wished-for content; but if my food be no better than such amorous dreams, Venus at the year's end shall find me but a lean lover. Yet do I take these follies for high fortunes, and hope these feigned affections do divine some unfeigned end of ensuing fancies.'

'And thereupon', quoth Aliena, 'I'll play the priest: from this day forth Ganymede shall call thee husband, and thou shall call Ganymede wife, and so we'll have a marriage.'

'Content', quoth Rosader, and laughed.

'Content', quoth Ganymede, and changed as red as a rose: and so with a smile and a blush, they made up this jesting match, that after proved to a marriage in earnest, Rosader full little thinking he had wooed and won his Rosalynde.

But all was well: hope is a sweet thing to harp on, and therefore let the forester awhile shape himself to his shadow, and tarry fortune's leisure, till she may make a metamorphosis fit for his purpose. I digress: and therefore to Aliena, who said, the wedding was not worth a pin, unless there were some cheer, nor that bargain well made that was not stricken up with a cup of wine: and therefore she willed Ganymede to set out such cates as they had, and to draw out her bottle, charging the forester, as he had imagined his loves, so to conceit these cates to be a most sumptuous banquet, and to take a mazer of wine and to drink to his Rosalynde; which Rosader did, and so they passed away the day in many pleasant devices. Till at last Aliena perceived time would tarry no man, and that the sun waxed very low, ready to set, which made her shorten their amorous prattle, and end the banquet with a fresh carouse; which done, they all three arose. . . .

One of the things Shakespeare keeps is the human touch, in that Rosalind's game is clearly designed to hold Orlando in her company, but it is by no means the game that is played by Lodge's young folk, whose fun is carefully underlined by the author with words like 'smiling' and 'merry', to ensure that the reader takes it as it is meant. 'Love is merely a madness', says Rosalind, 'and I tell you deserves as well a dark house and a whip as madmen do: and the reason why they are not so punished and cured is that the lunacy is so ordinary that the whippers are in love too.' To Orlando's inquiry 'Did you ever cure any so?' she replies:

Yes, one, and in this manner. He was to imagine me his love, his mistress; and I set him every day to woo me. At which time would I, being but a moonish youth, grieve, be effeminate, changeable, longing and liking, proud, fantastical, apish, shallow, inconstant, full of tears, full of smiles, for every passion something and for no passion truly anything, as boys and women are for the most part cattle of this colour: would now like him, now loathe him; then entertain him, then forswear him; now weep for him, then spit at him; that I drave my suitor from his mad humour of love to a living humour of madness, which was, to forswear the full stream of the world and to live in a nook merely monastic. And thus I cured him, and this way will I take upon me to wash your liver as clean as a sound sheep's heart, that there shall not be one spot of love in't.

The key word here, which points to Lyly, is 'moonish', meaning inconstant. In 1597 Lyly's only verse play, *The Woman in the Moon*, appeared in quarto. It had been entered in SR in 1595. It is genuinely amusing in many ways, but does not at first suggest Shakespeare, except in its pastoral idiom and the Lylyan touch observable in much of Shakespeare's early comedy.

Lyly's play begins in a Utopia inhabited solely by shepherds, who implore Nature to provide a female of their kind. Nature creates Pandora, robbing each of the planets to ensure that she shall be 'composed of every heavenly excellence' (cf. *AYL* iii ii. 135-49). The angry planets take it in turn to subject her to their influence, to which she responds with complete automatism. Her shepherd lovers never know in what mood they will find her next, reflecting in expanded action the way in which Rosalind promises to treat Orlando. In the end it is not they who are driven mad, though they are cured of love. Under the influence of Luna, Pandora becomes lunatic. Nature declares that she shall be placed permanently in the sphere of one planet, but she evades the threatened constancy. She chooses the moon, for

> *Cynthia* made me idle, mutable,
> Forgetfull, foolish, fickle, franticke, madde;
> These be the humours that content me best,
> And therefore I will stay with *Cynthia*.

So Nature places Woman in the moon.

> Now rule, *Pandora*, in fayre Cynthias steede,
> And make the moone inconstant like thy selfe;
> Raigne thou at women's nuptials, and their birth;
> Let them be mutable in all their loues,
> Fantasticall, childish, and foolish in their desires,
> Demanding toyes:
> And starke madde when they cannot haue their will.

The formalism of some of the dialogue in *As You Like It*, notably at v. ii. 84ff., with its antiphonal 'And so am I . . .', 'If this be so . . .', can be matched many times in *The Woman in the Moon*. See II. i. 133ff., IV. i. 11ff. and v. i. 276, where the seven planets beg that Pandora may be theirs.

Sat.   O Nature! place Pandora in my sphere,
         For I am old, and she will make me young.
Jup. With me! and I will leaue the Queene of heauen.
Mars. With me! and Venus shall no more be mine.
Sol.   With me! and Ile forget fayre Daphnes loue.
Venus. With me! and ile turne Cupid out of doores.
Mer. With me! and Ile forsake Aglauros loue.

This kind of thing is characteristic enough of Lyly's dramatic style, but is less to be expected in a mature play by Shakespeare.

Other parallels are trivial in themselves or appear in contexts so remote from Shakespeare's that they may hardly seem worth listing, yet they are there to be listed. They chiefly occur in the latter part of Shakespeare's play, beginning with the love-cure at III. ii. Warwick Bond sees a parallel with Lyly's 'sing vnto the wilde birdes note' (II. ii. 168) when Amiens promises to 'turn his merry note / Unto the sweet bird's throat' (*AYL* II. v. 3–4). At III. ii. 270 Lyly has a play on 'incontinent' which Shakespeare plays on with much more point at v. ii. 37–8. In Lyly's second act the shepherds are sent off by Pandora to hunt a boar and at II. i. 180 they come in carrying its head as a trophy (cf. *AYL* IV. ii). In the first scene of Act IV Pandora falls down in a feigned swoon at l. 85 (cf. *AYL* IV. iii. 156) and shortly after sends one of her lovers a 'bloody napkin' (cf. *AYL* IV. iii. 93 and 138) to convince them she has killed herself. Many of Lyly's plays carry reminders of *As You Like It* but none in quite this way, and none so independently of Lodge.

There is good reason to think that Lodge had already gone to Lyly's *Gallathea* (played 1586–7, printed 1592) for some of his cross-loves. In this play two girls, disguised as boys to avoid becoming victims to a sea-monster, fall mutually in love, and their happiness is only achieved when, at the last possible moment, Venus effects a sex-change. The theme can be traced back to Ovid's Iphis and Ianthe (*Metam.* ix, 666–797). The virgin sacrifice was common in Italian pastoral drama and the love of two girls, made viable by a sex-change, in Italian Renaissance comedy (see A. B. Lancashire, *Gallathea*, 1970, p. xvii). At iii. ii. 9–10 one of the girls, conscious of her disguised sex, says to the supposed boy she loves, 'I doe not wish thee to be a woman, for then I should not loue thee, for I haue sworne neuer to loue a woman', an irony which Shakespeare uses when Rosalind sighs 'for no woman'. At iv. iv. the mock-wooing is instituted.

Phil. Seeing we are both boyes, and both louers, that our affection may haue some showe, and seeme as it were loue, let me call thee Mistris.
Galla. I accept that name.

Lyly's plot has less of common humanity than either Lodge's or Shakespeare's, and only a metamorphosis can produce the dénouement. An added complication is the havoc wrought by the supposed boys among Diana's nymphs, who confess their love one after another in a scene (iii. i) so like *LLL* iv, iii that it is plain Shakespeare knew Lyly's play as well as the reflection of it in Lodge. It also parallels the Rosalind/Phebe situation, which Lodge had already borrowed.

Another of Lyly's plays, *Sapho and Phao* (1584), begins with a praise of country life which Shakespeare may have had in mind when he drew the contrast between court and country in *As You Like It*. Whether or no he was remembering this speech, with its celebration of honest toil, freedom from envy and ambition, the comfort of a thatched cottage, and the wind the only enemy, it is an interesting statement of the pastoral ideal, which he must have met in many similar passages in his reading, to be absorbed and reproduced, as he absorbed and reproduced so much of his age's thinking.[1]

1 It is also an example of an elegant and not over-elaborate euphuism by the first of the euphuists.

Phao. Thou art a Ferriman, Phao, yet a free man, possessing for riches content, and for honors quiet. Thy thoughts are no higher then thy fortunes, nor thy desires greater then thy calling. Who climeth, standeth on glasse, and falleth on thorne. Thy hearts thirste is satisfied with thy hands thrift, and thy gentle labours in the day, turne to sweete slumbers in the night. As much doth it delight thee to rule thine oare in a calme streame, as it dooth Sapho to swaye the Scepter in her braue court. Enuie neuer casteth her eie lowe, ambition pointeth alwaies vpwarde, and reuenge barketh onely at starres. Thou farest dilicately, if thou haue a fare to buy any thing. Thine angle is ready, when thine oar is idle, and as sweet is the fish which thou gettest in the ryuer as the fowle which other buye in the market. Thou needst not feare poyson in thy glasse, nor treason in thy garde. The winde is thy greatest enemy, whose might is withstoode with pollicy. O sweete life, seldom found vnder a golden couert, often vnder a thached cottage.

R. B. Sharpe, in *The Real War of the Theatres* (1935), pointed to the publication in 1600 of an anonymous pastoral-mythological play, *The Maydes Metamorphosis*,[1] from the repertory of Paul's Boys, and of Lyly's *Love's Metamorphosis*, in 1601, said to have been performed by the Children of the Chapel Royal. He thinks that the popularity of these pieces influenced Shakespeare to write *As You Like It*, in spite of the fact that pastoral was 'essentially distasteful to him'. In Lyly's play three foresters, a departure from the usual shepherds, woo three disdainful nymphs of Ceres. The setting is wholly artificial, and it is hard to see the ceremonial decking of Ceres' tree with garlands and poetical 'posies' as likely material for parody in *As You Like It*, where the 'odes upon hawthorns and elegies on brambles' are amusing because they appear in a realistic context. Lyly's nymphs and foresters belong to their own self-contained world of sentimental fantasy, which is laughable only when it is mistaken for real. The Renaissance accepted it as serious and delightful, and G. K. Hunter declares *Love's Metamorphosis* 'one of the best of Lyly's plays' (op. cit., p. 206).

The Maydes Metamorphosis alternates rhymed couplets with songs and comic prose, and tells a story of adventure in which gods and mortals mingle. There are flickers in the tale's entanglements which make one think of Shakespeare, and of Lodge as well, since they are a common currency of pastoral romance. The heroine is forced from the court of Duke Telemachus because the young prince has fallen in love with her and she is of 'meane

1 *Works* of Lyly, ed. W. Bond, III.

discent'. She is wooed in her retirement by a shepherd and a forester and finally by Apollo himself. She escapes the god only when he honours the request he has promised to grant her. She asks him to turn her literally into a man. He is angry that she has eluded him and a curse goes with the gift.

> And though thou walke in chaunged bodie now,
> This pennance shall be added to thy vow:
> Thy selfe a man, shalt loue a man, in vaine:
> And louing, wish to be a maide againe.[1]
>
> III. i. 225–8.

Happily her princely lover recognizes her despite her metamorphosis and when he interests the Muses in his plight, they persuade Apollo to restore her to him in her true shape. The woodland hermit, who tells the prince where to look for the missing maiden, is himself a prince in exile. Apollo reveals that he is the girl's father and she becomes an eligible bride.

viii *Nomenclature*

Shakespeare was already supplied by Lodge with names for many of his characters. The changes he made seem to have been in a search for something short, simple, distinctive, euphonious, and if possible in current use. He rejects the grandiloquent and unfamiliar Torismond and Gerismond which Lodge had taken from Tasso's play *Il Re Torismondo* (1587).[2] The usurping duke has no name in speech headings. He is Frederick in three places in the text, one of them disputable. Shakespeare himself can hardly have been at a loss for a name. He has already found a suitably French name for Dennis, and the girls have a waiting gentlewoman called Hisperia, who is never on stage. It was no part of a scribe's business to provide a name where an author was silent, so the other duke becomes Duke Senior.

Lodge's names for the three brothers, Saladyne, Fernandyne and Rosader, are fantastic. He found Saladyne in Greene's *Penelope's Web* (SR 1587). Rosader, artfully designed to chime with Rosalind, chimes a little too well for a play, where if it caused no other confusion it would make havoc of speech headings. Roland and Oliver were already linked in the legendary history of France. By giving Orlando an alternative form of his father's

---

1 *Works* of Lyly, ed. W. Bond, III.
2 P. A. Burnett, 'Thomas Lodge, *Rosalynde*', unpublished B.Litt. thesis, Oxford, 1968.

name, Shakespeare linked them alliteratively as well. Sisson says Orlando was not infrequent as an English Christian name. The musician Orlando Gibbons bore it, for one. In literature it was familiar from Tasso's *Orlando Furioso* and Greene's play of that name. It is musical and distinctive, with romantic associations, a little out of key with the young man's very unitalianate character. There is no risk of confusing Oliver with Sir Oliver Martext. All the emphasis falls on the parson's significant surname, and in any case he is a very minor character. He may owe his Oliver to Touchstone's snatch of popular song, 'O sweet Oliver', perhaps supplied by the actor, not by the author. An intelligent clown was presumably permitted to make a few spontaneous gestures at rehearsal.

Lodge's pastoral names, Corydon, Montanus and Phoebe, might well have stood unchanged. Phoebe does stand. It has the kind of simplicity Shakespeare seems to have been seeking and its association with Diana fits a cold maiden. As Corin, Corydon is less pretentious. He is an honest, elderly countryman. Theocritus and Virgil had popularized the name Corydon, and Virgil had given it associations of simple rusticity. In Nashe's *Summer's Last Will* (played *c.* 1592), Harvest, coming in with sickle and scythe, is hailed as 'Thou Coridon' (l. 820). But it was inevitably stamped as 'literary'. The name Corin appears in Lyly's *Midas* (1592) and in a play dating back to the seventies, *Sir Clyomon and Clamydes*,[1] first published in 1599. It also recalls Colin, which although it has literary associations could be said to belong to the more realistic side of pastoral. Silvius is a name proper to a woodlander, paralleled by Silvio, the name of the 'ranger' in the anonymous *Maydes Metamorphosis*. It must surely owe something to Montemayor's Sylvanus, who suffered so much at the hands of Diana, and something to the Silvias and Silvios of Sannazaro, Tasso and Guarini. These link it unmistakably with the literary pastoral.

Rosalind keeps the name Lodge gave her, apparently adapted from the Rosmonda of Tasso's *Il Re Torismondo*. It was a favourite with Shakespeare, who had already used it, in the form Rosaline, for Berowne's lady in *Love's Labour's Lost*, and for the object of Romeo's calf-love. It seems from the rhymes in Orlando's verses and in Touchstone's parody that it was pronounced with a long [ai]. Lodge rhymes it with 'mind' and 'unkind'. The modern stage tends to treat Orlando's rhymes as a joke, an ungifted

1 See p. lvi above.

amateur's distortion of normal pronunciation. It is unlikely that they sounded so to an Elizabethan. Shakespeare could find Celia's name in Montemayor, in Lyly's *Love's Metamorphosis*, and doubtless elsewhere. Alinda (apparently the Olynda of Greene's *Penelope's Web*) was not sufficiently distinguished from Rosalinda. He retained Ganymede and Aliena, as having reference to the girls' estates. J. H. Walter sees a significance in the Renaissance equation of Ganymede with intelligence and in particular with wisdom and joy.

In speech headings, Touchstone is regularly Clown, a generic title for the company's comedian, without reference to the particular part he may be playing. The direction 'Clown, alias Touchstone' at his entrance at II. i is not likely to imply a change of name comparable with 'Rosalind for Ganymede and Celia for Aliena'. He has not yet been given a name and it would be a needless complication if he had.[1] 'Touchstone' appears to be an extension of Tutch, the name of the comic servant whom Armin played with great acclaim in his own piece, *Two Maids of Moreclacke*.[2] 'Touch' signifies cotton impregnated with oil, which was used with tinder to get a quick flame. It is also the first element of the 'touchstone' with which jewellers tested the quality of metals, and which became an emblem of their trade. When his plotting is discovered, Tutch says, 'Now am I try'd on my own tutch, O I am true metall one way, but counterfeit another.' As the name by which Armin was introduced to the audience at the Globe, Touchstone was trebly appropriate. Armin had written the part of Tutch, played the part of Tutch, and was by trade a goldsmith.

'Clown' is reserved in stage directions for Touchstone. William always has his name. If William Shakespeare played this small but rewarding part the name becomes a mild theatrical in-joke. W. M. Jones has extracted all and rather more than it is worth from this idea, first suggested by T. W. Baldwin.[3] William and Audrey have no pretensions to be other than English. Audrey's name is an abbreviation of the Anglo-Saxon saint, Etheldreda. Adam's name goes back to Adam the spencer, or steward, in *The Tale of Gamelyn*, and even further, to that gentle labourer in Eden, our unfallen forefather.

1 But cf. p. xii.
2 See L. Hotson, *Shakespeare's Motley*, pp. 114–15 and C. S. Felver, 'Robert Armin. Shakespeare's source for Touchstone', *Shakespeare Quarterly*, VII (1956), pp. 135–7.
3 'William Shakespeare as William in *As You Like It*', *Shakespeare Quarterly*, XI (1960), pp. 228–31.

The name of the melancholy Jaques is disyllabic, Jake-is or Jack-is. Kökeritz favours [dʒeːkis] in preference to the more customary [dʒeikwiz] (p. 330). As an English first name and surname it is a monosyllable and indistinguishable from Elizabethan jakes = a privy. When he gave it a French accentuation, appropriate to the play, Shakespeare avoided an otherwise irresistible quibble. Touchstone does not resist it. His 'Good master What-ye-call't' at iii. iii. 66 is the only time the name is punned on throughout the play. Evidence of disyllabic pronunciation is supplied at ii. i. 26: 'The melancholy Jaques grieves at that' and at v. iv. 193: 'Stay, Jaques, stay'. There is a similar instance in *LLL* ii. i. 42. It is worth comparing the way the French name Parolles is treated in *All's Well*, where it is a trisyllable. This does not mean that either name is to be pronounced precisely in the French manner. The pronunciation is anglicized, but not to the point of sacrificing the final syllable. Greene uses Jaques in *James IV* as the name of a comic French bravo and constantly incorporates it in heavily stressed verse. Grotesque and unsympathetic as he is, Greene's character is spared any vulgar jesting on his name. The resemblance to jakes did not apparently strike Elizabethan ears. In Greene's *Friar Bacon and Friar Bungay* both spelling and metre point to a disyllable, e.g. ii. iv. 815–16: 'a Germane of esteeme, / Whose surname is Don Iaquesse Vandermast' and iii. ii. 1095: 'What is thy iudgment, Iaquis Vandermast'. Nineteenth-century players seem to have popularized the pronunciation Jakewiss or Jakeweez, because they and their audiences were all too conscious of the meaning of jakes.

In so far as prose rhythms are discernible, it would seem that the name of Jaques de Boys is pronounced in the English way on the one occasion when it is mentioned, at i. i. 5: 'My brother Jaques he keeps at school.' If this is so, it clears Shakespeare of a maladroit duplication of names. If, on the other hand, the names by some oversight were identical, there is little harm done. When Jaques de Boys comes on at the end of the play, by which time the audience is familiar with the other Jaques, he is called Second Brother and announces himself simply and clearly, 'I am the second son of old Sir Rowland'.

Shakespeare is responsible for Amiens, Le Beau and De Boys, all genuine French names. There was a family named De Boys at Weston-in-Arden in the middle ages, and Sisson has found the name in London in Shakespeare's time.

The title of the play is typically Shakespearian, titillating the audience, giving nothing away, promising pleasure, avoiding pretension, and gently soliciting approval by implying that approval is important. It closely parallels *What You Will*, the alternative title of *Twelfth Night*. It is generally supposed to have its source in a casual phrase used by Lodge in his address to the readers of his *Rosalynde*, 'If you like it, so' (Greg, p. xxix). It is particularly suited to the do-as-you-please atmosphere of Arden, a place where a very mixed collection of people very happily go their own various ways. Bernard Shaw, to whom romantic comedy was antipathetic, fancies Shakespeare flinging it contemptuously in the face of his audience, indicating that the play is a specimen of the kind of 'pleasant and cheap falsehood' they enjoyed, 'one of the most effective samples of romantic nonsense in existence'.[1] He at least pays tribute to its effectiveness and takes the trouble to try and solve the riddle of its title.

IV. PEOPLE AND THEMES

As You Like It is a pastoral play but it does not confine the simple life to keeping sheep. The native inhabitants of Arden are shepherds. The banished Duke and his followers are outlaws, camping in caves. About the Duke's pursuits there is an aristocratic air and a good deal of the holiday spirit. He must frequently have hunted for recreation where now he hunts to live. Peter Alexander says that he introduces 'a Sherwood Forest note of independence and natural justice that protects, as it were, the pastoral peace of the shepherds'.[2] It has become a critical commonplace that his pleasure in the wild woods is an object of Shakespeare's satire, an affectation. He may say he is enjoying himself, but we know better. At the end of the play he and all his company return 'with a most ingenuous alacrity' to the life they had abjured forever.[3] 'I would not change it', says Amiens, and then he does. Touchstone had the rights of it after all. 'Now am I in Arden, the more fool I. When I was at home I was in a better

---

1 *London Daily News*, 17 April 1905, reprinted in *Shaw on Shakespeare* ed. E. Wilson, 1962, p. 1.

2 *Shakespeare's Life and Art* (1939), p. 133.

3 J. Palmer, *Comic Characters of Shakespeare* (1946), p. 42. W. H. Auden, 'Music in Shakespeare', *Encounter* IX (1957), finds the Duke 'a bit of a humbug', since the life he praises was not of his own choosing. R. B. Pierce in 'The moral language of Rosalynde and *As You Like It*', *Studies in Philology* LXVIII (1971), p. 73, says 'both smugness and contrivance come through his first speech'. M. Taylor, in '*As You Like It*: the penalty of Adam', *Critical Quarterly* XV (1973), p. 76, declares it 'a bathetic expansion of impulses from a vernal wood'.

place.' There is a return to good sense and normality comparable with the break up of Navarre's 'little Academe' at the end of *Love's Labour's Lost*.

To argue so is to overlook some basic discrepancies. The refugees who flee to Arden are escaping but they are not escapists. They have death at their heels and old Adam barely survives. The references to the hardships of life lived close to nature are not there to show up the folly of the Duke, as though the audience knows something he does not. It is he who has endured shrewd days and nights and owns it. Arden makes demands on both physical and moral courage. Its virtue is that it is free from human malice; the worst it can show is winter and rough weather, and these furnish matter for the Duke's gentle philosophy and for the songs of Amiens. The best pastoral has always been aware of the weather, and of harder things, that nobody in *As You Like It* is called upon to endure, though Adam narrowly escapes. Life in Arden is natural and happy and wholesome and all good men flourish there. One after another the refugees from the world's unkindness arrive drooping and the forest revives them. The Duke is already established, so with him we do not actually see the process of acclimatization. We are not to dismiss the speaker as a tedious bore, who perhaps deserved to lose his dukedom. At the end of the play the company return refreshed and invigorated to take up their ordinary duties, after what has been a life-enhancing and not a self-deluding interlude. The fact that they return so promptly and so cheerfully is what validates their experience. It would be time to look for satire if they had not done so. Their feeling, so long as they are in Arden, that it is wonderful, and that they wouldn't mind if it went on for ever, is simply a holiday feeling and can raise only the shadow of a smile at their expense. It is entirely right and natural.

So far the tale has dispensed with supernatural assistance, and all it will ever have is Rosalind's make-believe at the end. Yet 'the circle of this forest' is a magic circle even though the magic does not take material forms as it does in *A Midsummer Night's Dream* and *The Tempest*. The power of Arden to heal may be referred to fresh air and happy accidents. Its power to convert surpasses nature. When Oliver enters its confines he completely changes his character and in the twinkling of an eye becomes a fit lover for Celia. The usurping Duke fails even to enter. He lets fall his weapons as though there were some invisible barrier which evil cannot pass. This is the point at which we must acknowledge that we are in the world of Shakespearian romance, and by now we should be conditioned to accept it, however strange. We have been watching something very like it actually happen before our eyes. At the end we are asked to take it on trust, 'and greater wonders yet', the Masque of Hymen, which momentarily crystallizes the ideal patterns and declares them not only to be happy but holy.

Walter R. Davis has described the pastoral pattern, in relation to Sidney's *Arcadia*, in a way which is equally applicable to *As You Like It*:

The heroes of the Renaissance pastoral romances are always *sojourners* in the Arcadian preserve, never native shepherds. This fact, together with the continuing contrast between the pastoral land and other places necessary to exhibit its meaning, makes the settings of the Renaissance pastoral romances always *multiple*. The pattern formed by the subdivisions of this setting may be graphically if roughly imaged as a center with two concentric circles surrounding it, implying a kind of purification of life proceeding inward; from the gross and turbulently naturalistic outer circle, to the refined pastoral inner circle, and then to the pure center of the world. The center is always supernatural, usually either a shrine like the Cave of the Nymphs or the dwelling of a magician. It may be the actual dwelling place of the god.[1]

Jaques has another way of putting it: 'Sure', he says, 'there is another Flood towards, and all these couples are coming to the ark.'

However audiences may take them, readers, who have more time for thought, have seldom been altogether happy about the rapid conversions at the end of *As You Like It*. We have been aware of no principle of goodness in the persons concerned from which they might come, though in retrospect we must accept that it was there. That nature, the character we are born with, can master fortune, wresting some kind of compensation from the most unfavourable circumstances, is the subject of a perceptive essay by John Shaw.[2] The first arrivals do something to deserve their good fortune. Duke Senior has been wronged. *The Tempest* gives an inkling of how Prospero came to lose his dukedom. In *As You Like It* it is a datum. Shakespeare is not interested in how the Duke came to lose his dukedom but in how little he regretted it. There is no dejection or repining. The Duke makes the best of his situation, exerting a virtue highly regarded in a century when

1 *A Map of Arcadia. Sidney's Romance in its Tradition* (1965), pp. 34, 35.
2 'Fortune and nature in *As You Like It*', *Shakespeare Quarterly*, VI (1955), pp. 45–50.

misfortunes of all sorts were less remediable than they are now. He summons patience to meet his troubles, and he is at once rewarded. He finds he is enjoying himself.

Rosalind, like her father, is deprived of her rightful inheritance and the life to which she is accustomed. In Arden she finds her freedom. She is no longer living on sufferance at the usurper's court, and in doublet and hose she is no longer confined to a woman's limited role. Her own temperament frees her from the restrictions of romantic love-cults. 'Men have died from time to time and worms have eaten them, but not for love.' This does not mean that she is in the least destructive of love itself or resentful of its compulsive tides, in which she is happily drowning. Rosalind, says Mark Van Doren, has found that 'there is only one thing sillier than being in love, and that is thinking it silly to be in love'.[1] What she will not countenance is an affected and humourless intensity, the besetting fault of Elizabethan love-cults. Once in the forest, it is she who takes control—even of her father, to whom she makes herself known in her own good time—and Shakespeare puts the dénouement into her capable hands. Without her earlier misfortunes she might seem almost too managing, but when we first meet her she is sad, so that it is a pleasure to watch her spirits bubble up. She comes into her own and into a better heritage than she has lost.

Orlando is deprived in much the same way and that is why the two waifs drift together, drawn by a natural sympathy. He is not one of Shakespeare's usual comedy heroes, those well-found and rather exquisite young men, Bassanio, Orsino, Claudio and Bertram. He has none of the sharp wit Benedick shares with Berowne, nor their irrepressible itch to be talking. He is a very English young man, who prefers wrestling to rapier, who is down on his luck, and who is tender to subordinates. He falls in love at first sight, writes indifferent verses, and is led by the nose by a clever girl, who will see to it that nobody else ever gets the better of him. He comes from the folk-tale of Gamelyn and not from a polished novella. This helps to ensure that the love-play of what Lodge calls 'the amorous boy-girl', however sexually ambiguous, can give no offence. The relation between Ganymede and Orlando is deliciously but not perilously balanced. In any case, the play is so busy with love that it has little or no time for sex.

The goodness and loyalty of old Adam are his passport to

1 *Shakespeare* (1941), p. 159.

Arden. He has lived by its values all his life, no benefits forgot. The part can be very touching when it is well played. It was traditionally Shakespeare's. Capell reported the tradition, in his *Notes to Shakespeare* I, i, 1774, as current then in Stratford. Steevens supported it in 1778, from the papers of the eighteenth-century antiquary, William Oldys.[1] According to Oldys a younger brother of Shakespeare, asked at an advanced age what he could remember about him, and doubtless pressed hard, dredged up some dim recollection of seeing him on the stage. The hearers identified the play as *As You Like It* and the part as Adam, after which they may very well have tailored their reports to fit more exactly, for they fit suspiciously well. The old man, says Oldys, produced

the faint, general, and almost lost ideas he had of having once seen [his brother] act a part in one of his own comedies, which being to personate a decrepit old man, he wore a long beard, and appeared so weak and drooping and unable to walk, that he was forced to be supported and carried by another person to a table, at which he was seated among some company, who were eating, and one of them sung a song.

Celia, like Adam, also wins her right of entry by unselfishness and loyalty. Once in the forest she has the important function, which only she can perform, of displaying Rosalind in her double character of pretended boy and true girl. Her pulling of her cousin's feathers is one way in which the boy-girl cockiness is muted into something acceptable in a woman. Celia can make the retorts Orlando cannot and is the one person whom Rosalind does not command. When she wins Oliver we must assume she has won a prize. She has earned one.

Touchstone enters by virtue of his invincible good humour. The girls think he will be useful to them on their travels. His arm is strong, however weak his head, and they sorely need a real man in the party. Since he is a person in a play we can have no psychologist's report on his mental capacity. When he raises a laugh by pseudo-syllogisms the laughter is all the play demands. We are not to reflect that nobody could be so outrageously illogical without being a bit of a logician. It is Shakespeare's wit that gives Touchstone something entertaining to say, just as it is Shakespeare's metrical skill that supplies blank verse to his characters. They are not poets in their own right, and Touchstone is not as clever as his creator.

1 See E. K. Chambers, *Shakespeare*, II, pp. 278–9, 289.

The origin of the role of the 'allowed fool' or licensed jester goes back to a time when a fool's low mentality was what earned him his place as a kind of household pet. He was dressed and indulged like a child, ordered about, scolded, and punished like a child, and protected from the full stream of a world too hard for him to meet on ordinary terms. He was not incapable of exploiting his own gift for raising laughter. To hold a place at court he had to be in effect a professional entertainer. Touchstone has his own kind of shrewdness, and his jester's skills, of which he is justly proud, but the play labels him fool and very rarely asks us to think of him otherwise. Rosalind calls him on his first entrance 'Nature's natural'. Later he is 'the clownish fool'. To a member of Duke Frederick's retinue, not perhaps in the best of tempers, he is 'the roynish clown'. Jaques recognizes him by his dress as 'a motley fool' and is amused by his pretensions to learning, his 'strange places cramm'd / With observation, the which he vents / In mangl'd forms'. Valuing him rather as one might value a parrot with an altogether exceptional vocabulary, he affords him exactly the benevolent, protective guidance appropriate to a weaker intellect. His warning, 'thy loving voyage / Is but for six months victualled', rings uncomfortably true.

Touchstone is sufficiently three-dimensional to satisfy the requirements of the play and to give an actor scope to exert comic charm. Audiences like him, but as a person he will not stand up to much investigation. He is a functional character and his function is to play the fool. Many commentators, struck by his name, give him an important part as a critic within the play.[1] His prosaic common sense and the momentarily deflating effect of his wit are a gauge by which others are measured and found wanting. 'He *tests* all that the world takes for gold, especially the gold of the golden world of pastoralism.'[2] Fair comment enough, provided it is allowed that the golden world stands the test, just as Prospero's island stands the drunken tramplings of Trinculo and Stephano, proving thereby that it is firmly founded. Arden absorbs Touchstone quite happily. After all, it bred William and Audrey. It does not dissolve when he enters it. To argue that his touch shows the gold counterfeit is another matter. The pastoral world is no more disturbed when he announces that his legs are weary than

---

[1] E.g. E. Welsford, *The Fool* (1935), p. 249, J. Palmer, *Comic Characters of Shakespeare* (1946), p. 35, and F. W. Sternfeld, *Music in Shakespearian Tragedy* (1963), p. 110.

[2] J. D. Wilson, *Shakespeare's Happy Comedies* (1962), p. 156.

when the Duke admits that he has shrunk with cold. As for 'when I was at home I was in a better place', that is possibly true for Touchstone—even Lear's devoted fool would have compromised for 'court holy water in a dry house'—but it is not, for so long as their story extends, true for anybody else in the play. If it were a straight statement of fact it would cease to be funny. His measured answer to Corin's 'How like you this shepherd's life, Master Touchstone?' is a piece of elaborate nonsense, designed upon probing to burst like a toy balloon. It appears to have a meaning, in that it is structured significantly, but in point of fact it has none, since the key words are not antithetical. It is comparable with the sham logic with which he blinds William. His joke about the 'old cuckoldly ram' in no way invalidates Corin's statement of the shepherd's creed. His bawdy couplets, his wooing of Jane Smile, his admission that 'wedlock would be nibbling' are not Shakespeare's bold assertion of biological fact in the face of romantic fancy. When Jaques warns him against the ignorant Sir Oliver, 'this fellow will but join you together as they join wainscot', his sly aside that there are advantages in a wedding ceremony irregularly conducted is not to be taken as an attack on the institution of marriage.

The values of romantic love, which are what the play endorses, are strengthened rather than undermined by the presence of Touchstone. His prose acts as a foil to the poetry. The mistake is to suppose that in a play called *As You Like It* either one is meant to be destructive of the other. No affectation could survive the fool's eye view, which infallibly sees and says when the emperor has no clothes, but Touchstone, as satirist, is not required in Arden. All is well there. His part in the play can be summed very adequately by saying that among courtly persons he appears awkward and among country people he appears courtly. This is not satire. It is an agreeable exploitation of incongruities. Touchstone in Arden can enjoy the very great pleasure of giving himself airs. For once, he is among people in some ways simpler than himself. His learning slides off Audrey and terrifies William. He lectures Corin on good manners, though Corin is one of nature's gentlemen, and receives with complacency the title of Master Touchstone. When, on the other hand, he is with Celia and Rosalind and the talk is of love, he abandons his pretensions to refinement and remembers Jane Smile and the kissing of the cow's dugs her pretty chapped hands have milked. He knows, with the accuracy of the *enfant terrible*, what is the inappropriate thing to say. He brings a note of humanity into the usurper's court when he inquires since when rib-breaking was a sport for ladies, and he justifies his choice of Audrey in the face of Duke Senior, and indeed in the face of all the world. 'An ill-favoured thing, sir, but mine own' is the true wisdom of the Shakespearian fool.

Jaques, when he is with Touchstone, treats him with great courtesy, from which we may deduce that Jaques hits only those who are his own size. He is, in his way, an equally incongruous figure in a pastoral. The pair are complementary. Both are fish out of water in that they are satirists in a milieu proof against satire. In the eyes of the rest of the woodlanders Jaques is a bit of a fool, and he displays a bent for clowning (at II. v) before ever he asks for a motley coat. The experience on which he ruminates is alien to Arden. He is the very essence of sophistication, has experimented with everything and found none of it very good, and he can import his sensitivity to the cruelty and injustice of man's world even into the world of nature. But his shafts fall harmlessly off a company who are armoured in complete happiness. Nobody troubles to contradict his cynical Seven Ages of Man. The whole atmosphere of the place contradicts it. He has hardly finished, when in comes Orlando supporting old Adam and 'as if to rebuke the melancholy jester . . . old age is found to be not second childishness, but fidelity, loyalty and long-enduring affection'.[1] At the same time, his railing against the wicked ways of the world keeps before us the truth that, outside the charmed circle, the ways of the world are wicked. It is only in Arden that his cynicism looks ridiculous. At Elsinore it would be a different matter.

The Seven Ages is a fine speech, which has suffered from being too much praised; that is, from praise too frequent and mechanical. It has not been admired beyond its merits, not least of which is the way in which the verse is adapted to the natural, speaking voice, the easy, cultivated voice of a man who not only repudiates verse for himself but will not even engage in conversation with a verse speaker. Though the passage of time has faded some of the characters Jaques is sketching, at least the infant, 'mewling and puking' and the schoolboy, creeping 'like snail unwillingly to school', are as fresh as when he first skewered them on his pin; and however inappropriate the last line may be to Arden, few hearts have not been chilled by the dead march of its cruel monosyllables. It is an instance of a highly rhetorical structure successfully expressing a truth which would seem too stark for

1 Dowden, *The Comedies of Shakespeare* (1911), p. 669. Hunter saw it as a ratification not as a rebuke, *New Illustrations*, II (1845), p. 338.

rhetoric. For one moment we are allowed to glimpse the skull, with its epigraph *et in Arcadia ego*.[1]

Were Jaques the cheap and selfish cynic he is sometimes said to be, Arden would repudiate him, for it accepts only the good and true. He breathes its air easily and enjoys it. He flowers there. Because its atmosphere is highly permissive he is allowed his idiosyncrasies. After all, they do nobody any harm. They have an astringency, which the mood of the play softens by making him the object of affectionate laughter. At bottom, he and the Duke believe in the same things. It is not for nothing that George Sand fell in love with him and in her remaking of the play rewarded him with Celia's hand.[2] He has dignity and a sardonic charm, is wholly contemptuous of Orlando's drawn sword, genuinely anxious that Touchstone should get a good priest who can tell him what marriage is, and unlike the true exiles and fugitives he has no reason, beyond his loyalty to the Duke, to sleep out of his bed. He is himself the butt of his parody of 'Under the greenwood tree', a bit of genial banter which both confesses and conceals a sentimental foible. Of all the denizens of the forest Jaques is the one who can claim to have made a deliberate choice and therefore to be most faithful to the pastoral ideal. This is what gives him the right to speak the final benisons. His interest in Duke Frederick's conversion is genuine. It was shared by Dr. Johnson, who regretted that Shakespeare had not seen fit to expatiate upon it. 'Out of these convertites / There is much matter to be heard and learned.'

The power of Arden to bestow blessing is confined to those who come to it as a refuge from the pressures outside. To be born there need not confer any special insights. This aspect of the play's logic is one reason why readers have felt that there is something wrong with Shakespeare's presentation of pastoral values, or that he is deliberately critical of them. Except for Corin, the shepherds make a poor showing. Corin is the one instance in Arden of a simple life conferring simple wisdom and simple goodness. He has a small part and it is too often played as though he were no more than a feed for Touchstone. Touchstone successfully runs him out of breath but he is only the apparent victor in their wit-combats, into which Corin enters with some enthusiasm because, like William and with better reason, he takes a countryman's pride

1 See E. Panofsky, *'Et in Arcadia ego'*, in *Philosophy and History. Essays Presented to Ernst Cassirer*, eds. R. Klibansky and H. J. Paton (1936), pp. 223–54.

2 *Comme il vous plaira. Tirée de Shakespeare et arrangée par George Sand*, Paris (1856).

in a pretty wit. Asked by Touchstone to justify his faith, he can give a good account of himself. 'Sir, I am a true labourer: I earn that I eat, get that I wear; owe no man hate, envy no man's happiness; glad of other men's good, content with my harm; and the greatest of my pride is to see my ewes graze and my lambs suck.' Shakespeare's purpose was neither to state nor to analyse the pastoral ideal, but to use it. The sixteenth century was well accustomed to it and didn't have to be told.

The twentieth century might like to hear the shepherd's creed restated by a contemporary sociologist. James Littlejohn, in his survey of life in the Cheviots, observes that

A few elderly working class men, however, seemed liberated from society itself—money, status, convention, ambition, none of these touched them heavily. Among them serious (quite un-pretentious) discussion of man's history and destiny can be heard. They are much less bound down by time than other people. . . . They do not think of themselves, some of these elderly shepherds, as employees getting a wage by selling a skill to an employer but hold that shepherds are in the world to look after sheep, which could not survive without shepherds. If this is questioned they say there never has been a time when there were sheep without shepherds to look after them, as the Bible shows.[1]

Warwickshire lies further south and Corin does think of himself as an employee, with an ungenerous master. Alongside this tribute to the roots of the pastoral in real life, at least one Elizabethan courtier and poet has left us his unguarded opinion of a shepherd's standing. Ralegh, soldiering in Ireland, says of a position he thinks beneath him, 'I would disdayn it as miche as to keap sheepe' and of an application for the governorship of Jersey, 'if ther be neather honor nor profit I must begynn to keep sheep bytyme'.[2]

William and Audrey and Sir Oliver Martext are caricatures. They no more show the country as it really is than do Silvius and Phebe, who are so far from being idealized figures that Rosalind the outsider has to come in and straighten out their affairs. Rosalind teases Orlando because she loves him, and because she is absurdly happy, and because she knows that swinging on the branches can't possibly break the tree, or if she isn't perfectly sure of it she's going the best way towards finding out. Phebe teases Silvius because she doesn't know what love is. She is first cousin

1 *Westrigg, The Sociology of a Cheviot Parish* (1963), p. 106.
2 E. Edwards, *Life and Letters of Sir Walter Ralegh* (1868), II, pp. 17 and 203.

to 'cruel Barbry Allen' and he is the victim of her unawakened heart. The well-established literary convention which made the day-long leisure of shepherds an excuse for the endless analysis of different amorous situations was ready to Shakespeare's hand, and Lodge had already deployed it. The shepherd, spared the misery of greatness, cannot escape natural passion and natural grief. Love the incalculable and death the inevitable are the two great troublers of his peace, the motivation of pastoral lyric and pastoral elegy. Scornful shepherdesses exist to give shepherds something to complain about. In some ways they parallel the inaccessible ladies of *amour courtois* but love in a court setting and love in the sheep-walks of Arden are not quite the same thing. A shepherdess may reject a wooer because she is vain of her beauty, loves another, is vowed to virginity, or quite simply is ignorant of love. Lodge's Phoebe has a touch of the vowed virgin. She holds Diana 'for the goddess of her devotion', and thinks it 'as great an honour to triumph over fancy as over fortune'. Shakespeare's Phebe is conceived on a lower and more realistic plane. She thinks love silly and makes game of Silvius.

> Now I do frown on thee with all my heart,
> And if mine eyes can wound, now let them kill thee.
> Now counterfeit to swoon: why now fall down,
> Or if thou canst not, O for shame, for shame,
> Lie not, to say mine eyes are murderers.

Rosalind, by attacking her vanity, establishes her as a coquette, to whom a lover's distress is a source of amusement. It is a character extremely rare in Shakespeare's comedies. She meets the punishment reserved for those who scorn the power of love. She is visited by a monstrous passion. Her unkind treatment of Silvius would be impossible to the *cuor gentil*, and in this she perhaps parallels Spenser's Mirabella, who 'Of meane parentage and kindred base . . . scornd them all, that loue vnto her ment'.[1] The Elizabethans were always torn between their admiration for the simple life and their conviction that there is a special worth in gentle blood and a classical education. They could never give themselves quite wholeheartedly to a congenital shepherdess.

Silvius, the love-sick swain, is a simpler conception. It is he, rather than the more realistically conceived Phebe, who is a pastoral stereotype, made to look ridiculous in Rosalind's Arden. But even here the balance is very delicate, for though we see that

1 *The Faerie Queene*, VI, vii, 28 and 29.

love has made Silvius a tame snake we are not invited to mock the passion itself, but only its more foolish manifestations. Love is very comical, as Rosalind demonstrates, but if we find Silvius merely ridiculous we are making the same mistake as Phebe, who is told 'Down on your knees / And thank heaven, fasting, for a good man's love'. The lesson is typical of the good sense which always ballasts the romance of *As You Like It*. The play's abiding attraction lies in the marriage it effects between sense and sensibility, criticism and celebration.

It is a play in which, at a superficial level, very little seems to happen. This fact, together with the way in which, like all pastoral, it approaches simplicity from a standpoint of sophistication, may explain why such a favourite school play is favoured more by the teachers than the taught. It is, however, precisely when the play moves to the greenwood, to a timeless world in which it is the act of a fool to consult a watch, that it establishes its true character and becomes truly delightful. '*As You Like It*', says Anne Barton, 'derives much of its classical stability and poise from the fact that its plot barely exists.'[1] This, she argues, is what Shakespeare has been steadily moving towards. It is a play which seems to Harold Jenkins 'to exhibit, most clearly of all the comedies, Shakespeare's characteristic excellences in this kind'.[2] For Helen Gardner it is the 'most consistently played over by a delighted intelligence . . . Shakespeare's most Mozartian comedy'.[3]

The first act establishes the hardness of the world outside the forest, the injustices, ennuis and fears that accompany life on the manor and at the court, both of them places where man is treacherous and ungrateful. It is devoted to evoking a moral climate and rousing a warm sympathy for the good people, who are manifestly oppressed. We are told in so many words that Orlando and Rosalind are hated for no better reason than that they are exceptionally likeable. The distinction between good and bad is clear-cut. Nobody suggests that Oliver was wronged (as he undoubtedly was in the source book), that Rosalind might make a dynastically dangerous marriage (as Lodge's Torismond fears), or that Duke Senior (little as some people like him) deserved his fate. Shakespeare is careful not to let us know the facts about his exile, only that it was unjust. When it is re-enacted, with his guiltless daughter as the victim, our sympathies are warmly engaged.

1 '*As You Like It* and *Twelfth Night*: Shakespeare's sense of an ending', *Shakespearian Comedy*, Stratford-upon-Avon Studies 14, pp. 160–80.

2 '*As You Like It*', *Shakespeare Survey 8*, ed. A. Nicoll (1955), p. 43.

3 '*As You Like It*', *More Talking of Shakespeare*, ed. J. Garrett (1959), p. 18.

Goodness leaves the court when the good Duke goes, and Charles the wrestler tells us very early on that he is creating a golden world elsewhere. In Duke Frederick's world, injustice rules unchecked and it is not confined to the main characters. Old Adam is outrageously abused: 'Is old dog my reward?'. Le Beau dare hardly give his natural right feelings rein.

> The Duke is humorous; what he is indeed
> More suits you to conceive than I to speak of.

The currents of the play are running so strongly in one direction, towards the innocents and against the oppressors, that at first it lacks something of dramatic tension. Our moral choices have been made for us, and we are not going to crane forward in our seats to watch a stage wrestling match.[1]

When the play moves to the forest, manners take over from morals and attitudes from action. We are presented with a pattern of differing threads which, matching and contrasting, knitting and parting, make up the texture of the play. Violent occurrences would break the intricate and delicate web. They do from time to time take place—old Adam lies down to die, Orlando draws his sword, serpent and lioness threaten Oliver, the embattled usurper marches on the forest—but as the play unfolds them these are non-events. Anxiety is dissipated before it can grip. The audience knows what kind of reception Orlando will meet with. It knows that Oliver survives both the perils of the wood and of Orlando's natural resentment, since he is alive to tell the tale. Jaques de Boys gives the news of Duke Frederick's conversion in the same breath as he tells that he has taken up arms. Adam's plight is softened by Orlando's undaunted courage and tender concern, and we know there will be no need for him to engage with wild beasts for food. We have just seen the Duke's banquet spread.

When Shakespeare first began to weave dramatic patterns he had a model in Lyly, who had a special gift for this kind of writing, in which an elegant formalism is of first importance. By 1599 his textures were more complex and his colours more subtle,

---

1 It is plain from the frequency with which Shakespeare resorts to physical man-to-man encounters that they were successful at the Globe, doubtless with something of the effect they have on the cinema screen, where the smashing blows tell in a way they rarely do on the modern stage. But see John Doebler, 'Orlando: athlete of virtue', *Shakespeare Survey 26* (1973), pp. 111–17: 'This stage image of the wrestling match is always a memorable part of the current theatre experience of the play.'

far beyond the simplicities of high and low, young and old, fortunate and unfortunate, pert and grave, vulgar and refined. In *As You Like It* the distinctions are particularly various, and reside for the most part in individual character, which is why a survey of the play in terms of character is effective, and why it differs from Lyly's more mathematical formulae. In *Love's Labour's Lost*, Shakespeare's most Lylyan play, the four lovers and their four ladies set to partners in ranks like dancers, with Rosaline and Berowne as leaders, the rest following suit. Moreover, though the ladies carry the day, it is the gentlemen who hold the stage. Rosalind is vastly more interesting than Rosaline, whereas Orlando, even when sympathetically played, lags behind the witty Berowne. In *As You Like It* everyone has his own standpoint, so that what looks like a piece of purely formal parallelism, as for instance the lovers' quartet at Act v, scene ii

> *Sil.* And so am I for Phebe.
> *Phebe.* And I for Ganymede.
> *Orl.* And I for Rosalind.
> *Ros.* And I for no woman

is in fact, as Harold Jenkins demonstrates, different for every speaker.[1] Celia is not a copy of Rosalind but very much a person in her own right. The commentators, the fool and the scholar-courtier, could not be more unlike. There are not only gentlefolk and country folk, but there are three distinct kinds of country folk, the elderly, sober Corin, the type of 'the good old shepherd', the lovelorn Silvius and Phebe, only distantly connected with sheep, and the broadly comic William and Audrey. Audrey at least pays some attention to her goats, in themselves grotesque animals and notoriously pungent. Their sexual potency pervades the wooing scene between her and Touchstone. There is even a village parson, who can owe nothing to Virgil and Theocritus, and who anchors the scene firmly in contemporary life.

These people behave 'in character', in accord both with their status, their situation, and their personal idiosyncrasies. Their individuality is defined by their often casual meetings with other people, and enhanced by the uninhibited life they are leading. The forest, the still centre, with its atmosphere of endless afternoon, confers on them an opportunity to be themselves and to find 'true contents'.

Some critics would lay a heavier emphasis on finding, a lesser on being.[2] Before they can be themselves people must realize,

1 Op. cit., p. 42–3.   2 E.g. J. Shaw, op. cit.

under stress if need be, who and what they are, and this the play helps them to discover. The metal they are made of is tested and tempered by the blows of fate, which leave them fending for themselves in an environment that is demanding as well as rewarding. There is no better way to show a person's resilience and power to adapt than to place him as a refugee from one milieu in quite a different one. In *As You Like It* the new milieu has the great advantage of being 'natural'. Looked at from one point of view the forest stands for things as they most profoundly are and ought to be. To adapt to it is to be 'true'.

It is a moot point how much of criticism there is in the play. Were there none it would be cloying. There are certainly lessons to be learnt. The Duke has to accustom himself to winter and rough weather. Phebe must learn what love is and accept Silvius thankfully. Rosalind tests Orlando's love and finds it pure gold. Orlando forgives Oliver, even before he learns of his repentance. Oliver discovers Celia, and this selfish and status-conscious young man will take her dowerless. It is true, he has not much on his side to give, no height left to stoop from, but that is part of the lesson. Touchstone, employed to act as every courtier's butt, can play the courtier himself for a change, and he finds in Audrey at least one person who doesn't think him a fool. Jaques argues that the fool's métier has its value and the Duke praises the skill with which Touchstone exercises it. When he laments that his jesting is as little appreciated in Arden as Ovid's poetry among the Goths, that is only his learned fun. He is having the time of his life. Jaques is too busy teaching to learn very much. He must find his pupils singularly unreceptive, but he goes off happily at the end to study at first hand Duke Frederick's conversion.

This is not the procedure of satire, which tends to school the audience at the expense of the persons on the stage. They are derided and lured into traps so that they can be exposed to ridicule. The nearest thing to a trap in Arden is laid by Rosalind for Phebe. Phebe has tried to manipulate Silvius only to fall into the hands of an arch-manipulator, but it is to her advantage in the end. She learns to love and wins a lover. Nobody in Arden meets the full force of ridicule. Martext and William are very lightly sketched in, and there is something touching about Martext's concern for his calling. It is one of those momentary flashes of sympathy, evoked for Shakespeare's very minor characters, like that accorded to the curate in *Love's Labour's Lost*, absurdly miscast as Alexander. If William is a fool to run from Touchstone's turkey-cock rufflings, the laughter is divided, for Touchstone is very comical when he struts. His hostile display is effective because William is a simple soul, not because Touchstone is a complex one. In Ben Jonson's comedies the fools and knaves are properly paid home for their folly and their knavery, but they do not change their ways, still less their hearts. The changes wrought in *As You Like It* are happy and lasting ones, and the play deals in rewards and not in punishments.

The matching and crossing of threads inevitably involves contrasts. Their purpose is artistic not corrective. We are not to prefer red to blue, but to observe how the one throws up the other, harmonizes, or mingles with it to produce a new colour altogether. Rosalind's romantic love-pangs set beside Touchstone's reminiscences, her weary spirits countered with his weary legs, are entertaining juxtapositions. The sides we take in such encounters, if we take sides at all, are to a great extent dictated by our own inclinations. There are critics who allow that Touchstone scores over the lovers and brings them down to earth, but not that Jaques, in a more educated accent, launches an equally devastating attack. He is answered in something like his own language. Touchstone can be silenced with 'Peace, you dull fool'. If we are disinclined to take sides, we can simply enjoy. 'One must not say that Shakespeare never judges, but that one judgment is always modified by another. Opposite views may contradict one another, but of course they do not cancel out. Instead they add up to an all-embracing view far larger and more satisfying than any one of them by itself.'[1]

This larger view is what *As You Like It* permits when it offers its people the freedom of the forest. To say it is about the opposition of court and country is only a half truth. Basically it is about right values and the good life. Paradoxically, and momentarily, the good life is found in the woods. It should be found in the court and when Duke Senior resumes his sway it will be found in the court again. We see his essentially civilized attitude when Orlando bursts violently in on what he takes to be a robbers' feast only to let fall his sword when the Duke assures him

> True is it that we have seen better days,
> And have with holy bell been knoll'd to church
> And sat at good men's feasts, and wip'd our eyes
> Of drops that sacred pity hath engender'd.

1 H. Jenkins, op. cit., p. 45.

These 'better days' may seem to contradict the Duke's earlier opinion:

> Hath not old custom made this life more sweet
> Than that of painted pomp? Are not these woods
> More free from peril than the envious court?

But he is speaking of a corrupt court and in any case making a comparison. The woodland life is *more* sweet. Considered absolutely it is not the best of all possible lives. The woods are still, in one sense,

> this desert inaccessible
> Under the shade of melancholy boughs.

We are reminded of Orlando's promise to civilize them. They need it, but it will not be achieved by hanging indifferent verses on the boughs. The Duke's little commune civilizes them, and so does Corin's careful husbandry. We are further reminded of Touchstone's comic routine, with which he answers Corin's 'How like you this shepherd's life, Master Touchstone?'

> In respect that it is solitary, I like it very well; but in respect that it is private, it is a very vile life. Now in respect it is in the fields, it pleaseth me well; but in respect it is not in the court, it is tedious. As it is a spare life, look you, it fits my humour well; but as there is no more plenty in it, it goes much against my stomach.

It might look as though every sentiment presented us is liable at any moment to be undermined. But it is not so. There are two ways of looking at everything. The contradictions are offered as part of a life which is in fact full of them, but is livable all the same, even enjoyable. Its flexibility comes of its allowing contradictions and we live by being adaptable. This is what makes Shakespeare's version of pastoral acceptable where other writers' more selective varieties proclaim a manifest falseness and can only feed our fantasy life. This is not in itself an improper thing for literature to do, but it is not what Shakespeare is doing.

If the play does not strike all readers as quite so optimistic, touching as it does on follies and evils and delusions, that is the sadness never very far from the surface of any of Shakespeare's romantic comedies. It is a sadness inherent in pastoral, which delineates life as we know it is not, but as we wish it were, and the emphasis can easily fall upon the negative side. *As You Like It* is not a play based on effete conventions—what is too silly to be said anywhere else can be said in a pastoral—but on ideas at once more serious and more true. It is not a solemn play, not a didactic play, but it gains in depth by having behind it, like oaks in the forest, some of the great moral assumptions which underlie the pastoral mode—about the old simple virtues, conceived of as preserved among those who live a simple life, about freedom from ambition and envy and avarice, and the treachery that goes with them. Even profounder than that is the dream of Eden recovered, a world of natural innocence. In smaller things, the pastoral celebrates the pleasure of being unceremonious and the very real joy of summer days in the country.

V. STAGE HISTORY

As You Like It appears to have been written for the newly opened Globe Theatre where, in 1599, the first Jaques told the audience that 'all the world's a stage'. In August 1600 it was entered in the Stationers' Register 'to be stayed', which can be interpreted as evidence of its success, on the grounds that the company would not be anxious to protect an unpopular play (Intro., pp. ix–x). There are no extant references to it or quotations from it in the literature of the time to confirm this speculation. It set no fashion, but came in, itself, on the wave of a temporary vogue for pastoral and woodland plays (Intro., p. xxvi). There is a tradition that it was revived in 1603 and played before James I and his court at Wilton (Intro., pp. ix–x). After that, there is no more heard of it for over a century. It made no appeal when the theatres reopened after the Restoration. Its satire, if it can be called satire, was perhaps too genial for the court of Charles II, just as its pastoralism was perhaps insufficiently high-flown for the neoplatonizing court of Charles I.

In 1723 Charles Johnson rifled a number of Shakespeare's comedies to make an acting version of what is substantially *As You Like It* for Drury Lane.[1] Some of the less extravagant adaptations were retained for a long time. It is unlikely that Oliver and Orlando ever again quarrelled in the words of Bolingbroke and Mowbray, from *Richard II*, or that Quince and his company performed *Pyramus and Thisbe* to entertain the banished duke. The extraneous comic matter was inserted at the expense of Touchstone, Audrey, William, Phebe and Corin, whose parts were omitted. But the idea that Jaques was in love with Celia occurred,

---

1 The fate of the play in the eighteenth century is traced by C. B. Hogan, in *Shakespeare in the Theatre 1707–1800* (1952). Harold Child provides a stage history up to 1920, in *NCS*, pp. 167–171, to which this account is indebted.

INTRODUCTION lxxxvii

no doubt independently, to George Sand, and the First Lord's speech on the sobbing deer, at II. i, was appropriated by many an actor for Jaques in person. Booth played in this travesty, as the banished Duke, with Mrs Booth as Rosalind, Wilks as Orlando, and Cibber as Jaques. It was put on again in 1741 in Dublin, with Quin's Jaques, and possibly in London.

The first revival of the play with a text near to what Shakespeare wrote was in 1740 at Drury Lane, with Dr Arne's music. Along with it came revivals of *The Merchant of Venice* and *Twelfth Night*, inspired it is said by Macklin, though he did not play Touchstone till 1741.[1] Chapman was the first Touchstone, in 1740, with Quin as Jaques, Mrs Pritchard as Rosalind and Mrs Clive as Celia. Celia sang the Cuckoo Song from *Love's Labour's Lost*, but thereafter and for a very long time it was liable to be claimed by any Rosalind who had a singing voice, and was used as a vocal extension of her mockery of men and marriage.

Throughout the rest of the eighteenth century the play was popular, largely because it offered parts for a succession of gifted and charming actresses. Critics tend to greet a good Celia with surprise, as though Shakespeare had not written a good part for her. It is a part Kitty Clive made specially her own, and she went on acting it till 1763. From 1741 to 1750 Mrs Pritchard and Mrs Woffington were rival Rosalinds. Peg Woffington was playing Rosalind on her last appearance at the Haymarket. Mrs Bland had the part in 1753 and 1755, Mrs Yates in 1761, Mrs Dancer was much admired in it in 1767, Mrs Robinson in 1780 and Miss Kemble in 1785. Mrs Jordan was the most admired Rosalind of them all, playing the part from 1787 to 1814, at Drury Lane. Even Mrs Siddons tried it, in 1785 and 1786, but the public could not be persuaded to accept a tragedy-queen in comedy and complained that she did not know how to be arch. There were competent actors to take Jaques and Touchstone. Quin, Ryan, Cibber, Sparks, Berry and Burton played Jaques, followed by Aikin, Henderson, Palmer and Harley. Chapman, Macklin, Woodward, Shuter and Yates played Touchstone, a part which from 1767 to 1802 King made his own. *As You Like It* was more frequently acted at Drury Lane, from 1776 to 1817, than any other Shakespeare play.[2] In 1824 and 1825 there were operatic versions, but they had little to commend them, in spite of Madame Vestris making her first appearance as Rosalind.

1 G. C. D. Odell, *Shakespeare from Betterton to Irving* (1920), I, p. 228.
2 Ibid., II, p. 20.

What the nineteenth century had to contribute was a new scenic magnificence, ultimately a better text, and some new Rosalinds. They included Helen Faucit (1845), Mary Anderson (Stratford, 1885, New York, 1888), Ada Rehan (New York, 1889, The Lyceum, 1890), Lily Langtry (1890) and Julia Neilson (1896). Ellen Terry never had the part. A Touchstone or a Jaques by Irving would have upset the balance of the play. H. B. Irving played Jaques in a few scenes contributed to the Anniversary Celebrations at Camberwell in 1896. It was a part J. P. Kemble and Macready had played before him. Barry Sullivan was to take it in 1855 and Phelps at Sadler's Wells in 1867. Lionel Brough played Touchstone in 1880, John Hare in 1885.

In 1842 Macready put on a very carefully considered production at Drury Lane, with Stanfield's scenery, omitting the persistent Cuckoo Song, and restoring the description of Jaques and the deer to the First Lord. Charles Kean presented it in 1851 at the Princess's, and Sullivan in 1855 at the Haymarket. In 1885 the Kendals, at the St James's, lavished their utmost art on the play. There was new music by Alfred Cellier, unhappily undistinguished. The scenery had great acclaim. 'The brook rippling among the sedges' seems to have been real water, not painted canvas. The approach of the actors, however, Kendal as Orlando, Mrs Kendal as Rosalind, Arthur Cecil as Touchstone and Hermann Vezin as Jaques, was declared to be too prosaic. The essential quality of the play was missing.

In December 1896 George Alexander put on what was virtually the full text. It took four hours in performance, which suggests that scene-shifts were elaborate. This was a notable production. Bernard Shaw, who had a love-hate relationship with the play, after deploring Touchstone's feeble wit, Duke Senior's 'pious twaddle', and the stale commonplaces of Jaques, admitted that *As You Like It* is nonetheless fascinating,[1] H. W. Vernon was a good Jaques, Esmond was Touchstone, and Irving played Oliver, 'much like Iago'. Julia Neilson's Rosalind accounted for some of the fascination. Fay Davis was Celia and Dorothea Baird, whose Rosalind at Camberwell in the Anniversary Celebrations Shaw disliked, made a pretty Phebe. Edward German had composed music for the masque of Hymen, and the little scene in which the two boys sing 'It was a lover and his lass' was restored and proved charming. In 1897 Shaw rejected Augustin Daly's showy and popular production at the Grand Theatre, Islington, in which

1 George Bernard Shaw, *Our Theatre in the Nineties* (1932), 11, pp. 267-70.

soft music accompanied the great speeches. He said it was 'As You Like It just as I don't like it', though he allowed that Ada Rehan was an incomparable Rosalind.[1]

As You Like It in the present century has kept its place among the comedies regularly performed. It has proved a perfect outdoor play, which puts it high on the list at the Open Air Theatre in Regent's Park (e.g. under Robert Atkins in 1956; Leslie French, 1958) and in college gardens (e.g. OUDS in Magdalen Grove, under Thea Holme, with Nova Pilbeam fresh from Peter Pan, 1936; under Neville Coghill, Worcester College garden, 1955). It is an attractive play for amateurs, since it offers a wide and varied range of parts, which can be attempted at a variety of levels and which reward the player's efforts. Against this must be set the fact that it is hackneyed, that the pastoral mode is unfamiliar and its kind of sweetness less and less acceptable to present-day taste. Moreover the play's magic can absent itself entirely when it is unsympathetically performed. Rosalind remains one of the best Shakespearian parts available to an actress, and the new stage settings, which encourage something like the swift scene-shifts of the Elizabethans, are greatly to the play's advantage. The management of the Maddermarket Theatre, Norwich, which is an early reproduction of an Elizabethan stage, chose to open with it, the actors nameless in consonance with Elizabethan practice. In 1951 Kenneth McClellan produced it at the George Inn, Southwark, on an inn-yard stage, and in 1961 Ellen Pollock did it in the round at Croydon.

More conventional London performances, at the beginning of the century, were when Oscar Asche put it on in 1907 at His Majesty's, and when Phyllis Neilson-Terry made her début as Rosalind in 1911, with Miriam Lewis's Celia. In 1936 Nigel Playfair at the St James's 'produced it with originality and a fine dramatic economy', with Athene Seyler for Rosalind.[2] A particularly memorable *As You Like It* was directed by Esmé Church at the Old Vic in 1936 (New Theatre 1937), with Edith Evans as a Rosalind of calculated and enchanting mannerisms. The costumes, designed *à la Watteau* by Molly McArthur, displayed the pale satins of the ladies and the hunting costumes of the gentlemen against a brown forest background. According to Muriel St Clare Byrne, 'By transferring it from the less-known Elizabethan convention to the better known eighteenth-century convention, it

1 Ibid., II, p. 208.
2 H. Child, op. cit., p. 171.

was made more essentially itself for the average spectator.'[1] In 1950 Salvador Dali made use of eighteenth-century styles, interpreted surrealistically, for a performance in Rome. The play was presented Watteau-style in Oslo in 1955.

It is not possible to do justice to the fifty and more productions in the United Kingdom recorded in *Shakespeare Survey* between 1950 and 1965. They include performances at Stratford, directed by Glen Byam Shaw, in 1952 and 1957; at Hammersmith, by Donald Wolfit, in 1953, and in the same year at the Mermaid by Bernard Miles; at the Old Vic by Robert Helpmann in 1955, and Wendy Toye in 1957; by the Marlowe Society at Cambridge in 1957 and 1963; at Harrow School under Ronald Watkins in 1955; at Bristol Old Vic under Alan Davis in 1950 and John Moody in 1958; and John Russell Brown's production for Birmingham University Theatre Guild in 1961.

Glen Byam Shaw's Stratford production in 1957 had Peggy Ashcroft as Rosalind and Patrick Wymark as Touchstone. Motley had designed delicately pretty Arcadian settings, which seemed to Richard David to be 'too appropriate', and for him the magic began to evaporate.[2] The play needs something to strive against. Michael Elliot's production for the National Shakespeare Company in 1961 supplied it. It was notable for the way it underlined the sadness implicit in a tale of precarious happiness snatched from misfortune. Vanessa Redgrave was Rosalind, Max Adrian, Jaques, and Colin Blakely, Touchstone. In 1962, at the Aldwych, Patrick Wymark took over Touchstone. The costumes and the leafless trees made it plain at the beginning that the Duke's company were enduring shrewd days and nights. Miss Redgrave was no carefree, confident Rosalind, stage-managing affairs in the forest, but a waif who unsealed springs of pathos in the part, her gaiety and courage the more admirable because a little tremulous. It was a reading perhaps akin to the one Mrs Siddons was not permitted to establish, and very touching. In 1967 Dorothy Tutin provided a tomboy Rosalind, with David Jones directing at Stratford. Roy Kinnear was Touchstone, Alan Howard, Jaques, and Janet Suzman, Celia. In 1968 Janet Suzman took over Rosalind, and Patrick Stewart, Touchstone.

In 1967 the National Theatre made stage history by putting on

1 'Fifty years of Shakespearian production: 1898–1948', *Shakespeare Survey 2* (1949), p. 16.
2 'Actors and scholars: a view of Shakespeare in the modern theatre', *Shakespeare Survey 12* (1957), p. 86.

the play with an all-male cast, directed by Clifford Williams. The programme notes acknowledge that Ben Greet was actually first in the field, staging an all-male performance on 23 April 1920 at the Central YMCA Buildings, 'for the mere joy of the thing'. It was in Elizabethan dress, Duncan Yarrow as Rosalind, Leslie French as Celia, Andrew Leigh as Audrey, 'assuming the customary red wig', and Anton Dolin as Phebe. *The Stage* reported with relief that 'neither in attire nor in tone was there the slightest cause for offence'. In 1967 Ronald Pickup played Rosalind and Charles Kay, Celia. They wore modern dress and played straight, though in minor matters, an effeminate Jaques, a fascist Duke Frederick, an Audrey from pantomime and a Phebe from the early cinema, the production tried for contemporary 'relevance'. The director said he was not seeking ambiguities and innuendoes, but hoped to evoke 'an atmosphere of spiritual purity which transcends sensuality in the search for poetic sexuality'. Audiences enjoyed the experience. In 1973 Buzz Goodbody directed a performance for the Royal Shakespeare Company, with Eileen Atkins a Rosalind in jeans, David Suchet her Orlando, Derek Smith as Touchstone and Richard Pasco as Jaques.

ABBREVIATIONS

The following abbreviations are used in the collations and explanatory notes.

F	*Mr. William Shakespeares Comedies, Histories, & Tragedies.* 1623.
F2	*Mr. William Shakespeares Comedies, Histories, and Tragedies.* 1632.
F3	*Mr. William Shakespear's Comedies, Histories, and Tragedies . . . The third Impression.* 1664.
F4	*Mr. William Shakespear's Comedies, Histories, and Tragedies . . . The fourth Edition.* 1685.
Rowe	*The Works of Mr. William Shakespear . . . Revis'd and Corrected . . . by N. Rowe Esq.* (Vol. II) 1709.
Rowe³	*The Works of Mr. William Shakespear . . . Revis'd and Corrected By N. Rowe Esq.* (Vol. I) 1714.
Pope	*The Works of Shakspear . . . Collected and Corrected . . . by Mr. Pope.* (Vol. II) 1723.
Pope²	*The Works of Shakespear . . . Collected . . . by Mr. Pope.* (Vol. II) 1728.
Theobald	*The Works of Shakespeare . . . Collated with the Oldest Copies, and Corrected; With Notes . . . By Mr. Theobald.* (Vol. II) 1733.
Theobald²	*The Works of Shakespeare . . . Collated . . . and Corrected: With Notes . . . By Mr. Theobald. The Second Edition.* (Vol. I) 1740.
Hanmer	*The Works of Shakspear . . . Carefully Revised and Corrected by the former Editions.* (Vol. II) Oxford, 1744.
Warburton	*The Works of Shakespear. The Genuine Text . . . settled . . . By Mr. Pope and Mr. Warburton.* (Vol. II) 1747.
Johnson	*The Plays of William Shakespeare . . . To which are added Notes by Sam. Johnson.* (Vol. II) 1765.
Capell	*Mr William Shakespeare his Comedies, Histories, and Tragedies* [edited by Edward Capell]. (Vol. III) [1768].
Steevens	*The Plays of William Shakespeare . . . To which are added notes by Samuel Johnson and George Steevens.* (Vol. III) 1773.
Steevens²	*The Plays of William Shakespeare . . . The Second Edition, Revised and Augmented.* (Vol. I) 1778.
Rann	*The Dramatic Works of Shakespeare . . . with notes by Joseph Rann.* (Vol. II) Oxford, 1787.
Malone	*The Plays and Poems of William Shakespeare . . . with . . . notes By Edmond Malone.* (Vol. III) 1790.
Steevens³	*The Plays of William Shakespeare . . . The Fourth Edition.* (Vol. VI) 1793.

Caldecott   *Hamlet and As You Like It. A Specimen of a new edition of Shakespeare* [By T. Caldecott]. 1819.

Malone[2]   *The Plays and Poems of William Shakespeare . . . with the corrections and illustrations of various commentators . . . by the late Edmond Malone.* (Vol. VI) 1821.

Harness   *The Dramatic Works of William Shakespeare; with Notes . . . by the Rev. William Harness.* (Vol. III) 1825.

Singer   *The Dramatic Works of William Shakespeare with Notes . . . by Samuel Weller Singer.* (Vol. III) 1826.

Knight   *The Pictorial Edition of the Works of Shakspere. Edited by Charles Knight. Comedies.* (Vol. III) [1839].

Collier   *The Works of William Shakespeare . . . with the various readings, notes . . . by J. Payne Collier.* (Vol. III) 1842.

Halliwell   *The Complete Works of Shakspere, revised . . . by J. O. Halliwell. Comedies.* London and New York [1852].

Halliwell[2]   *The Works of William Shakspere . . . from a New Collation of the Early Editions . . . by James O. Halliwell.* (Vol. VI) 1856.

Singer[2]   *The Dramatic Works of William Shakespeare . . . with notes by Samuel Weller Singer F.S.A. The Life of the Poet and Critical Essays on the Plays by William Watkiss Lloyd.* 1856.

Dyce   *The Works of William Shakespeare . . . The Text revised by the Rev. Alexander Dyce.* (Vol. II) 1857.

Grant White   *The Works of William Shakespeare . . . edited . . . by Richard Grant White.* (Vol. IV) Boston, 1857.

Collier[2]   *Shakespeare's Comedies, Histories, Tragedies, and Poems. Edited by J. Payne Collier.* (Vol. II) 1858.

Staunton   *The Plays of Shakespeare. Edited by Howard Staunton.* (Vol. II) 1858.

Camb.   *The Works of William Shakespeare edited by William Aldis Wright . . . and John Glover.* (Vol. II) Cambridge and London, 1863.

Globe   *The Works of William Shakespeare edited by William George Clark and William Aldis Wright.* 1864.

Keightley   *The Plays of William Shakespeare Carefully edited by Thomas Keightley.* (Vol. II) 1864.

Dyce[2]   *The Works of William Shakespeare. The Text Revised by the Rev. Alexander Dyce.* (Vol. III) 1866.

Neil   *Shakespeare's Comedy of As You Like It. With Introductory Remarks . . . Notes, etc., by S. Neil.* 1876.

Wright   *As You Like It, edited by William Aldis Wright.* Oxford, 1877.

Hudson   *The Complete Works of William Shakespeare . . . edited by the Rev. Henry H. Hudson.* (Vol. V) Boston, 1881.

Grant White[2]   *Mr William Shakespeare's Comedies, Histories, Tragedies and Poems. The text newly edited . . . by Richard Grant White. I. Comedies.* 1883.

Rolfe   *Shakespeare's Comedy of As You Like It. Edited, with Notes, by William J. Rolfe.* New York, 1894.

Furness   *As You Like It. A New Variorum Edition of Shakespeare edited by Horace Howard Furness.* Philadelphia, 1890.

Holme   *As You Like It. Edited by J. W. Holme. The Arden Shakespeare.* 1914. (Fourth edition, revised, 1940).

NCS   *As You Like It. Edited . . . by Sir Arthur Quiller-Couch and John
               Dover Wilson. The New Shakespeare.* Cambridge, 1926. (With
               corrections 1957.)
Kittredge   *As You Like It by William Shakespeare. Edited by George Lyman
               Kittredge.* Boston, 1939.
Alexander   *William Shakespeare. The Complete Works . . . edited . . . by Peter
               Alexander.* 1951.
Sisson   *William Shakespeare. The Complete Works . . . Edited by Charles
               Jasper Sisson* [1954].
Walter   *As You Like It. Edited by J. H. Walter.* 1965.
Oliver   *As You Like It. Edited by H. J. Oliver.* Penguin Books. 1968.

REFERENCE BOOKS

Abbott   E. A. Abbott, *Shakespearian Grammar*, 3rd ed., 1870.
Baldwin *Five-Act*   T. W. Baldwin, *William Shakespere's Five-Act Structure*, 1947.
Structure
Baldwin   T. W. Baldwin, *William Shakespere's Small Latine and lesse
Small Latine   Greeke*, 2 vols, Urbana, 1944.
Becket   A. Becket, *Shakespeare's Himself Again*, 2 vols, 1815.
Capell   E. Capell, *Notes and Various Readings to Shakespeare*, 3 vols,
               1779.
Cotgrave   R. Cotgrave, *A Dictionarie of the French and English Tongues*,
               1611.
Curtius   E. R. Curtius, *European Literature and the Latin Middle Ages*,
               1953.
Drayton   M. Drayton, *Works (Polyolbion, Vol. IV)*, ed. J. W. Hebel,
               1933.
Douce   F. Douce, *Illustrations of Shakespeare*, Vol. I, 1807.
Farmer   R. Farmer, *An Essay on the Learning of Shakespeare*, Cambridge,
               1787.
Fleay   F. G. Fleay, *A Chronicle History of the Life and Work of William
               Shakespeare*, 1886.
Greene   R. Greene, *Plays and Poems*, ed. Churton Collins, 2 vols, 1905.
Gould   G. Gould, *Corrigenda and Explanations of the Text of Shakspere*,
               1881.
Heath   [B. Heath] *A Revisal of Shakespeare's Text*, 1765.
Hinman   C. Hinman, *The Printing and Proof-reading of the First Folio
               of Shakespeare*, 1963.
Hotson   J. L. Hotson, *Shakespeare's Motley*, 1952.
Hulme   H. Hulme, *Explorations in Shakespeare's Language*, 1962.
Hunter   J. Hunter, *New Illustrations of the Life, Studies, and Writings of
               Shakespeare* (Part II. The Comedies), 1845.
Jackson   Z. Jackson, *Shakespeare's Genius Justified*, 1819.
JEGP   *Journal of English and German Philology.*
Jervis   S. Jervis, *Proposed Emendations of the Text of Shakespeare's
               Plays*, 1860.
Jonson   B. Jonson, *Works*, eds. C. H. Herford and Percy and Evelyn
               Simpson, 11 vols, Oxford, 1925–52.
Kökeritz   H. Kökeritz, *Shakespeare's Pronunciation*, New Haven, 1953.
Lettsom   W. N. Lettsom, see Walker, W. S.

Lodge	T. Lodge, *Lodge's 'Rosalynde' being the original of Shakespeare's 'As You Like It'*, ed. W. W. Greg, 1897.
Lyly	John Lyly, *The Complete Works*, ed. R. Warwick Bond, 3 vols. 1907.
Marston *Malcontent*	J. Marston, *The Malcontent*, ed. B. Harris, 1967.
Mason	J. M. Mason, *Comments on the Last Edition of Shakespeare's Plays*, 1785.
MLN	*Modern Language Notes.*
Nashe	T. Nashe, *The Works . . . from the original texts*, ed. R. B. McKerrow, Rev. F. P. Wilson, 5 vols, Oxford, 1958.
OED	*A New English Dictionary on Historical Principles*, eds. Murray, Bradley, Craigie, Onions, 1884–1928.
Onions	C. T. Onions, *A Shakespeare Glossary*, 1911.
Ovid	*Metamorphoses*, trs. William Golding, 1565–7.
Pliny	*Natural History*, trs. Philemon Holland, 1601.
PMLA	*Publications of the Modern Language Association of America.*
Ray	J. Ray, *A Compleat Collection of English Proverbs*, 3rd ed., 1737.
Ritson	[J. Ritson] *Cursory Criticisms on the edition of Shakespeare published by Edmond Malone*, 1792.
Schmidt	A. Schmidt, *A Shakespeare Lexicon*, 1874.
Sisson	C. J. Sisson, *New Readings in Shakespeare*, 2 vols, 1956.
Sidney *Arcadia*	Sir Philip Sidney, *The Complete Works*, ed. A. Feuillerat, Cambridge, 1912.
Sidney *A Defence of Poetry*	*Miscellaneous Prose of Sir Philip Sidney*, eds. K. Duncan-Jones and J. van Dorsten, Oxford, 1973.
Tilley	M. P. Tilley, *A Dictionary of the Proverbs in England in the Sixteenth and Seventeenth Centuries*, Ann Arbor, 1950.
TLS	*The Times Literary Supplement.*
Tyrwhitt	T. Tyrwhitt, *Observations and Conjectures upon some Passages of Shakespeare*, Oxford, 1766.
Walker	W. S. Walker, *A Critical Examination of the Text of Shakespeare*, ed. W. N. Lettsom, 3 vols, 1860.
Whiter	[W. Whiter] *A Specimen of a Commentary on Shakespeare*, 1794.
Whiting	J. B. Whiting, *Proverbs, Sentences, and Proverbial Phrases*, Ann Arbor, 1968.

The abbreviations of the titles of Shakespeare's plays and poems are those of C. T. Onions, *A Shakespeare Glossary*. All quotations from Shakespeare (except from *As You Like It*) use the text and lineation of *Works*, ed. Peter Alexander (1951).

AS YOU LIKE IT

DRAMATIS PERSONÆ

DUKE SENIOR, *living in exile.*
DUKE FREDERICK, *his brother and usurper of his dominions.*
LE BEAU, *a courtier attending on Frederick.*
CHARLES, *Duke Frederick's wrestler.*
TOUCHSTONE, *a Fool at the Duke's court.*
OLIVER,
ORLANDO, } *sons of Sir Rowland de Boys.*
JAQUES,
DENNIS,
ADAM, } *servants to Oliver.*
AMIENS,
JAQUES, } *lords attending on the banished Duke.*
CORIN,
SILVIUS, } *shepherds in the Forest of Arden.*
WILLIAM, *a country fellow.*
SIR OLIVER MARTEXT, *vicar of a country parish.*
ROSALIND, *daughter to Duke Senior.*
CELIA, *daughter to Duke Frederick.*
PHEBE, *a shepherdess.*
AUDREY, *a goat-herd.*
Lords attending on the Dukes, with pages and other attendants.

*DRAMATIS PERSONÆ] This edition, based on Rowe, the first to supply such a list.
See Intro., pp. lxv–lxvi, for commentary on the sources and pronunciation of names. For
Capell's introduction of* a person representing Hymen *see* v. iv. 105 SD note.

2

AS YOU LIKE IT

ACT I

SCENE I

Enter ORLANDO *and* ADAM.

Orl. As I remember, Adam, it was upon this fashion
bequeathed me by will but poor a thousand crowns,
and, as thou sayst, charged my brother on his blessing to breed me well; and there begins my sadness.
My brother Jaques he keeps at school, and report   5

ACT I

Scene I

ACT I. Scene I] *Actus primus. Scæna Prima. F.* [Location] *Oliver's Orchard.*
Theobald; not in F.   1–2. this fashion bequeathed] *F*; this my Father bequeath'd *Hanmer*; this, my Father bequeath'd *Warburton*; this fashion he
bequeathed *conj. Ritson*; this fashion. He bequeathed *Malone, conj. Blackstone*;
this fashion,—bequeathed *Dyce¹*; this fashion,—he bequeathed *Dyce²*; this
fashion: a' bequeathed *NCS, conj. Dyce, conj. Greg.*   2. me by] *F*; me. By
Johnson. poor a] *F*; a poore *F2.*

2. *bequeathed me*] Most editors have
felt the need to supply a subject for
bequeathed. NCS records a conjecture
by W. W. Greg that the unnecessary *a*
of *poor a thousand* could be *a*=he,
jerked out of the printer's chase during
the insertion of the ornamental
capital for *As*, and put back in the
wrong place. The curious syntax may
be meant to reinforce the impression
of a conversation of which the audience only overhears the end. Shakespeare has been charged with letting
Orlando tell Adam something of
which he can hardly be ignorant.
Sisson contends that Orlando has
been explaining the circumstances
rather than stating the facts. *It was
upon this*=this was why my father be-

queathed me so little. The reason,
imparted off-stage, is never disclosed.
In Lodge's *Rosalynde* the youngest
brother has the greatest portion because his father has noted his excellent
qualities. Thus Rosader (Orlando) is
introduced as a favourite and a bit of
a prig, and Saladyne (Oliver) wins
some sympathy.

2. *poor a thousand*] See Abbott 85.

3. *charged*] [it was] charged, understood after *it was bequeathed.*

5. *Jaques*] probably pronounced
Jakes, and distinguished thus from
the other Jàques in the play. See
Intro., p. lxviii.

keeps] maintains, as distinct from
stays=detains.

school] university. Cf. *Ham.*, I. ii.

3

speaks goldenly of his profit: for my part, he keeps
me rustically at home, or, to speak more properly,
stays me here at home unkept; for call you that
keeping for a gentleman of my birth, that differs
not from the stalling of an ox? His horses are bred 10
better; for besides that they are fair with their feeding, they are taught their manage, and to that end
riders dearly hired: but I, his brother, gain nothing
under him but growth, for the which his animals on
his dunghills are as much bound to him as I. 15
Besides this nothing that he so plentifully gives me,
the something that nature gave me his countenance
seems to take from me. He lets me feed with his
hinds, bars me the place of a brother, and, as much
as in him lies, mines my gentility with my educa- 20
tion. This is it, Adam, that grieves me, and the spirit
of my father, which I think is within me, begins to
mutiny against this servitude. I will no longer endure it, though yet I know no wise remedy how to
avoid it. 25

Adam. Yonder comes my master, your brother.

Enter OLIVER.

Orl. Go apart Adam, and thou shalt hear how he will
shake me up.

Oli. Now sir, what make you here?

Orl. Nothing. I am not taught to make anything. 30

26. SD *Enter Oliver*] This ed; *F* (after 25); *Collier* (after 28).

113, 'going back to school in Witten-
berg', and modern American usage.

6. *profit*] progress, commonly used of
learning.

12. *manage*] 'the actions and paces
to which a horse is trained' (*OED*
sb. 1, quoting *AYL*).

17. *countenance*] the style of living he
allows me (Walker, III, p. 59).

19. *hinds*] servants, generally farm-
servants. Oliver is a landed gentleman
living on his manor, not a courtier.

bars me] forbids me. Cf. v. iv. 124:
'I bar confusion.'

20. *mines*] undermines. 'He counter-

acts the advantages of my good birth
by the bad education he gives me'
(Holme).

28. *shake me up*] Cf. *Rosalynde*: 'As
thus he was ruminating of his melancholy passions in came Saladyne with
his men, and seeing his brother in a
brown study, and to forget his wonted
reverence, thought to shake him out
of his dumps thus . . .' (Greg, p. 11).

29. *sir*] the peremptory *sir*, as to a
dog. Both brothers use *you* but Charles
the wrestler is *thou* when Oliver wants
to ingratiate himself.

what make you] What are you doing?

Oli. What mar you then sir?

Orl. Marry sir, I am helping you to mar that which God
made, a poor unworthy brother of yours, with
idleness.

Oli. Marry sir, be better employed, and be naught 35
awhile.

Orl. Shall I keep your hogs and eat husks with them?
What prodigal portion have I spent that I should
come to such penury?

Oli. Know you where you are sir? 40

Orl. O sir, very well: here in your orchard.

Oli. Know you before whom sir?

Orl. Ay, better than him I am before knows me. I know
you are my eldest brother, and in the gentle condition of blood you should so know me. The 45
courtesy of nations allows you my better, in that you
are the first-born, but the same tradition takes not
away my blood, were there twenty brothers betwixt
us. I have as much of my father in me as you, albeit
I confess your coming before me is nearer to his 50
reverence.

Oli. [*striking him*] What, boy!

Orl. [*putting a wrestler's grip on him*] Come, come, elder
brother, you are too young in this.

50–1. your . . . is . . . reverence] *F*; you . . . are . . . revenue *Hanmer*; your . . .
is . . . revenue *Warburton*. 52. SD *striking him*] *This ed*; *menacing with his hand.*
Johnson; *Strikes at him Grant White²*; not in *F*. 53. SD *putting a wrestler's grip on
him*] *This ed*; *collaring him Johnson*; *Takes him by the throat Grant White²*; not in *F*.

35–6. *be naught awhile*] 'Be hang'd
to you!' (Capell). *Awhile* has no
particular meaning in the context.
There is a general sense of 'make
yourself scarce' .Gifford (in his ed. of
Jonson's *Bartholomew Fair* (1897), p.
165) classes the phrase with 'petty and
familiar maledictions'.

38. *prodigal portion*] Luke 15.

45. *so know me*] acknowledge me for
your brother.

46. *courtesy of nations*] conventions
of the civilized world. Lodge has
Rosader say 'I am thine equal by
nature, though not by birth' (Greg,

p. 12). Jurists distinguished between
the man-made 'law of nations' and the
universal law of nature. Cf. *Lr*, I. ii.
3–4: 'and permit / The curiosity of
nations to deprive me'.

51. *reverence*] the respect due to him.
Sisson dismisses Warburton's popular emendation 'revenue' as too
crudely provocative. The quarrel
turns very much upon status.

52. *What, boy!*] an insult rather than
a description. Cf. *Ado*, v. i. 79, 83, 91,
94 and *Cor.*, v. vi. 101, 104, 117.

54. *too young in this*] inferior to the
youngest-born when it comes to

Oli. Wilt thou lay hands on me villain?   55

Orl. I am no villain. I am the youngest son of Sir
Rowland de Boys: he was my father, and he is
thrice a villain that says such a father begot
villains. Wert thou not my brother, I would not
take this hand from thy throat till this other had   60
pulled out thy tongue for saying so. Thou hast
railed on thyself.

Adam. Sweet masters be patient. For your father's re-
membrance, be at accord.

Oli. Let me go I say.   65

Orl. I will not till I please: you shall hear me. My
father charged you in his will to give me good
education: you have trained me like a peasant, ob-
scuring and hiding from me all gentleman-like
qualities. The spirit of my father grows strong in   70
me, and I will no longer endure it. Therefore allow
me such exercises as may become a gentleman, or
give me the poor allottery my father left me by
testament; with that I will go buy my fortunes.

Oli. And what wilt thou do? Beg when that is spent?   75
Well sir, get you in. I will not long be troubled with
you; you shall have some part of your will. I pray
you leave me.

Orl. I will no further offend you than becomes me for my
good.   80

Oli. Get you with him, you old dog.

Adam. Is old dog my reward? Most true, I have lost my
teeth in your service. God be with my old

57. Boys] *F*; Bois *Steevens*³.   68. me] *F*; me up *F3*.

wrestling. Lodge makes Saladyne say,
when he incites Rosader to the
wrestling match, 'For myself thou
knowest, though I am eldest by birth,
yet never having attempted any
deeds of arms, I am youngest to perform any martial exploits, knowing
better how to survey my lands than to
charge my lance' (Greg, p. 15). Cf.
'He has made a younger brother of
him', Ray's *Proverbs* (1737), p. 11, and

Mac., III. iv. 144: 'We are yet but
young in deed.'

55. *villain*] a man who is (1) low-
born; (2) wicked (Oliver's usage).

73. *allottery*] share, what was
allotted (*OED*, quoting this as a rare
usage).

77. *your will*] (1) testament; (2)
desire.

master!—he would not have spoke such a word.

Exeunt Orlando [and] Adam.

Oli. Is it even so? Begin you to grow upon me? I will   85
physic your rankness, and yet give no thousand
crowns neither. Holla Dennis!

Enter DENNIS.

Dennis. Calls your worship?

Oli. Was not Charles the Duke's wrestler here to speak
with me?   90

Dennis. So please you, he is here at the door and impor-
tunes access to you.

Oli. Call him in. [*Exit Dennis.*] 'Twill be a good way.
And tomorrow the wrestling is.

Enter CHARLES.

Cha. Good morrow to your worship.   95

Oli. Good Monsieur Charles! What's the new news at
the new court?

Cha. There's no news at the court sir, but the old news.
That is, the old Duke is banished by his younger
brother the new Duke, and three or four loving   100
lords have put themselves into voluntary exile
with him, whose lands and revenues enrich the
new Duke, therefore he gives them good leave to
wander.

Oli. Can you tell if Rosalind the Duke's daughter be   105
banished with her father?

Cha. O no; for the Duke's daughter her cousin so loves
her, being ever from their cradles bred together,
that she would have followed her exile, or have

91. SD *Dennis goes* NCS; *Dennis goes to the door* Sisson (*after 90*); *not in* F.   93.
SD *Exit Dennis*] Johnson; Sisson (*after 92*); *not in* F.   96. Good] F; Good
morrow *Dyce²*, conj. *Walker*.   109. she] *F3*; hee F.

85. *grow upon me*] (1) encroach, take
liberties; (2) grow up.

86. *physic your rankness*] cure your
insolence. *Rankness* carries on the
sense of overlush vegetation in *grow*

upon me. Cf. *2H4*, IV. i. 64: 'To diet
rank minds sick of happiness'; *H5*,
v. ii. 50: 'Wanting the scythe, all
uncorrected, rank'.

died to stay behind her. She is at the court, and no   110
less beloved of her uncle than his own daughter,
and never two ladies loved as they do.

Oli. Where will the old Duke live?

Cha. They say he is already in the Forest of Arden, and
a many merry men with him; and there they live   115
like the old Robin Hood of England. They say
many young gentlemen flock to him every day,
and fleet the time carelessly as they did in the
golden world.

Oli. What, you wrestle tomorrow before the new Duke?   120

Cha. Marry do I sir. And I came to acquaint you with a
matter. I am given, sir, secretly to understand that
your younger brother Orlando hath a disposition
to come in disguised against me to try a fall. Tomorrow, sir, I wrestle for my credit, and he that   125
escapes me without some broken limb shall acquit
him well. Your brother is but young and tender,
and for your love I would be loath to foil him, as I
must for my own honour if he come in. Therefore
out of my love to you, I came hither to acquaint   130
you withal, that either you might stay him from
his intendment, or brook such disgrace well as he

---

114. *Forest of Arden*] the Ardennes, on the border of Belgium and Luxemburg. The region gains some romantic associations from an incident in Ariosto's *Orlando Furioso* set in 'Ardenna woods' (Harington's translation, XLII, 44) and from a reference in Spenser's *Astrophel* (l. 96) to 'famous Ardeyn'. Shakespeare, and no doubt many of his audience, could identify it easily with those parts of Warwickshire still known as Arden, though no forest of that name survived.

116. *Robin Hood*] In 1598 the Rose Theatre staged plays on the life and death of Robin Hood. Intro., p. xxvi.

118. *fleet the time*] a very rare transitive use of *fleet* (*OED* vb, 10d).

118–19. *the golden world*] Pastoral writers look back to the classical Golden Age, which preceded the Iron Age of Saturn. Cf. Ovid, *Metamorphoses*, trs. W. Golding. XV, 103ff.: 'that same auncient age / Which we have named the golden world'. There were no ploughshares, no animals were slaughtered, and nobody had to work for a living. Charles gives an idyllic picture of the forest life. The Duke, who is actually living it and liking it, knows the other side too. See II. i. 1ff. and Jaques on the sobbing deer at l. 26.

124. *disguised*] Orlando conceals his name until directly challenged by Duke Frederick at I. ii. 210.

132. *intendment*] intent.

shall run into, in that it is a thing of his own
search, and altogether against my will.

Oli. Charles, I thank thee for thy love to me, which   135
thou shalt find I will most kindly requite. I had
myself notice of my brother's purpose herein, and
have by underhand means laboured to dissuade
him from it; but he is resolute. I'll tell thee
Charles, it is the stubbornest young fellow of   140
France, full of ambition, an envious emulator of
every man's good parts, a secret and villainous
contriver against me his natural brother. Therefore use thy discretion; I had as lief thou didst
break his neck as his finger. And thou wert best   145
look to't; for if thou dost him any slight disgrace,
or if he do not mightily grace himself on thee, he
will practise against thee by poison, entrap thee
by some treacherous device, and never leave thee
till he hath ta'en thy life by some indirect means   150
or other. For I assure thee—and almost with
tears I speak it—there is not one so young and so
villainous this day living. I speak but brotherly of
him, but should I anatomize him to thee as he is, I
must blush and weep, and thou must look pale and   155
wonder.

Cha. I am heartily glad I came hither to you. If he come
tomorrow, I'll give him his payment. If ever he go
alone again, I'll never wrestle for prize more. And
so God keep your worship.   160

Oli. Farewell good Charles. *Exit [Charles].* Now will I
stir this gamester. I hope I shall see an end of him;
for my soul—yet I know not why—hates nothing
more than he. Yet he's gentle, never schooled and

---

161. *Oli.*] *F2; not in F.* SD *Exit Charles*] *Capell; F (after 160).*

138. *underhand*] unobtrusive.

140. *it is*] a contemptuous use of *it*
for 'he'.

143. *natural brother*] blood brother.

148. *practise*] plot.

154. *anatomize*] dissect, a common

Elizabethan term for a thorough and
methodical disclosure of moral faults.

158–9. *go alone*] walk without
crutches.

162. *gamester*] (1) athlete; (2) gay
young dog.

yet learned, full of noble device, of all sorts en-   165
chantingly beloved, and indeed so much in the
heart of the world, and especially of my own
people, who best know him, that I am altogether
misprised. But it shall not be so long; this wrestler
shall clear all. Nothing remains but that I kindle   170
the boy thither, which now I'll go about.   *Exit.*

SCENE II

Enter ROSALIND *and* CELIA.

Celia. I pray thee Rosalind, sweet my coz, be merry.
Ros. Dear Celia, I show more mirth than I am mistress
      of, and would you yet I were merrier? Unless you
      could teach me to forget a banished father, you
      must not learn me how to remember any extra-   5
      ordinary pleasure.
Celia. Herein I see thou lov'st me not with the full weight
      that I love thee. If my uncle thy banished father
      had banished thy uncle the Duke my father, so thou
      hadst been still with me, I could have taught my   10
      love to take thy father for mine; so wouldst thou,
      if the truth of thy love to me were so righteously
      tempered as mine is to thee.

Scene II

Scene II] *Scæna Secunda. F.* [Location] *an Open Walk, before the Duke's Palace.*
Theobald; not in F. Celia] F (*Cellia*), *F2.*   2. *Celia*] F (*Cellia*), *F2.*   3. I
were] *Rowe³*; were F.

165–6. *enchantingly*] He charms
them.

168–9. *I am altogether misprised*] a
favourite motivation for a Shakespearian villain. Cf. Duke Frederick's
jealousy on Celia's behalf at I. iii. 76–
8.

Scene II

1. *coz*] an abbreviated form of
cousin, used as an endearment to both
kinsfolk and friends. Duke Senior uses
cousin to Amiens at II. vii. 173. Duke
Frederick uses it with high formality
when he banishes Rosalind, his niece,

at I. iii. 38.

2–3. *I show . . . merrier*] 'The mirth
which I already show is more than I
really feel; and do you still insist I
shall be merrier?' (Allen). Un-
emended the text can mean 'I wish
you at least were merrier, whatever
be my feelings' (Oliver). F has no
question mark.

5. *learn*] teach, a usage which survives as a regional vulgarism.

12–13. *righteously tempered*] propor-
tioned so virtuously. To temper=to
mix.

Ros. Well, I will forget the condition of my estate, to
    rejoice in yours.   15

Celia. You know my father hath no child but I, nor none
    is like to have; and truly when he dies, thou shalt
    be his heir; for what he hath taken away from thy
    father perforce, I will render thee again in affection.
    By mine honour I will, and when I break that oath,   20
    let me turn monster. Therefore my sweet Rose, my
    dear Rose, be merry.

Ros. From henceforth I will, coz, and devise sports. Let
    me see, what think you of falling in love?

Celia. Marry I prithee do, to make sport withal. But love   25
    no man in good earnest, nor no further in sport
    neither, than with safety of a pure blush thou mayst
    in honour come off again.

Ros. What shall be our sport then?

Celia. Let us sit and mock the good hussif Fortune from   30
    her wheel, that her gifts may henceforth be bes-
    towed equally.

Ros. I would we could do so; for her benefits are mightily
    misplaced, and the bountiful blind woman doth
    most mistake in her gifts to women.   35

Celia. 'Tis true, for those that she makes fair, she scarce

---

30. hussif] *This ed*; houswife *F*.

27. *a pure blush*] *pure* = (1) mere;
(2) free of guilt. Cf. Ray's *Proverbs*,
p. 81; 'Blushing is virtue's colour',
and Lyly, *Euphues and his England*, p.
101, ll. 5ff.: 'I thinke if a fayre
woeman hauing heard the suite of a
louer, if she blush at ye first brunt,
and shew hir bloud in hir face,
sheweth a well dysposed minde: so as
vertuous woemenne I confesse are for
to bee chosen by the face, not when
they blushe for the shame of some
sinne committed, but for feare she
should comitte any.'

30. *the good hussif Fortune*] who
changes men's lives with the turning
of her emblematic wheel, here
derisively equated with a domestic
spinning-wheel. Cf. *Ant.*, IV. xiv. 43–

4: 'let me rail so high / That the false
huswife Fortune break her wheel.'
Celia is a little uncomfortable about
her own good fortune. The strife
between nature and fortune was a
medieval commonplace deriving ultimately from Seneca, through Boe-
thius, and constantly recurring in
Shakespeare. Lodge describes old
Sir Rowland as a knight 'whom fortune had graced with many favours,
and nature honoured with sundry
exquisite qualities, so beautified with
the excellence of both, as it was a
question whether fortune or nature
were more prodigal in deciphering
the riches of their bounties' (Greg, p.
1). For the spelling *hussif* cf. IV. iii. 27
where F reads *huswiues*.

makes honest; and those that she makes honest, she
makes very ill-favouredly.

Ros. Nay now thou goest from Fortune's office to
Nature's; Fortune reigns in gifts of the world, not   40
in the lineaments of Nature.

Celia. No? When Nature hath made a fair creature, may
she not by Fortune fall into the fire? Though Nature
hath given us wit to flout at Fortune, hath not
Fortune sent in this fool to cut off the argument?   45

Enter TOUCHSTONE.

Ros. Indeed, there is Fortune too hard for Nature, when
Fortune makes Nature's natural the cutter-off of
Nature's wit.

Celia. Peradventure this is not Fortune's work neither,
but Nature's, who perceiveth our natural wits too   50
dull to reason of such goddesses, and hath sent this
natural for our whetstone; for always the dullness
of the fool is the whetstone of the wits. How now
Wit, whither wander you?

Touch. Mistress, you must come away to your father.   55

Celia. Were you made the messenger?

Touch. No by mine honour, but I was bid to come for you.

Celia. Where learned you that oath, fool?

Touch. Of a certain knight, that swore by his honour they
were good pancakes, and swore by his honour the   60

---

38. ill-favouredly] illfauouredly *F*; ill-favoured *Rowe*[3].   45. SD *Enter*] *Dyce*; *F*
(*after 41*). *Touchstone*] *Malone*; *Touchstone, a Clown Theobald*[2]; *Clowne F* (*so
throughout the play*).   50. perceiveth] *F*; perceiving *F2*.   51. and hath]
Malone; hath *F*.

37. *honest*] chaste.

38. *ill-favouredly*] in an ugly fashion
(*NCS*).

47. *natural*] a congenital idiot.

50. *perceiveth*] word-endings such as
-*eth* and -*ing* can cause confusion, the
more so because they were often
contracted in manuscript. F2's emendation may be justified.

51. *reason*] talk. Cf. French
'raisonner'.

54. *Wit, whither wander you?*] a

catchphrase, here in allusion to the
wandering wits of the fool. See Tilley
(W570).

56. *messenger*] *NCS*, noting that
messenger was commonly used of a
pursuivant (*OED3*), says Touchstone
is pretending Celia has asked if he has
come to arrest her. It is characteristic
of Touchstone, himself addicted to
magniloquence, to mock other
people's language.

mustard was naught. Now I'll stand to it, the pancakes were naught and the mustard was good, and
yet was not the knight forsworn.

Celia. How prove you that in the great heap of your
knowledge?   65

Ros. Ay marry, now unmuzzle your wisdom.

Touch. Stand you both forth now: stroke your chins, and
swear by your beards that I am a knave.

Celia. By our beards, if we had them, thou art.

Touch. By my knavery, if I had it, then I were. But if you   70
swear by that that is not, you are not forsworn. No
more was this knight, swearing by his honour, for he
never had any; or if he had, he had sworn it away
before ever he saw those pancakes or that mustard.

Celia. Prithee, who is't that thou mean'st?   75

Touch. One that old Frederick your father loves.

Celia. My father's love is enough to honour him. Enough,
speak no more of him; you'll be whipped for
taxation one of these days.

Touch. The more pity that fools may not speak wisely   80
what wisemen do foolishly.

76. Frederick] *F*; Ferdinand *Collier²*, *conj. Capell*; Fernandine *conj. Capell*.
77. *Celia*] *Theobald*; *Ros. F.* him. Enough] *Alexander*; him enough; *F*; him:
enough! *Hanmer*; him. *Gould, conj. Keightley*.   81. wisemen] Wisemen *F*;
Wise men *F3*.

63. *not . . . forsworn*] This seems to
have been a well-worn joke.

76. *old Frederick*] F gives the reply
to Rosalind. It is Celia who has asked
the question and her father's name is
Frederick. *Old* must be read as a
colloquial familiarity, resented by the
daughter when used of her father. Cf.
Lucio's disrespectful allusion to 'the
old fantastical Duke of dark corners',
Meas., IV. iii. 163–4. Alternatively,
as Steevens suggests, Celia checks
Touchstone for his own sake, before
he can really go over the line. Intro.,
pp. xxx–xxxi. Capell's conjectural
'Ferdinand' or 'Fernandine', for
Frederick (*Notes*, I, pp. 55–6), supposes
that Shakespeare changed the second
brother's name to Jaques because he

wanted Lodge's Fernandyne, or
something like it, for Duke Senior.
'Old Frederick', he says, 'will be
forever a stumbling-block to those
who read with attention.' Malone was
impressed by a possible confusion
between *Fer.* and *Fre.*

79. *taxation*] fault-finding (*OED* 3,
quoting *AYL*).

81. *wisemen*] F prints as one word,
the rhythm requiring the stress on the
first element. Cf. v. i. 30–1. See also
blind woman at l. 34 above, *wild-goose*,
at II. vii. 86, and the common spelling
and accentuation of 'madman',
'freshman', 'goodman' etc. Furness
would distinguish this usage from F's
wise men at l. 84 below.

Celia. By my troth thou sayest true. For since the little
wit that fools have was silenced, the little foolery
that wisemen have makes a great show. Here comes
Monsieur Le Beau.   85

Enter LE BEAU.

Ros. With his mouth full of news.
Celia. Which he will put on us, as pigeons feed their
young.
Ros. Then shall we be news-crammed.
Celia. All the better; we shall be the more marketable.   90
Bon jour Monsieur Le Beau. What's the news?
Le Beau. Fair Princess, you have lost much good sport.
Celia. Sport? Of what colour?
Le Beau. What colour madam? How shall I answer
you?   95
Ros. As wit and fortune will.

84. wisemen] *This ed*; wise men *F*.   85. Le Beau] *Steevens³*; the *Beu F*; *Le Beu
F2*. SD *Enter Le Beau] F; Dyce, Grant White (after 90); Sisson (after 84)*.
91. Le Beau] *Steevens³; le Beu F (so throughout)*.   92. Fair Princess . . . sport.]
as Pope (prose); Fair Princesse, / you . . . sport. / *F*.

83. *silenced*] Johnson suggests that
licensed jesters were beginning to be
less tolerated. They were certainly a
dying race. Wright sees a reference to
the closing of the theatres, Fleay, in
The Life of Shakespeare (1886), p. 208,
to the burning of satirical books in
June 1599. There may be some
significance in Celia's *Here comes
Monsieur Le Beau*. The girls have
silenced the official jester only to be
plagued by a ceremonious courtier.
Whatever Le Beau is really like (and
he shows to advantage when he is
warning Orlando at the end of this
scene) Rosalind and Celia make him
a figure of fun.
87. *put on us*] force on us, whether
we will or no.
87–8. *as pigeons feed their young*] They
stuff them with predigested food,

which they produce from their crops.
Cf. *news-crammed*, l. 89 below.

90. *the more marketable*] a recently
fed bird weighs heavier.

93. *colour*] kind or nature, as in 'a
horse of another colour'. 'Of what
colour?' was a catchword of the day.
See Tilley (H665). Le Beau may be
puzzled by the slang of the younger
generation, or else his hesitation is
part of his courtly manner, which
makes him pause to choose his words
fastidiously. This foible, if he has it,
he shares with Polonius. Collier
suggests that he provokes Celia by
pronouncing *sport* as 'spot', with an
affected French accent. Le Beau
however is no more French than anyone else in the play. Even so minor a
character as Charles is called *Monsieur*.

Touch. Or as the Destinies decrees.

Celia. Well said! That was laid on with a trowel.

Touch. Nay, if I keep not my rank—

Ros. Thou losest thy old smell.   100

Le Beau. You amaze me ladies. I would have told you of
     good wrestling, which you have lost the sight of.

Ros. Yet tell us the manner of the wrestling.

Le Beau. I will tell you the beginning, and if it please
     your ladyships, you may see the end, for the best is   105
     yet to do, and here where you are they are coming
     to perform it.

Celia. Well, the beginning that is dead and buried.

Le Beau. There comes an old man, and his three sons—

Celia. I could match this beginning with an old tale.   110

Le Beau. Three proper young men, of excellent growth
     and presence—

Ros. With bills on their necks: 'Be it known unto all
     men by these presents'—

97. decrees] *F*; decree *Pope.*   99. rank—] *Rowe*; ranke. *F.*   109. sons—]
sons,— *Theobald*; sons. *F.*   112. presence—] presence;— *Theobald*; presence. F.
113–14. *Ros.* With . . . presents] *F*; *Ros.* With . . . necks. *Clo. Be . . . presents*
—*Warburton*; *Le Beau (cont.)* with . . . necks,— *Ros.* "Be . . . presents", *Dyce*,
conj. Farmer.   114. presents—] presents,— *Theobald*; presents. *F.*

97. *Destinies*] Lodge delights to
impute events in his story to destiny,
e.g. '"O my sons, you see that fate
hath set a period of my years, and
destinies have determined the final
end of my days"' (Greg, p. 2). The
theme of fortune is prominent in
Montemayor's *Diana.*

decrees] See Abbott 333–8 and
Wright. A third person plural in *-s*
is not uncommon. It may be due to a
misreading of the verbal suffix in
manuscript, though Abbott thinks it
was sometimes a distinct verbal form.

98. *laid on with a trowel*] slapped on
thick and without nicety, like mortar.
'An excellent random stroke' (Rann).
See Tilley (T539). Celia's '*Well said*' is
a commendation, which Touchstone
accepts complacently.

99. *keep not my rank*] fail to live up to

my common form, i.e. can't produce
a classical allusion at will.

100. *smell*] a quibble on *rank*=
malodorous. Cf. *Cym.*, II. i. 17–19.

101. *amaze*] perplex, put out.

111. *proper*] well-made.

113–14. *With bills . . . presents*]
Rosalind is still perpetrating atrocious
jokes, to the confusion of Le Beau.
Some editors make *with bills on their
necks* the end of Le Beau's speech, to
allow her at least the merit of a quick
retort, but the fun, for what it is
worth, is all of her contriving. She
imagines the party with *bills* balanced
across one shoulder, Dick Whittington
style. A bill, a hedging implement and
at need a weapon, was not the equipment of a wrestler but of a countryman making a journey. Cf. *Rosalynde*:
'taking his forest bill on his neck, he

Le Beau. The eldest of the three wrestled with Charles   115
    the Duke's wrestler, which Charles in a moment
    threw him and broke three of his ribs, that there is
    little hope of life in him. So he served the second,
    and so the third. Yonder they lie, the poor old
    man their father making such pitiful dole over   120
    them that all the beholders take his part with
    weeping.

Ros. Alas!

Touch. But what is the sport monsieur, that the ladies
    have lost?   125

Le Beau. Why this that I speak of.

Touch. Thus men may grow wiser every day. It is the
    first time that ever I heard breaking of ribs was
    sport for ladies.

Celia. Or I, I promise thee.   130

Ros. But is there any else longs to see this broken music
    in his sides? Is there yet another dotes upon rib-
    breaking? Shall we see this wrestling, cousin?

Le Beau. You must if you stay here, for here is the place
    appointed for the wrestling, and they are ready to   135
    perform it.

Celia. Yonder sure they are coming. Let us now stay and
    see it.

131. see] *F*; set *Theobald*; feel *Dyce²*, *conj. Johnson.*   138. SD *Frederick] Rowe*;
junior | Capell; *not in F.*

trudgeth in all haste' (Greg, p. 124)
and Sydney's *Arcadia* (1590): 'comes
master Dametas with a hedging bill
in his hand'; 'Dametas . . . with . . . a
forrest-bill on his neck' (Feuillerat, I,
pp. 87 and 117). The association
stems from *There comes an old man, and
his three sons* and Celia's comparing it
to the beginning of an old tale. Lodge,
following *Gamelyn*, assigns the old man
two sons, which is less obviously in the
folk tradition. Rosalind picks up the
phrase *of excellent presence* and uses it to
quibble on bills = (1) labels; (2) legal
bills and their conventional opening
'Be it known unto all men by these

presents'. She is in an irresponsible
mood, the manic side of her previous
depression, where everything becomes
hilarious. As Johnson says, 'where
meaning is so very thin, as in this vein
of jocularity, it is hard to catch.'

131. *broken music*] The phrase has
various technical meanings. It is
generally interpreted here as 'part
music', i.e. music played by a number
of different instruments. *NCS* sees a
reference to the broken ribs of a lute.
Warburton emended *see* to 'set' because he thought a musical term
agreed with the rest of the imagery.

Flourish. Enter DUKE [FREDERICK], *lords,*
ORLANDO, CHARLES *and attendants.*

Duke F. Come on. Since the youth will not be entreated,
his own peril on his forwardness.   140
Ros. Is yonder the man?
Le Beau. Even he, madam.
Ros. Alas, he is too young. Yet he looks successfully.
Duke F. How now daughter and cousin? Are you crept
hither to see the wrestling?   145
Ros. Ay my liege, so please you give us leave.
Duke F. You will take little delight in it, I can tell you,
there is such odds in the man. In pity of the chal-
lenger's youth, I would fain dissuade him, but he
will not be entreated. Speak to him ladies; see if   150
you can move him.
Celia. Call him hither, good Monsieur Le Beau.
Duke F. Do so. I'll not be by.
Le Beau. Monsieur the challenger, the Princess calls for
you.   155
Orl. I attend them with all respect and duty.
Ros. Young man, have you challenged Charles the
wrestler?
Orl. No fair Princess: he is the general challenger.
I come but in as others do, to try with him the   160
strength of my youth.
Celia. Young gentleman, your spirits are too bold for

139. *Duke F.*] *Malone*; *Duke F.*   139–40. Come . . . forwardness.] *As Pope*
(*prose*); Come . . . intreated / . . . forwardnesse. *F.*   144–5. How . . . wrestling?] *As Pope* (*prose*); How . . . Cousin: / . . . wrastling? / *F.*   148. man] *F*;
men *Hanmer.*   154. Princess calls] Princesse cals *F*; Princesses call *Theobald*;
princess' call *Dyce.*   156. them] *F*; her *Rowe.*

148. *odds*] superiority, referring to
the sinewy Charles. Lodge makes much
of the great size and strength of the
wrestler. See II. iii. 8 note.

154. *Princess*] There is no need to
emend to a plural because Orlando
uses *them* at l. 156. Le Beau observes
protocol and recognizes only one
princess. To Orlando, both ladies are
princely, Rosalind especially. He

does not yet know which is daughter
to the banished Duke. See ll. 259–60
below. Dyce's *princess'* is a plural,
which he compares with *Tem.*, I. ii.
173.

159. *general challenger*] Bales, in
Winning of a Golden Pen (MS Harley
675), describes himself as 'generall
Chalenger' for the pen (Hulme, p.
145). Charles will take on all comers.

your years. You have seen cruel proof of this man's
strength; if you saw yourself with your eyes or
knew yourself with your judgement, the fear of   165
your adventure would counsel you to a more equal
enterprise. We pray you for your own sake to em-
brace your own safety and give over this attempt.

Ros. Do young sir; your reputation shall not therefore
be misprized: we will make it our suit to the Duke   170
that the wrestling might not go forward.

Orl. I beseech you, punish me not with your hard
thoughts, wherein I confess me much guilty to
deny so fair and excellent ladies anything. But let
your fair eyes and gentle wishes go with me to my   175
trial; wherein if I be foiled, there is but one shamed
that was never gracious; if killed, but one dead
that is willing to be so. I shall do my friends no
wrong, for I have none to lament me; the world no
injury, for in it I have nothing; only in the world I   180
fill up a place which may be better supplied when
I have made it empty.

Ros. The little strength that I have, I would it were
with you.

Celia. And mine to eke out hers.   185

Ros. Fare you well. Pray heaven I be deceived in you!

Celia. Your heart's desires be with you!

Cha. Come, where is this young gallant that is so
desirous to lie with his mother earth?

Orl. Ready sir, but his will hath in it a more modest   190
working.

164–5. your eyes . . . your judgement] *F*; our eyes . . . our judgment *Hanmer*;
your own eyes . . . your judgment *Johnson.*   176. wherein] *F*; Therein *conj.*
Johnson; herein *Dyce², conj. Capell.*   187. *Celia*]. *Cel. F; Orla. Theobald.*

164–5. *your eyes . . . your judgement*]
One cannot see one's self. Orlando
is dangerously unaware of what is
obvious to everyone else, his own
youth and slenderness contrasted with
the mature and muscular Charles.
Cf. *Troil.*, III. iii. 103ff.: 'The beauty
that is borne here in the face / The
bearer knows not, but commends itself/
To other's eyes.' See Tilley E342.

176. *wherein* etc.] I admit I deserve
your hard thoughts, but none the less,
do not think hardly of me. *Wherein*=
though (*NCS*). Cf. *Wint.*, I. i. 8 and
MND, III. ii. 179.

177. *gracious*] in anyone's good
graces, in favour.

191. *working*] endeavour, with
modest referring back to Charles's
witticism in the line above.

Duke F. You shall try but one fall.

Cha. No, I warrant your Grace you shall not entreat
    him to a second, that have so mightily persuaded
    him from a first.   195

Orl. You mean to mock me after: you should not have
    mocked me before. But come your ways.

Ros. Now Hercules be thy speed, young man!

Celia. I would I were invisible, to catch the strong
    fellow by the leg.   [*They*] *wrestle.*   200

Ros. O excellent young man!

Celia. If I had a thunderbolt in mine eye, I can tell who
    should down.   *Shout.* [*Charles is thrown.*]

Duke F. No more, no more.

Orl. Yes, I beseech your Grace, I am not yet well   205
    breathed.

Duke F. How dost thou Charles?

Le Beau. He cannot speak my lord.

---

196. You] *F*; An you *conj. Theobald*; If you *Rann, conj. Mason*; And you *conj.*
Camb.   200. SD *They wrestle.*] *F3*; *Wrestle. F.*   203. SD *Charles is thrown.*]
Rowe; not in F.   207–8. How . . . lord.] *Capell* (*prose*); *F* (*prose or verse*);
Keightley (*verse, one line*).   209. SD *Charles is borne out.*] *Steevens³; not in F.*

196–7. *You mean . . . before*] Don't
crow over me until you have in fact
won the victory you expect. The
emendation *And you mean* is justified
by the Cambridge editors on the
assumption that the compositor has
misread 'Orl. And' as the speech
heading *Orland*. The usual form of
the heading in F is *Orl.*

198. *Hercules be thy speed*] bring you
success. Hercules is invoked as a demi-
god, the apotheosis of physical
strength. Shakespeare may also have
had in mind his wrestling with
Antaeus, who renewed his strength at
every contact with the earth. Cf. ll.
188–9 above.

204–10. It is possible to set all this
as blank verse, though the spectators' comments on a wrestling match
seem hardly formal enough to warrant
it. *NCS* begins to set verse at l. 207.

There must be business at some
point with the speechless Charles,
which interrupts the flow. The obvious place is after *Bear him away*,
where F breaks the Duke's speech but
does not give a direction. Pope puts
the speech together again as one
blank-verse line. It is impossible to
know whether he thought the pre-
ceding two speeches were to be read,
with Keightley, as another blank-
verse line. Orlando, at l. 211,
answers in prose. He has to speak his
father's name and proper names are
not always metrically amenable.
Thereafter the scene settles down to
verse.

205–6. *well breathed*] adequately
exercised, fully extended. (*OED*
'breathe' 11). Cf. *Cor.*, I. v. 17: 'My
work hath yet not warm'd me' and
Per., II. iii. 101: 'Here is a lady that
wants breathing too.'

Duke F. Bear him away.   [*Charles is borne out.*]
    What is thy name, young man?   210
Orl. Orlando my liege, the youngest son of Sir Rowland
    de Boys.
Duke F. I would thou hadst been son to some man else.
    The world esteem'd thy father honourable,
    But I did find him still mine enemy.   215
    Thou should'st have better pleas'd me with this deed,
    Hadst thou descended from another house.
    But fare thee well, thou art a gallant youth—
    I would thou hadst told me of another father.
                    Exeunt Duke, [*Le Beau and train.*]
Celia. Were I my father, coz, would I do this?   220
Orl. I am more proud to be Sir Rowland's son,
    His youngest son, and would not change that calling
    To be adopted heir to Frederick.
Ros. My father lov'd Sir Rowland as his soul,
    And all the world was of my father's mind.   225
    Had I before known this young man his son,
    I should have given him tears unto entreaties,
    Ere he should thus have ventur'd.
Celia.   Gentle cousin,
    Let us go thank him and encourage him.
    My father's rough and envious disposition   230
    Sticks me at heart. Sir, you have well deserv'd.
    If you do keep your promises in love
    But justly, as you have exceeded all promise,
    Your mistress shall be happy.
Ros. [*giving him a chain from her neck*] Gentleman,   235
    Wear this for me; one out of suits with fortune,

209–10. Bear . . . man?] *Capell (prose)*; Beare . . . awaie: / . . . man? / *F*; *Pope
(verse, one line).*   219. SD *Exeunt . . . train.*] *Exit Duke, with his Train. Theobald;
Exit Duke. F.*   233. you have exceeded all] *F*; you've here exceeded *Hanmer*;
you have exceeded *Capell*; y'have here excell'd all *conj. Walker.* promise] *F*; in
promise *F2*; promise here *Keightley.*   235. SD *giving . . . neck*] *Theobald; not in F.*

215. *still*] always.
222. *calling*] name, a rare usage
(*OED* vbl sb. 1† 4, quoting *AYL*).
231. *Sticks me at heart*] grieves me
deeply.

236. *out of suits with fortune*] no
longer in fortune's livery. (*OED* 'suit'
sb. III. †13d. ?not in the uniform of,
hence, out of favour with). Malone
compares 'turning these jests out of

That could give more but that her hand lacks means.
Shall we go coz?
Celia.   Ay. Fare you well, fair gentleman.
Orl. Can I not say, 'I thank you'? My better parts
Are all thrown down, and that which here stands up 240
Is but a quintain, a mere lifeless block.
Ros. He calls us back. My pride fell with my fortunes;
I'll ask him what he would. Did you call sir?
Sir, you have wrestled well, and overthrown
More than your enemies.
Celia.   Will you go coz?   245
Ros. Have with you. Fare you well. *Exeunt [Rosalind and Celia.]*
Orl. What passion hangs these weights upon my tongue?
I cannot speak to her, yet she urg'd conference.

Enter LE BEAU.

O poor Orlando, thou art overthrown!
Or Charles, or something weaker masters thee.   250
Le Beau. Good sir, I do in friendship counsel you
To leave this place. Albeit you have deserv'd
High commendation, true applause, and love,
Yet such is now the Duke's condition
That he misconsters all that you have done.   255
The Duke is humorous; what he is indeed

237. could] *F*; would *Hanmer.*   248. SD *Enter Le Beau] F*; Halliwell *(after 250).*

service' at I. iii. 23–4. Whiter quotes *H5*, IV. iii. 117–19: 'pluck / The gay new coats o'er the French soldiers heads / And turn them out of service'.

237. *could give*] has the will to give. Cf. II. iv. 3, 'could find in my heart'.

240. *all thrown down*] Orlando's mind runs on wrestling. Cf. ll. 249–50 below. So does Rosalind's at ll. 242 and 244.

241. *quintain*] a post at which riders practising tilting directed their lances. It might be in a roughly human likeness, holding out a shield on a hinged arm. A second arm was so constructed as to swing round and

strike the rider if he did not disengage adroitly. See J. Stow, *A Survey of London* (1603), p. 95, 'Sports and pastimes of old time used in this Citie', with a woodcut.

255. *misconsters*] a form of 'misconstrues', with the accent on the second syllable.

256. *is humorous*] is temperamental, is not to be relied on. Holme thinks Le Beau is speaking in a fashionable jargon and implying that the Duke has a Jonsonian 'humour' of obstinacy. Humour was a word with wide connotations, which is perhaps why the cautious Le Beau uses it.

More suits you to conceive than I to speak of.
Orl. I thank you sir; and pray you tell me this,
Which of the two was daughter of the Duke
That here was at the wrestling?   260
Le Beau. Neither his daughter, if we judge by manners,
But yet indeed the taller is his daughter.
The other is daughter to the banish'd Duke,
And here detain'd by her usurping uncle
To keep his daughter company, whose loves   265
Are dearer than the natural bond of sisters.
But I can tell you that of late this Duke
Hath ta'en displeasure 'gainst his gentle niece,
Grounded upon no other argument
But that the people praise her for her virtues,   270
And pity her for her good father's sake;
And on my life his malice 'gainst the lady
Will suddenly break forth. Sir, fare you well.
Hereafter, in a better world than this,
I shall desire more love and knowledge of you.   275
Orl. I rest much bounden to you. Fare you well.

                                              [*Exit Le Beau.*]

---

262. taller] *F*; shorter *Rowe*[3]; smaller *Malone*; lower *Staunton*; lesser *Globe, conj.*
Spedding; less taller *Keightley.*   276. SD Exit Le Beau] *Capell*; *Rowe (after* 275); *not in F.* 279. Rosalind] *F (Rosaline), Rowe.*

262. *taller*] The Folio reading here
is contradicted by the fact that it is
Rosalind who dresses as a boy because she is 'more than common tall',
I. iii. 111, and Celia, as Aliena, is
'low / And browner than her brother',
IV. iii. 87–8. The Elizabethans used
'lower', 'lesser' and 'shorter' of a
person's height, none of them words
which could easily be misread as
taller. There is no evidence that they
used 'smaller' except in the very
general sense in which a child is
smaller than a grown-up. Sisson
argues for *smaller* as a possible rare
usage, which if it were initially blotted
or torn would inevitably be trans-
mitted as 'taller'. It is unlikely that the
players would go on saying 'taller'
with the contrary evidence before
their eyes, though they were hard-
worked people, as was the prompter,
who might not have taken the trouble
to make so small a correction had he
noticed the error. H. Brooks supplies
an instance in Massinger's *Believe as
you List* of an author's original error
being retained in a prompt book.
Taller may then go back to Shakespeare, setting down an antonym, as a
hurried writer will. For stage pur-
poses, 'shorter' seems the best substi-
tute. *Taller* is retained here on the
assumption that it is what Shakespeare wrote. See Intro., pp. xxix–xxx.
      269. *argument*] reason.

Thus must I from the smoke into the smother,
From tyrant Duke unto a tyrant brother.
But heavenly Rosalind!   *Exit.*

SCENE III

Enter CELIA *and* ROSALIND.

Celia. Why cousin, why Rosalind! Cupid have mercy,
    not a word?
Ros. Not one to throw at a dog.
Celia. No, thy words are too precious to be cast away
    upon curs. Throw some of them at me; come lame   5
    me with reasons.
Ros. Then there were two cousins laid up, when the one
    should be lamed with reasons and the other mad
    without any.
Celia. But is all this for your father?   10
Ros. No, some of it is for my child's father. O how full of
    briers is this working-day world!
Celia. They are but burs, cousin, thrown upon thee in
    holiday foolery; if we walk not in the trodden paths
    our very petticoats will catch them.   15
Ros. I could shake them off my coat: these burs are in
    my heart.

Scene III

Scene III] *Scena Tertius. F.* [Location] *an Apartment in the Palace Theobald*; *not in F.*
Rosalind] F (Rosaline), Rowe.   1. Rosalind] *F (Rosaline), Rowe.*   11. child's
father] *F*; Father's Child *Rowe*[3].

277. *smoke into the smother*] from bad
to worse. See Tilley (S570). *Smother* =
thick, choking smoke.

Scene III

8–9. *mad without any*] because she
has thrown them all at Celia, and
if one loses one's reason one is mad.
   11. *my child's father*] the man I shall
marry. Editorial delicacy has sometimes reversed the last two words.
   12. *working-day*] equivalent to the
modern 'ordinary everyday'. Celia's

holiday carries on the imagery (*NCS*).
   13. *burs*] the prickly, clinging
flower-heads of the burdock, am-
munition for the mischievous. See
Nicholas Culpeper, *The English Physi-
tian* (1652), 'The Bur-Dock . . . well
known even to the little Boys who pul
off the Burs to throw and stick upon
one another'. Cf. Marston, *The
Malcontent*, II. iii. 31–3: 'Thou burr,
that only stickest to nappy fortunes';
Troil., III. ii. 108–9: 'They are burs...
they'll stick where they are thrown';
MND, III. ii. 260; *Meas.*, IV. iii. 173.

Celia. Hem them away.

Ros. I would try, if I could cry hem and have him.

Celia. Come, come, wrestle with thy affections.   20

Ros. O they take the part of a better wrestler than myself.

Celia. O a good wish upon you! You will cry in time, in
     despite of a fall. But turning these jests out of
     service, let us talk in good earnest. Is it possible, on
     such a sudden, you should fall into so strong a liking   25
     with old Sir Rowland's youngest son?

Ros. The Duke my father loved his father dearly.

Celia. Doth it therefore ensue that you should love his son
     dearly? By this kind of chase, I should hate him,
     for my father hated his father dearly; yet I hate not   30
     Orlando.

Ros. No faith, hate him not, for my sake.

Celia. Why should I not? Doth he not deserve well?

Ros. Let me love him for that, and do you love him be-

22. cry] *Sisson;* trie *F.*   33. I not?] *F;* I? *Theobald;* I hate? *conj. Theobald.*
34–5. Let . . . Duke.] *As Pope (prose);* Let . . . him / Because . . . Duke. / *F.*

18. *Hem them away*] because they are
burs=a thickening of the voice, and
because the heart may be thought of
as sufficiently near the throat to be
affected by *hemming*=clearing.

19. *cry hem and have him*] Commentators have seen a reference to the
public crying of something lost.
Kittredge says the emphasis is on *hem*
and *have*, not on *hem* and *him*. Kökeritz (p. 114) says *cry*=to proclaim, to
call for, perhaps even to proclaim the
marriage banns of. Warburton claims
the phrase as proverbial. Harold
Brooks thinks the primary meaning
resides in *cry hem* interpreted as 'to
give a privy signal'. Rosalind would
be perfectly happy if she could call
Orlando to her in the secret language
of lovers. Circumstances thwart her,
not any doubt that Orlando would
come at her call. Cf. *Oth.,* IV. ii. 29:
'Cough, or cry "hem", if anybody
come', and *2H4,* III. ii. 212–13: 'Our
watchword was "Hem, boys!"'

22. *cry in time*] cry when your time

comes, i.e. your labour throes.
Sisson's emendation depends on the
strong resemblance between *t* and *c*
in an English secretary hand. Celia is
picking up Rosalind's reference to
my child's father, cry hem, and *wrestler,*
and she does in fact bestow *a good wish*
on her cousin, for a timely delivery.
Cf. Golding's *Ovid,* IX, 294: 'He came
untoo his wyfe then big and ready
downe to lye, / And sayd: twoo things
I wish thee. Tone, that when thou out
shalt cry, / Thou mayst dispatch with
little payne: the other that thou have /
A Boay . . .

25. *liking*] the speaker can't quite
bring herself to say love.

29. *chase*] (1) chain of arguments;
(2) hunt.

33. *Why should I not?*] Why should
I not do as you ask? i.e. love Orlando.
Sisson prefers 'Why should I not hate
him? Has he not deserved hatred, as
I have explained?'

34. *for that*] his deserts.

cause I do. Look, here comes the Duke.   35

Enter DUKE [FREDERICK] *with lords.*

Celia. With his eyes full of anger.

Duke F. Mistress, dispatch you with your safest haste
    And get you from our court.

Ros.   Me uncle?

Duke F.   You cousin.
    Within these ten days if that thou be'st found
    So near our public court as twenty miles,   40
    Thou diest for it.

Ros.   I do beseech your Grace,
    Let me the knowledge of my fault bear with me.
    If with myself I hold intelligence,
    Or have acquaintance with mine own desires,
    If that I do not dream, or be not frantic,   45
    As I do trust I am not, then dear uncle,
    Never so much as in a thought unborn
    Did I offend your Highness.

Duke F.   Thus do all traitors.
    If their purgation did consist in words,
    They are as innocent as grace itself.   50
    Let it suffice thee that I trust thee not.

Ros. Yet your mistrust cannot make me a traitor.
    Tell me whereon the likelihood depends.

---

35. SD *Enter Duke Frederick with Lords.*] *This ed*; *F* (*after 33, without Frederick*); *Steevens*[3] (*after 36*); *Collier* (*after* I do *at* 35).   53. likelihood] *F2*; likelihoods *F.*

37. *safest haste*] the haste that will best ensure your safety, i.e. it will be dangerous to delay.

43. *If . . . intelligence*] If I know what I'm talking about (and since the subject is my own feelings and actions, I ought to). To hold intelligence = to communicate (*OED* sb. 5, rare or obsolete).

49. *purgation*] 'the action of clearing oneself of an accusation or suspicion of crime or guilt' (*OED* 4). The Saxons employed purgation by oath, supported by a number of compur-gators, who testified to their belief in the honesty of the oath. In major criminal cases they had recourse to various forms of ordeal. These primitive methods of finding out the truth by invoking the justice of God were obsolete in the sixteenth century, not because they were no longer legal but because more sophisticated procedures were available. They were not formally abolished till the early nineteenth century. W. S. Holdsworth, *A History of English Law*, I (1956), pp. 305–12. Cf. Touchstone and purgation at v iv. 43–4.

Duke F. Thou art thy father's daughter, there's enough.

Ros. So was I when your Highness took his dukedom,   55
   So was I when your Highness banish'd him.
   Treason is not inherited, my lord,
   Or if we did derive it from our friends,
   What's that to me? My father was no traitor.
   Then good my liege, mistake me not so much   60
   To think my poverty is treacherous.

Celia. Dear sovereign, hear me speak.

Duke F. Ay Celia, we stay'd her for your sake,
   Else had she with her father rang'd along.

Celia. I did not then entreat to have her stay;   65
   It was your pleasure and your own remorse.
   I was too young that time to value her,
   But now I know her. If she be a traitor,
   Why so am I. We still have slept together,
   Rose at an instant, learn'd, play'd, eat together,   70
   And whereso'er we went, like Juno's swans,
   Still we went coupled and inseparable.

Duke F. She is too subtle for thee, and her smoothness,
   Her very silence, and her patience
   Speak to the people and they pity her.   75
   Thou art a fool; she robs thee of thy name,
   And thou wilt show more bright and seem more virtuous
   When she is gone. Then open not thy lips.
   Firm and irrevocable is my doom
   Which I have pass'd upon her; she is banish'd.   80

Celia. Pronounce that sentence then on me, my liege.
   I cannot live out of her company.

Duke F. You are a fool. You, niece, provide yourself.
   If you outstay the time, upon mine honour,
   And in the greatness of my word, you die.   85

   Exeunt Duke [Frederick] and train.

67. *too young*] suggesting a longer lapse of time than the facts of the play have so far seemed to warrant. See Intro., p. xxix.

69. *still*] always.

71. *Juno's swans*] Swans traditionally drew the chariot of Venus. Here Shakespeare assigns them, not in-appropriately, because they are royal birds, to the queen of the gods (H. Brooks). Cf. Kyd, *Soliman and Perseda*, IV. i. 70 (Oliver).

76. *fool*] with some sense of 'too innocent'.

77. *virtuous*] having admirable qualities.

Celia. O my poor Rosalind, whither wilt thou go?
Wilt thou change fathers? I will give thee mine.
I charge thee be not thou more griev'd than I am.
Ros. I have more cause.
Celia.   Thou hast not, cousin.
Prithee be cheerful. Know'st thou not the Duke   90
Hath banish'd me his daughter?
Ros.   That he hath not.
Celia. No, hath not? Rosalind lacks then the love
Which teacheth thee that thou and I am one.
Shall we be sunder'd? Shall we part, sweet girl?
No, let my father seek another heir.   95
Therefore devise with me how we may fly,
Whither to go and what to bear with us,
And do not seek to take your change upon you,
To bear your griefs yourself and leave me out.
For by this heaven, now at our sorrows pale,   100
Say what thou canst, I'll go along with thee.
Ros. Why, whither shall we go?
Celia. To seek my uncle in the Forest of Arden.

85. SD *Exeunt . . . train*] *Exeunt Duke, etc. Theobald; Exit Duke etc. F.*   86.
Rosalind] *F (Rosaline), Rowe.*   92. Rosalind] *F (Rosaline), Rowe. No hath not?*]
F; No? hath not? Theobald; No hath not? Singer²; No 'hath not'. conj. Halliwell².
93. thee] *F; Me Theobald.* thou] she *Rann, conj. Capell.* am] are *Hanmer.*
98. your change] *F;* your charge *F2;* the charge *Singer².*   102–3. Why . . .
go? / . . . Arden. /] *As F;* Why . . . go? / . . . uncle / . . . Arden. / *Capell;* Why
. . . uncle? *Steevens³;* Why . . . uncle / . . . Arden. / *Collier.*

98. *your change*] change of fortune.
Cf. *Ant.,* III. vi. 33–4: 'He his high
authority abus'd / And did deserve
his change.' Kittredge, who notes this
parallel, prefers to read *charge,* with
F2. *Charge,* interpreted 'burden' or
'weight' of trouble to be borne, agrees
with Celia's *bear.* There seems to have
been continual confusion between *n*
and *r,* in both manuscript and printed
texts. Cf. *AYL,* III. ii. 138: 'Therefore
Heaven Nature charg'd', where
F2 has an unacceptable reading
'chang'd', and 410, where F2 reads
'wash . . . clear' for F's 'wash . . .
clean'. *Ant.,* I. ii. 4: 'must change his
horns with garlands' has been

emended upon Warburton's conjecture to 'must charge his horns'.
It was easy in manuscript to read
double-stemmed *r* as *n.* A compositor
who suspected such a misreading
might take it upon himself to correct
it. Singer reads 'the' for *your,* con-
jecturing that the contraction *yᵉ* was
misread as *yʳ*.

100. *pale*] in shocked sympathy. Cf.
I. i. 155.

103. *in the Forest of Arden*] This
phrase, which Steevens dismissed as
extra-metrical, may have been added
in rehearsal to make the topography
of the play quite clear. So far Arden
has been named once only, at I. i. 114.

Ros. Alas, what danger will it be to us,
    Maids as we are, to travel forth so far?   105
    Beauty provoketh thieves sooner than gold.
Celia. I'll put myself in poor and mean attire,
    And with a kind of umber smirch my face;
    The like do you. So shall we pass along
    And never stir assailants.
Ros.   Were it not better,   110
    Because that I am more than common tall,
    That I did suit me all points like a man?
    A gallant curtle-axe upon my thigh,
    A boar-spear in my hand, and in my heart,
    Lie there what hidden woman's fear there will,   115
    We'll have a swashing and a martial outside,
    As many other mannish cowards have
    That do outface it with their semblances.
Celia. What shall I call thee when thou art a man?
Ros. I'll have no worse a name than Jove's own page,   120
    And therefore look you call me Ganymede.
    But what will you be call'd?
Celia. Something that hath a reference to my state.
    No longer Celia, but Aliena.
Ros. But cousin, what if we assay'd to steal   125
    The clownish fool out of your father's court?
    Would he not be a comfort to our travel?
Celia. He'll go along o'er the wide world with me;
    Leave me alone to woo him. Let's away,
    And get our jewels and our wealth together,   130
    Devise the fittest time and safest way
    To hide us from pursuit that will be made
    After my flight. Now go we in content
    To liberty, and not to banishment.   *Exeunt.*

133. we in] *F2*; in we *F*.

108. *umber*] brown earth such as is used to make the paint called umber.

113. *curtle-axe*] cutlass.

116. *swashing*] swaggering.

outside] (1) a suit of clothes; (2) outward appearance. Cf. *Tw.N.*, II. ii. 16: 'Fortune forbid my outside have not charm'd her!'. The stress is on *out*. See Abbott 455.

124. *Aliena*] generally given an accent on the penultimate syllable, though the line can be scanned with a stress on the second, which produces a truer parallel to Alinda.

ACT II

SCENE I

Enter DUKE SENIOR, AMIENS, *and two or three lords like foresters.*

Duke Sen. Now my co-mates and brothers in exile,
Hath not old custom made this life more sweet
Than that of painted pomp? Are not these woods
More free from peril than the envious court?
Here feel we not the penalty of Adam,   5

ACT II
Scene 1

ACT II. Scene 1] *Actus Secundus. Scæna Prima. F.* [Location] *Arden Forest, Theobald; not in F.* Amiens] *Amyens | F (so throughout, except at 18).*   5. not] *F; but Theobald; yet conj. Staunton.*   5–6. Adam, | The] *F;* Adam, | *(line missing)* | The *conj. Keightley.*   6. difference,] *F;* difference; *Theobald;* difference? *NCS, conj. Anon. (Gentleman's Magazine, 1784].*

1–17. It is characteristic of the Duke, and in accord with the sentiments expressed in the songs of Amiens, that he should make a disadvantage appear advantageous. The play invites us to honour him for it, though critics today do not always accept the invitation. See Intro., p. lxix. The power of the elements to teach proud man what he really is will be explored more deeply in *King Lear*. See Intro., p. lvii for parallels between this speech and Seneca's *Hippolytus*.

2. *old custom*] denoting a considerable lapse of time, unless J. H. Walter's interpretation is accepted, that it has been customary of old to praise the simple life. That custom makes all things easy is proverbial. See Tilley (C933). Cf. also *Ham.*, v. i. 67–8 and *Oth.*, I. iii. 229–31.

5. *feel we not*] Not 'we have no sense of' but 'we are none the worse for',

just as a negative answer to 'Do you feel the draught?' need not mean that the speaker is unaware of it, only that he is not inconvenienced by it. The Duke goes on to explain why he can make this claim. Theobald's emendation of *not* to 'but', which has found such favour, has the same general sense, that the rigours of winter are mild in comparison with the rigours of court life. H. J. C. Grierson, in 'A note on the text of *As You Like It*', *Modern Language Review*, IX (1914), pp. 370–2, suggests that the Duke is asking a rhetorical question, and *NCS* puts a question mark after *difference*, following a conjecture first made in *The Gentleman's Magazine*, LIV (1784), p. 407. Sisson objects that 'We are free from painted pomp, are free from peril' does not parallel 'we are unfortunately subject to winter and wind', but the parallel is

The seasons' difference, as the icy fang
And churlish chiding of the winter's wind,
Which when it bites and blows upon my body
Even till I shrink with cold, I smile, and say
'This is no flattery. These are counsellors   10
That feelingly persuade me what I am'.
Sweet are the uses of adversity,
Which like the toad, ugly and venomous,
Wears yet a precious jewel in his head;
And this our life, exempt from public haunt,   15
Finds tongues in trees, books in the running brooks,
Sermons in stones, and good in everything.
Ami. I would not change it. Happy is your Grace,
That can translate the stubbornness of fortune

18. *Ami.* I] *F*; I *Dyce, Grant White, conj. Upton.* it. Happy] *F (subst.)*; it. | *Ami.*
Happy *Dyce, Grant White, conj. Upton.*

'we are free from flattery'. When
almost absolute power was vested in a
prince, he lived in a hothouse of self-
interested adulation. It is worth
noting here how many English
monarchs have taken a special delight
in field-sports as a relaxation from
court life.

the penalty of Adam] In Eden there
was eternal summer. After the Fall,
the earth shared the curse. See
Genesis 3:17: 'Cursed is the ground
for thy sake', and Romans 8:22: 'For
we know that the whole creation
groaneth and travaileth in pain
together until now.' The seasons
altered, the axis of the earth was
tilted and it became subject to
extremes of climate. See *Paradise Lost*,
X, 651ff. The Duke is generalizing
about the pains incident to the un-
idealized pastoral life. He is not
commenting on the weather at the
time of speaking, and we do not have
to suppose that the scene is set in
winter. Cf. the idealized picture that
Charles, who knew of it only by
hearsay, gives at I. i.

6. *difference*] (1) change; (2)
dissension.

as] for instance.

12. *uses*] profits. Halliwell[2] quotes
Henry Smith's *Sermons* (1609), p. 87:
'They are distinguished by the *use of
adversity*: for this is a proper and
peculiar marke of Gods children, to
profit by affliction.'

13. *the toad*] Cf. Lyly, *Euphues*
(Bond, I, p. 202), 'The foule Toade
hathe a fayre stoane in his head.'
Toads are not venomous, though they
were long thought to be so. See Pliny,
Natural History, XXV, and *R3*,
I. iii. 246. The jewel is imaginary and
the lore about it is confused. Its
value was medicinal, as an antidote
to venom, which fits the Duke's train
of thought. Cf. *H5*, IV. i. 4–5: 'There
is some soul of goodness in things evil,
/ Would men observingly distil it out.'

15. *public haunt*] resort of men.

18. *I would not change it*] In defiance
of F, this line is often given to the
Duke, but as Furness pertinently
observes, 'The Duke has asked a
question. Is no one to answer?' *NCS*
says that 'it crowns the Duke's speech
rhythmically and poetically', and
goes on to the dubious inference that
here Amiens's cue, i.e. the end of the

Into so quiet and so sweet a style.   20
Duke Sen. Come, shall we go and kill us venison?
    And yet it irks me the poor dappled fools,
    Being native burghers of this desert city,
    Should in their own confines with forked heads
    Have their round haunches gor'd.
First Lord.   Indeed my lord,   25
    The melancholy Jaques grieves at that,
    And in that kind swears you do more usurp
    Than doth your brother that hath banish'd you.
    To-day my Lord of Amiens and myself
    Did steal behind him as he lay along   30
    Under an oak, whose antique root peeps out
    Upon the brook that brawls along this wood,
    To the which place a poor sequester'd stag,
    That from the hunter's aim had ta'en a hurt,
    Did come to languish; and indeed my lord,   35

Duke's speech, has been inadvertently incorporated in his part.

22. *irks me*] makes me uncomfortable.

fools] innocent, vulnerable creatures. 'Poor dears' (*NCS*). Hotson refers the epithet *dappled* to the fool's motley (p. 41). Shakespeare generally ranges himself on the side of the quarry against the hunter. Cf. *LLL*, IV. i. 8 and 24–35, and the hunted hare in *Ven.* 679–708. The *sobbing deer* is a well-known topos, in which the attitude of the scholar (Jaques) is opposed to that of the courtier (the Duke and his retinue). But the Duke in Arden must hunt to live, and regrets the necessity. Courtiers were sometimes scholars, too. C. Uhlig, in '"The sobbing deer" . . . and the historical context', *Renaissance Drama* (1970), pp. 79–109, discusses Shakespeare's treatment of the subject, relating it to Sidney's *Arcadia* (Feuillerat, I, p. 61) and showing how strongly emblematic it is. Does this explain why it is presented pictorially, in reported speech, and not in action? See note on ll. 30–1 below.

23. *burghers*] Steevens notes that Sidney, *Arcadia*, 1590, and Drayton, *Polyolbion*, 1613, 65–6, use this periphrasis. Cf. also Lodge, *Rosalynde*, p. 116: 'The citizens of wood'; *Scillaes Metamorphosis*, 1590, sig. F^v, 'Poem in Commendation of the Solitarie Life': 'the citizens of Forest'; Nashe, *Pierce Pennilesse*, 1592: 'the nimble citizens of the wood'.

24. *forked heads*] barbed arrows, perhaps not in any very technical sense. Ascham says that a 'forkehead' has 'ii poyntes stretchyng forwarde' (*Toxophilus*, ed. Arber, p. 135).

26. *Jaques*] Pronounced as a disyllable. See Intro., p. lxviii.

30–1. *he lay along / Under an oak*] the stereotyped attitude of the pastoral moralist. In 1723 this speech was ingeniously transposed, so that the actor playing Jaques could speak for himself, a device long favoured by the stage. See, for example, J. P. Kemble's acting copy, 1812.

33. *sequester'd*] cut off from his fellows.

The wretched animal heav'd forth such groans
That their discharge did stretch his leathern coat
Almost to bursting, and the big round tears
Cours'd one another down his innocent nose
In piteous chase; and thus the hairy fool,   40
Much marked of the melancholy Jaques,
Stood on th'extremest verge of the swift brook,
Augmenting it with tears.
Duke Sen.   But what said Jaques?
Did he not moralize this spectacle?
First Lord. O yes, into a thousand similes.   45
First, for his weeping into the needless stream,
'Poor deer', quoth he, 'thou mak'st a testament
As worldlings do, giving thy sum of more
To that which had too much.' Then being there alone,
Left and abandon'd of his velvet friend,   50
''Tis right', quoth he, 'thus misery doth part
The flux of company.' Anon a careless herd,
Full of the pasture, jumps along by him
And never stays to greet him. 'Ay', quoth Jaques,
'Sweep on you fat and greasy citizens,   55

42. th'extremest] *F*; the extremest *Hanmer*.   49. much] *F2*; must *F*. there]
F; *not in F2*.   50. friend] *F*; Friends *Rowe*.

38. *tears*] It was a commonplace
that deer wept when distressed. Cf.
Ham., III. ii. 264: 'Why, let the
stricken deer go weep'; Golding's
Ovid, III, 240ff.; Sidney, *Arcadia*,
1590, p. 61; Drayton, *Polyolbion*,
XIII, 100–61.

44. *moralize*] expound in a moral
sense.

46–9. See T. W. Baldwin, *The
Literary Genetics of Shakespere's Plays*,
pp. 310–11, for a history of this
conceit, a favourite with Shakespeare,
which Baldwin traces to the *Adagia* of
Erasmus.

50. *velvet friend*] The velvet is that
of the stag's sleek coat. Nothing so
particular is meant as the 'velvet' of
his horns. Sisson explains it as
'horned', distinguishing the stag from
the doe. Most editors read *friends* to

agree with *herd*. Jaques is thinking
more of men than of deer, and the
intimate personal situation, the
successful man avoiding his bankrupt
friend, is appropriate. *Velvet* was an
epithet in regular use to indicate a
real or more often an assumed
superiority in status. Cf. Nashe,
Pierce Pennilesse, 1592 (I, p. 160):
'carterly vpstarts, that outface Towne
and Country in their Veluets', and
Greene, *A Quip for an Vpstart Courtier:
or, A quaint dispute between veluet
breeches and cloth-breeches*, 1592.

51. *part*] depart from.

55. *greasy*] (1) well supplied with
money and good fare; (2) soiled with
handling goods in shops or ware-
houses. Cf. Nashe, *Pierce Pennilesse*,
1592: 'the greasie son of a Cloathier',
I, p. 168.

'Tis just the fashion. Wherefore do you look
Upon that poor and broken bankrupt there?'
Thus most invectively he pierceth through
The body of country, city, court,
Yea, and of this our life, swearing that we   60
Are mere usurpers, tyrants, and what's worse,
To fright the animals and to kill them up
In their assign'd and native dwelling-place.

Duke Sen. And did you leave him in this contemplation?

Second Lord. We did my lord, weeping and commenting   65
        Upon the sobbing deer.

Duke Sen.   Show me the place:
I love to cope him in these sullen fits,
For then he's full of matter.

First Lord. I'll bring you to him straight.   *Exeunt.*

SCENE II

Enter DUKE [FREDERICK] *with lords.*

Duke F. Can it be possible that no man saw them?
It cannot be; some villains of my court
Are of consent and sufferance in this.

First Lord. I cannot hear of any that did see her.
The ladies her attendants of her chamber   5

59. of] *F*; of the *F2*.   65. *Second Lord.*] 2. *Lord. F*; *Ami. | Capell.*

Scene II

Scene II] *Scena Secunda. F.* [Location] *The Palace. Rowe*; *not in F. Frederick*] *Pope*;
junior | Capell; *not in F.*

59. *country*] Many editors prefer to
read 'the country', with *F2*, in order
to make the line metrically regular.
Malone thinks *country* might be read
as a trisyllable. A slight prolongation
of the natural pauses in the verse will
have the same effect. What jars on a
printer will not necessarily present any
problem to an actor.

62. *kill them up*] A common
Elizabethan usage, implying a whole-
sale slaughter, comparable with
modern 'kill off'.

67. *cope*] encounter, debate with.
Cf. *Ham.*, III. ii. 52–3: 'as just a man
| As e'er my conversation cop'd
withal.'

68. *matter*] ideas, matter for argu-
ments. Cf. 'He is too disputable',
II. v. 31–2, and 'A material fool',
III. iii. 28.

Scene II

2. *villains*] lower servants (Grant
White). Cf. I. i. 55.

Saw her abed, and in the morning early,
They found the bed untreasur'd of their mistress.
Second Lord. My lord, the roynish clown, at whom so oft
Your Grace was wont to laugh, is also missing.
Hisperia, the princess' gentlewoman,   10
Confesses that she secretly o'erheard
Your daughter and her cousin much commend
The parts and graces of the wrestler
That did but lately foil the sinewy Charles,
And she believes wherever they are gone   15
That youth is surely in their company.
Duke F. Send to his brother. Fetch that gallant hither.
If he be absent, bring his brother to me;
I'll make him find him. Do this suddenly;
And let not search and inquisition quail   20
To bring again these foolish runaways.   *Exeunt.*

SCENE III

Enter ORLANDO *and* ADAM [*meeting.*]

Orl. Who's there?
Adam. What my young master? O my gentle master,
O my sweet master, O you memory
Of old Sir Rowland! Why, what make you here?
Why are you virtuous? Why do people love you?   5
And wherefore are you gentle, strong, and valiant?
Why would you be so fond to overcome

17. brother] *F*; brother's *Capell.*

Scene III

Scene III] *Scena Tertia. F.* [Location] *Before Oliver's House. Capell; not in F.* SD
meeting] *Capell; not in F.*   8. bonny] *F* (bonnie); boney *Warburton.*

8. *roynish*] From French 'rogneux' =   19. *suddenly*] immediately.
scurvy, and hence 'coarse.' Cf. Nashe,   20. *quail*] slacken.
Strange Newes, 1592 (I, 324), 'clownish
and roynish ieasts'.
  13. *wrestler*] a trisyllable here.   *Scene* III
  17. *brother*] There seems no justifica-
tion for Capell's *brother's.* The elder   3. *memory*] memorial.
brother is told to yield the younger up.   7. *fond*] foolish. Preserved in
Gallant = Orlando.   northern dialect.

The bonny prizer of the humorous Duke?
Your praise is come too swiftly home before you.
Know you not master, to some kind of men,   10
Their graces serve them but as enemies?
No more do yours. Your virtues, gentle master,
Are sanctified and holy traitors to you.
O what a world is this, when what is comely
Envenoms him that bears it!   15

Orl. Why, what's the matter?

Adam.   O unhappy youth,
Come not within these doors; within this roof
The enemy of all your graces lives.
Your brother, no, no brother, yet the son—
Yet not the son, I will not call him son—   20
Of him I was about to call his father,
Hath heard your praises, and this night he means
To burn the lodging where you use to lie,
And you within it. If he fail of that,
He will have other means to cut you off.   25
I overheard him, and his practices.
This is no place: this house is but a butchery.
Abhor it, fear it, do not enter it.

Orl. Why whither Adam would'st thou have me go?

Adam. No matter whither, so you come not here.   30

Orl. What, wouldst thou have me go and beg my food,
Or with a base and boist'rous sword enforce
A thievish living on the common road?
This I must do, or know not what to do;

---

10. some] *F2*; seeme *F*.   16. *Orl.*] *F2*; *not in F*.   17. within this] *F*; beneath this *conj. Capell*.   29. *Orl.*] *F2*; *Ad. F*.

8. *bonny*] robust, sturdily built. Preserved in northern dialect. Cf. *Rosalynde*: 'a Norman, a man of tall stature and of great strength; so valiant, that in many such conflicts he always bare away the victory, not only overthrowing them which he encountered, but often with the weight of his body killing them outright' (Greg, p. 14).

humorous] See I. ii. 256, note.

17. *within*] cf. Chapman's *Odyssey*: 'Within your roofe', XIV, 279 (Dyce). Wright instances similar usages.

26. *practices*] plots.

27. *no place*] no appropriate, here 'no safe' place for you, a usage that goes back to the sixteenth century, and seems preferable to Steevens's 'Place'=a gentleman's house. See *OED* sb. iv. 12.

butchery] a slaughterhouse.

Yet this I will not do, do how I can.   35
I rather will subject me to the malice
Of a diverted blood and bloody brother.
Adam. But do not so. I have five hundred crowns,
The thrifty hire I sav'd under your father,
Which I did store to be my foster-nurse,   40
When service should in my old limbs lie lame,
And unregarded age in corners thrown.
Take that, and He that doth the ravens feed,
Yea providently caters for the sparrow,
Be comfort to my age. Here is the gold,   45
All this I give you. Let me be your servant.
Though I look old, yet I am strong and lusty;
For in my youth I never did apply
Hot and rebellious liquors in my blood,
Nor did not with unbashful forehead woo   50
The means of weakness and debility.
Therefore my age is as a lusty winter,
Frosty, but kindly. Let me go with you,
I'll do the service of a younger man
In all your business and necessities.   55
Orl. O good old man, how well in thee appears
The constant service of the antique world,
When service sweat for duty, not for meed.

---

57. service] *F*; favour *conj. Collier*²; duty *conj. Walker*; temper *conj. Lettsom*;
fashion *conj. Keightley*; virtue *conj. Neil.*   58. meed] *F*; neede *F2.*

37. *diverted blood*] a blood relationship taking an unnatural course.
39. *thrifty hire*] that part of my
wages that I have thriftily put by.
41. *should . . . lie*] This verb is to be
understood in the next line.
43–4. *ravens . . . sparrow*] Psalm
147:9. and Matt. 10:29.
49. *rebellious*] tending to overset the
proper government of body and
mind. Cf. Medwall's *Nature* (Whiting
D395): 'For hote drynkys and dely-
cate refeccyon / Causeth flesshely
insurreccyon.' Adam is a very careful
study of an old man. He has the old
man's foible of attributing his health
and longevity to some favourite form

of abstinence, in which he instructs
his hearers whether they want to
know of it or not.
57–8. *service*] Editors have doubted
whether Shakespeare would use this
word twice in consecutive lines, but
repetition is a feature of the whole
speech. *Service* occurs three times,
sweat and *having* twice. Orlando is
saying that men cease to be obliging
once their assiduity has won the
desired promotion. Service is no
longer disinterested.
58. *meed*] reward. Furness reports
that his copy of F plainly reads
'neede'. It appears that he was mis-
led by a minim erasure, presumably

Thou art not for the fashion of these times,
Where none will sweat but for promotion,   60
And having that, do choke their service up
Even with the having; it is not so with thee.
But poor old man, thou prun'st a rotten tree,
That cannot so much as a blossom yield,
In lieu of all thy pains and husbandry.   65
But come thy ways, we'll go along together,
And ere we have thy youthful wages spent,
We'll light upon some settled low content.
Adam. Master go on, and I will follow thee
To the last gasp with truth and loyalty.   70
From seventeen years, till now almost fourscore
Here lived I, but now live here no more.
At seventeen years, many their fortunes seek
But at fourscore, it is too late a week;
Yet fortune cannot recompense me better   75
Than to die well, and not my master's debtor.   *Exeunt.*

SCENE IV.

Enter ROSALIND *as* GANYMEDE, CELIA *as* ALIENA
and TOUCHSTONE.

Ros. O Jupiter, how weary are my spirits!
Touch. I care not for my spirits, if my legs were not weary.

71. seventeen] *Rowe;* seauentie *F.*

Scene IV

Scene IV] *Scena Quarta. F.* [Location] *the Forest of Arden. Theobald; not in F.* SD
*Rosalind] F (Rosaline), Rowe. Touchstone] Singer; Clowne, alias Touchstone F;
Touchstone, the Clown. Johnson.*   1. weary] *Theobald, conj. Warburton;* merry *F.*

made by a previous owner. See H. J.
Oliver, *Notes and Queries,* XIV (1967),
p. 136.

65. *In lieu of*] in return for.

71–6. *From . . . debtor*] F marks the
metrical pauses throughout this
passage, perhaps to reflect a characteristic rhythm in the old man's speech,
short-breathed and emphatic.

Scene IV

1. *O Jupiter*] Rosalind, having

taken the name of Jove's page,
swears by her master. Cf. l. 57 below,
and III. i. 152. The Elizabethans
carried the nice choice of oaths to
excess, and laughed at themselves for
it. See *Arcadia* (Feuillerat, I, p. 87 and
IV, p. 26), and Bobadil in Jonson's
Every Man in his Humour.

weary] emended from *merry,* on the
assumption that there has been an
m/w confusion, particularly easy if the
manuscript spelling was *werie.*

Ros. I could find in my heart to disgrace my man's
apparel and to cry like a woman. But I must comfort the weaker vessel, as doublet and hose ought   5
to show itself courageous to petticoat; therefore
courage, good Aliena.

Celia. I pray you bear with me. I cannot go no further.

Touch. For my part, I had rather bear with you than
bear you; yet I should bear no cross if I did bear   10
you, for I think you have no money in your purse.

Ros. Well, this is the Forest of Arden.

Touch. Ay, now am I in Arden, the more fool I; when I
was at home I was in a better place, but travellers
must be content.   15

Ros. Ay, be so, good Touchstone.

Enter CORIN *and* SILVIUS.

Look you, who comes here,
A young man and an old in solemn talk.

Corin. That is the way to make her scorn you still.

Silv. O Corin, that thou knew'st how I do love her!   20

Corin. I partly guess; for I have lov'd ere now.

Silv. No Corin, being old, thou canst not guess,
Though in thy youth thou wast as true a lover
As ever sigh'd upon a midnight pillow.
But if thy love were ever like to mine,   25
As sure I think did never man love so,
How many actions most ridiculous
Hast thou been drawn to by thy fantasy?

Corin. Into a thousand that I have forgotten.

---

8. cannot] *F*; can *F2*.   16. SD *Enter Corin and Silvius*] *Wright*; *F* (*after 15*);
Theobald (*after 18*).   16–18. Ay . . . Touchstone. / (*prose*). Look . . . here, /
. . . talk. / (*verse*)] *This ed*; I . . . talke. *F* (*prose*); Ay . . . here? / . . . talk. /
Capell (*verse*); Ay, / Be . . . here— / . . . talk. / *NCS, conj. Walker* (*verse*).

5. *weaker vessel*] 1 Peter 3:7.
8. *cannot*] Abbott 406.
10. *bear no cross*] Mat. 10:38.
Elizabethan silver coins were stamped
with crosses, which provided material
for simple jokes. Jesting apart, Celia
had money available. See I. iii. 130

and ll. 61 and 90–3 below.
16–18. *Ay . . . talk*] Rosalind answers
Touchstone in prose, and does not
change to verse until she announces
the entrance of Corin and Silvius,
who are going to be verse speakers.
28. *fantasy*] amorous desire.

Silv. O thou didst then never love so heartily.   30
     If thou remember'st not the slightest folly
     That ever love did make thee run into,
     Thou hast not lov'd.
     Or if thou hast not sat as I do now,
     Wearying thy hearer in thy mistress' praise,   35
     Thou hast not lov'd.
     Or if thou hast not broke from company
     Abruptly as my passion now makes me,
     Thou hast not lov'd.
     O Phebe, Phebe, Phebe!   *Exit.*   40
Ros. Alas, poor shepherd, searching of thy wound,
     I have by hard adventure found mine own.
Touch. And I mine. I remember when I was in love
     I broke my sword upon a stone, and bid him take
     that for coming a-night to Jane Smile; and I re-   45
     member the kissing of her batler, and the cow's dugs
     that her pretty chopt hands had milked; and I
     remember the wooing of a peascod instead of her,

---

30. never] *F*; ne'er *Rowe*.   35. Wearying] *F2*; wearing *F*.   41. thy wound]
Rowe; they would *F*; their wound *F2*.   46. batler] *F*; batlet *F2*.

30. *O*] Silvius's speech is very
broken and this moan of protest need
be no part of a regular blank-verse
line. Many editors prefer to ensure
regularity by abbreviating *never*.

35. *Wearying*] Midland records of
the sixteenth century show 'many
spellings of the gerund and present
participle in which the final *y* of the
verb stem is lost before the *-ing* ending' (Hulme, p. 319). Cf. *Ant.*, I. iv.
46, where for 'lacking' Theobald
reads 'lackeying'. In *AYL*, *defying* is
emended to 'deifying' at III. ii. 353.
The modern reader requires the *y* as
a guide to pronunciation. Hulme defends the F reading by quoting
Jonson, *The Gypsies Metamorphos'd*
(VII, l. 610): 'time and ears out-
wearinge'.

41. *searching*] probing.

thy wound] Sisson explains the F
reading by supposing that Shakes-

peare wrote *woude*. The digraph *de*
was misread as the digraph *ld* and *thy*
was then emended to agree with
would.

42. *by hard adventure*] unluckily for
me.

46. *batler*] a wooden bat for beating
clothes in the wash, sometimes
written *batlet*. Harold Brooks suggests
that Shakespeare passed from laundry
to milking by way of Golding's *Ovid*,
'udders full of batling (= nourishing)
milk', XV, l. 526.

47. *chopt*] chapped.

48. *wooing of a peascod*] By *peascod*
Touchstone means the whole plant,
of which the *cods* are the husks, from
cod = husk or bag. Cf. codpiece.
Touchstone, as a jester, underlines the
equivocal associations here. He describes himself acting a love scene in
the absence of the beloved, a caper
very common to lovers. J. O. Halli-

from whom I took two cods, and giving her them
again, said with weeping tears, 'Wear these for my   50
sake'. We that are true lovers run into strange
capers; but as all is mortal in nature, so is all nature
in love mortal in folly.

Ros. Thou speak'st wiser than thou art ware of.

Touch. Nay, I shall ne'er be ware of my own wit, till I   55
break my shins against it.

Ros. Jove, Jove! this shepherd's passion
Is much upon my fashion.

Touch. And mine, but it grows something stale with me.

Celia. I pray you, one of you question yond man, if he for   60
gold will give us any food. I faint almost to death.

Touch. Holla, you clown!

Ros. Peace fool, he's not thy kinsman.

Corin. Who calls?

Touch. Your betters sir.   65

Corin. Else are they very wretched.

Ros. Peace, I say. Good even to you friend.

Corin. And to you gentle sir, and to you all.

Ros. I prithee shepherd, if that love or gold

55–6. Nay . . . it.] *As F* (*prose*); Nay . . . wit, / . . . it. *Collier* (*verse*).   57–8.
Jove . . . passion / . . . fashion. /] *As F* (*verse*); *Pope* (*prose*).   60. yond] *Rowe*;
yon'd *F*; yon *Capell*.   60–1. I . . . death.] *This ed* (*prose*); I . . . / man, / . . .
foode, / . . . death. /*F* (*verse*).   61–3. I . . . kinsman.] *This ed* (*prose*); *F* (*verse
or prose*); I . . . death. / . . . kinsman. / *Steevens*³ (*verse*); I . . . clown. / . . .
kinsman. / *Keightley* (*verse*).   65–7. Your betters sir. / . . . wretched. / . . .
friend. /] *As F*; Your betters sir. / . . . say. / . . . friend. *Steevens*³ (*verse*); Your
. . . wretched. / . . . friend. / *Hudson* (*verse*).   68. you] *F2*; your *F*.

---

well says pea-pods were used as rustic
love-tokens and quotes Browne's
Britannia's Pastorals (1673) (B ii, Song
3, 93–6): 'The peascod greene oft
with no little toyle / Hee'd seeke for
in the fattest fertil'st soile / And rend
it from the stalke to bring it to her /
And in her bosome for acceptance
wooe her' (*Dictionary*, 1910, II, p.
610).

50. *weeping tears*] A common expression in Elizabethan English.
Halliwell² gives many parallels.

52–3. *all is mortal . . . folly*] The gist

is that as sure as mortality is a condition of life so is folly of love. Mortal
= (1) subject to death; (2) extreme (a
common intensitive).

54–5. *ware*] (1) aware; (2) cautious.

60–8. The dialogue at some point
modulates from Touchstone's prose
to a stately verse-exchange between
Rosalind and Corin. Celia's state of
collapse will not support the artifice
of verse. Cf. Rosalind's swoon at IV.
iii. 156, which swings a verse episode
abruptly into prose, and Othello's fit
at IV. i. 35–43. Line 60, ending at

Can in this desert place buy entertainment,   70
Bring us where we may rest ourselves and feed.
Here's a young maid with travel much oppress'd,
And faints for succour.

Corin.   Fair sir, I pity her,
And wish, for her sake more than for mine own,
My fortunes were more able to relieve her;   75
But I am shepherd to another man,
And do not shear the fleeces that I graze.
My master is of churlish disposition,
And little recks to find the way to heaven
By doing deeds of hospitality.   80
Besides, his cote, his flocks, and bounds of feed
Are now on sale, and at our sheepcote now
By reason of his absence there is nothing
That you will feed on. But what is, come see,
And in my voice most welcome shall you be.   85

Ros. What is he that shall buy his flock and pasture?

Corin. That young swain that you saw here but erewhile,
That little cares for buying anything.

Ros. I pray thee, if it stand with honesty,
Buy thou the cottage, pasture, and the flock,   90
And thou shalt have to pay for it of us.

Celia. And we will mend thy wages. I like this place,
And willingly could waste my time in it.

Corin. Assuredly the thing is to be sold.
Go with me; if you like upon report   95

92–3. And . . . place, / . . . it. /] *As Capell*; And . . . wages: / . . . could / . . . it. *F*; And . . . wages / . . . waste / . . . it. / *Rowe.*[3]

man in F, scans badly even with *question* a trisyllable. The quick exchanges at ll. 62–6 are better in prose than shuffled into a variety of awkward verse lines, to whose arrangement F gives no clue. It is true that Corin appears to be steadily attempting verse, but he fails to impose it on the scene until Rosalind addresses him in a complete and courteous pentameter at l. 67, to which he replies in kind. The scene proceeds so to the end, making it logical to arrange ll. 92–3 as regular blank verse.

79. *little recks*] takes no pains.

85. *in my voice*] so far as I have any say in the matter. *Voice* = vote.

87. *erewhile*] a short time ago.

89. *stand with honesty*] If you can do it without taking an unfair advantage of the love-sick Silvius.

93. *waste my time*] spend or pass the time, with no sense of making poor use of it. Cf. II. vii. 112.

The soil, the profit, and this kind of life,
I will your very faithful feeder be,
And buy it with your gold right suddenly.   *Exeunt.*

SCENE V

Enter AMIENS, JAQUES *and others.*

[*Amiens sings.*]

      Under the greenwood tree,
        Who loves to lie with me,
      And turn his merry note
        Unto the sweet bird's throat,
      Come hither, come hither, come hither.   5
        Here shall he see
        No enemy,
      But winter and rough weather.

Jaques. More, more, I prithee more.
Ami. It will make you melancholy, Monsieur Jaques.   10
Jaques. I thank it. More, I prithee more. I can suck
   melancholy out of a song, as a weasel sucks eggs.
   More, I prithee more.

Scene v

Scene v] *Scena Quinta. F.* [Location] *a desart Part of the Forest. Theobald; not in F.*
SD *Amiens sings.*] Song. *F.*   1. *Under*] F; *Ami. Under / Capell.*   3. *turn*] F
*(turne); tune Rowe.*³   6–7. *Here . . . enemy*] *As Pope; one line F. Here*] F; Cho.
Here / Capell.   11–13. *I . . . more.*] *As Pope (prose);* I . . . more, / . . . song,
/ . . . more. / F.

97. *feeder*] shepherd. *NCS* considers that Corin was attached to the farm, still in effect in a state of villeinage. Harold Brooks cannot see that the text suggests more than that it was natural for a new purchaser to retain the old shepherd. Silvius had no interest in dismissing him and it was manifestly advantageous for Rosalind and Celia to keep him.

98. *suddenly*] without delay.

Scene v

1. Under the greenwood tree] A stock phrase in ballads.

3. turn] adapt, follow the bird's

singing. Cf. Hall's *Satires*, ed. Davenport, vi. i. 195: 'Thred-bare Martiall turnes his merry note' (Singer). Bond claims a source in Lyly, *The Woman in the Moon*, iii. ii. 168: 'And we will sing vnto the wilde birdes notes.' There is no need to read *tunes* for *turnes*, although Shakespeare uses *tune* in *Gent.*, v. iv. 5–6: 'And to the nightingale's complaining notes / Tune my distresses' (Malone) and Lyly in *Campaspe*, v. i. 41: 'Poore Robin redbreast tunes his note' (H. Brooks).

11–13. In this scene, where all the conversation is in prose, four speeches by Jaques, here and at ll. 15–17, 31–4,

Ami. My voice is ragged, I know I cannot please you.

Jaques. I do not desire you to please me, I do desire you   15
to sing. Come, more, another stanzo. Call you 'em
stanzos?

Ami. What you will Monsieur Jaques.

Jaques. Nay, I care not for their names, they owe me
nothing. Will you sing?   20

Ami. More at your request than to please myself.

Jaques. Well then, if ever I thank any man, I'll thank
you; but that they call compliment is like th'encounter of two dog-apes. And when a man thanks
me heartily, methinks I have given him a penny and   25
he renders me the beggarly thanks. Come sing; and
you that will not, hold your tongues.

Ami. Well, I'll end the song. Sirs, cover the while: the
Duke will drink under this tree. He hath been all
this day to look you.   30

Jaques. And I have been all this day to avoid him. He is
too disputable for my company. I think of as many
matters as he, but I give heaven thanks and make
no boast of them. Come, warble, come.

[Amiens sings] Who doth ambition shun,   35
       And loves to live i' th' sun,

15–17. I . . . stanzos?] *As Pope (prose)*; I . . . me, / . . . sing: / . . . stanzo's? /
F.   31–4. And . . . come.] *As Pope (prose)*; And . . . him: / . . . companie: /
. . . giue / . . . them. / . . . come. / *F.*   36. *live*] *F*; lye *F4.*

43–4, and one by Amiens at l. 59 are
set as verse. It was presumably a
device of the printer to spread insufficient copy over more space than
it would normally require. It has not
been done to great purpose. Printed
as prose the copy would fill much the
same number of lines. Various
spreading devices have not been
attempted, notably wider spacing
before and after stage directions.

16. *stanzo*] Jaques in his character
of plain man and hater of compliment dismisses the term as an
affectation. He has it at his command,
though, as he has *sans.*

19. *names . . . owe*] *Nomina,* in

Thomas Cooper's *Thesaurus* (1573), is
glossed 'the names of debtes owen'.

24. *dog-apes*] baboons. Cf. *Tim.,*
I. i. 252–3: 'And all this courtesy!
The strain of man's bred out / Into
baboon and monkey.'

26. *beggarly thanks*] fulsome thanks
such as a beggar gives for alms.

28. *cover*] lay the table.

30. *look you*] look for you.

32. *disputable*] given to argument,
disputatious. Jaques prefers to initiate
argument himself.

36. live i' th' sun] Literally 'in the
open air', instanced by the picnic that
is being spread, but with a covert and
paradoxical allusion to the distinction

> Seeking the food he eats,
>   And pleas'd with what he gets,
>   Come hither, come hither, come hither.   All together
>   Here shall he see   here.   40
>   No enemy,
>   But winter and rough weather.

Jaques. I'll give you a verse to this note, that I made
   yesterday in despite of my invention.
Ami. And I'll sing it.   45
Jaques. Thus it goes.

>   If it do come to pass
>   That any man turn ass,
>   Leaving his wealth and ease,
>   A stubborn will to please,   50
>   Ducdame, ducdame, ducdame,

39. SD *All together here*] Song. Altogether heere. F (*before 35*); not in Theobald.   40–
1. *Here . . . enemy*] As Pope; one line F.   43–4. I'll . . . / . . . invention.] As Pope
(*prose*); Ile . . . note, / . . . Inuention. / F.   46. *Jaques.*] Iaq. F2; Amy. F.
goes.] F; goes. *Gives a paper. Amiens sings.* Sisson.   47–8. *If . . . ass*] As F3; one
line F.   51. *Ducdame*] Duc ad me / Hanmer.

between living easily, under a roof, and living rough, exposed to all weathers. Cf. the proverb 'Out of God's blessing into the warm sun', Tilley (G272). It is only very recently that a sunburnt complexion has become a mark of conspicuous leisure.

39. SD. F makes this direction apply to the whole stanza, and Jaques has been urging all to sing, but it seems more natural that Amiens should supply the solo part, and the rest join in the chorus, which they have learnt from the first stanza.

44. *in despite of my invention*] in spite of my lack of imagination, i.e. I am not by nature a poetic or fanciful man.

46. *Thus it goes*] F gives this speech to Amiens, who then has three speech headings in succession. Most editors give l. 46 to Jaques, but the stanza which follows is sometimes assigned to Amiens because he has promised to sing it. The words would come across better if they were spoken, and one would think no actor playing

Jaques would willingly part with them (though J. P. Kemble's acting version omits them, along with other comic matter). F prints the stanza in italic. All songs in the play are printed so, together with Orlando's verses, Touchstone's extempore parody and Phebe's love-letter. Songs are not assigned to singers. They are headed *Song*. It is significant in this scene that whereas the two previous stanzas both have such a heading, the third has not and is quite differently set out. It is not isolated from the dialogue by wide spacing, as the others are, even though the compositor seems to have been desperate to spread his copy. The lines are not indented alternately. The first and fifth lines are allowed an internal rhyme. Everything points to its being a speech by Jaques. Amiens's bewilderment over *ducdame* comes more naturally if he questions it before he sings it. Jaques does not stay to hear it sung.

51. *Ducdame*] Much ingenuity has

> *Here shall he see*
> *Gross fools as he,*
> *And if he will come to me.*

Ami. What's that 'ducdame'?　　　　　　　　　　55
Jaques. 'Tis a Greek invocation, to call fools into a circle.
　　I'll go sleep if I can; if I cannot, I'll rail against all

52–3. *Here . . . he*] *As Pope; one line F.*　　54. *to me*] *to Ami. Steevens³, conj. Farmer.*
55. *Ami.*] *F; not in Sisson.*

been bestowed to find the origin and significance of what may be sheer nonsense; though if it were, one might have hoped for a better rhyme. It is probably deliberate mystification. The word is generally taken to be a trisyllable, the accentuation matching *Come hither* and fitting the musical phrase to which *Come hither* is sung, but there are commentators who prefer to stress the last syllable. Two ancient British formulae, once current in children's games, have been suggested to explain it, Gaelic *Duthaic da mi* = This is my ground, and Cymric *Dewch da mi* = Come to me. (See Charles Mackay's *Glossary of Obscure Words*, 1877.) Had Latin *Duc ad me* been intended (Hanmer and Johnson) there seems no very good reason why it should have been garbled, and the mystification would be slight. *Notes and Queries, VIII* (1859), p. 284, suggests Italian *Duc dà me* = Lead him from me, take him away, i.e. a parodic opposite of *Come hither*. *NCS* pleads strongly for an approximation to Romani *Dukra me* = I tell fortunes, and links it with *Pedlars' Greek* and *the first born of Egypt*. The resemblance of the first element to 'Duke' has led to interpretations such as A. W. Verity's *duc damné* (Cambridge, 1902) and R. A. J. Knowles's *duc d'amis, duc d'âne(s)* and *duc d'âme(s), Shakespeare Quarterly, XVIII* (1967), pp. 435–41. *Dewch da mi* seems to hold the field as incontrovertibly appropriate, being simply *Come hither* in another language. H.

Brooks supports it by instancing Shakespeare's interest in Welsh in other plays between 1597 and 1599, e.g. the Welsh song in *1H4*, Sir Hugh Evans in *Wiv.* and Fluellen in *H5*. Jaques's stanzo is not mocking the Duke, who is an exile perforce, but the 'three or four loving lords', the speaker presumably among them, who have 'put themselves into voluntary exile with him', I. i. 100–2.

54. *to me*] The accent may be on *to*. Cf. Chaucer's *General Prologue*, l. 672, where 'Com hither, love, to me' rhymes with 'Romë', and the accentuation of 'O whistle and I'll come tae ye, my lad'.

56. *a Greek invocation*] Any incomprehensible gibberish can be called Greek, a language introduced by the sixteenth-century humanists and never so familiar as Latin. More precisely, rogues' cant was known as 'Pedlars' Greek', with an additional connotation of cunning and slyness.

56. *into a circle*] a magician invoking dangerous spirits inscribed a circle which they could not invade (or alternatively, to contain them). Jaques may refer to the safe circle of Arden into which the Duke and his followers have retreated. In stage performance the people to whom he is speaking often gather round him, lured by his mysterious and portentous manner, only to break up in some discomfiture as they realize that they have literally been drawn into a circle, and thus, in the manner of a playground joke, proved fools.

the first-born of Egypt.

Ami. And I'll go seek the Duke; his banquet is prepared.

Exeunt.

SCENE VI

Enter ORLANDO *and* ADAM.

Adam. Dear master, I can go no further. O I die for food.
Here lie I down, and measure out my grave. Farewell kind master.

Orl. Why how now Adam? No greater heart in thee?
Live a little, comfort a little, cheer thyself a little.   5
If this uncouth forest yield anything savage, I will

59. And . . . prepared.] *As Pope (prose)*; And . . . Duke, / . . . prepar'd. / *F.*

Scene VI

Scene VI] *Scena Sexta. F.* [Location] *Another part of the forest. Malone*[1]; *not in F.*
1–18. *As Pope (prose)*; Deere . . . further: / . . . downe, / . . . master. / . . . thee: /
. . . little. / . . . sauage, / . . . thee: / . . . powers. / . . . while / . . . presently,
/ . . . eate, / . . . diest / . . . labor. / . . . cheerely, / . . . liest / . . . thee / . . .
die / . . . dinner, / . . . Desert. / . . . Adam. / F.

58. *first-born of Egypt*] Exodus
12:29–30. The death of the first-born
caused a great cry in the night. It
also caused the exile of the Jews.
Jaques, who is not such a plain
speaker as he pretends, may simply
mean that nobody is to disturb his
nap. *NCS* sees a reference to Duke
Senior, himself a first-born, living the
life of a gipsy and forcing his unfortunate friends to do the same. But
see the final note at l. 51 above. The
Duke is not indulging a whim.

59. *banquet*] not 'banquet' in the
modern sense, but a light repast of
wine and fruit. At l. 29 we are told
'the Duke will drink under this
tree', and Orlando, breaking in on
the party at II. vii. 99, exclaims 'He
dies that touches any of this fruit'.
Jaques, with his pun on reasons /
raisins at l. 101, seems to be eating
grapes. There are difficulties in
serving venison on the stage. The
problem of what to do with the feast

for the duration of scene vi is discussed in Appendix A.

Scene VI

The whole of this prose scene is set
as though it were blank verse. The
compositor, who was having some
difficulty in the previous scene, is now
at his wits' end to make his copy fill
the column. Both scenes occur at Q6[v],
which was the work of compositor B.
See Intro., p. xix. Furness saw
copy was being deliberately spread
and conjectured that it was to avoid
Scæna Septima coming at the very
bottom of the page. A similar
manoeuvre, at III. iv. 1–16, he
imputes to 'piecemeal printing',
having some inkling, before Hinman,
that F was not set in successive pages.

4. *thee*] Orlando's use of the familiar
thee gives the scene a stiffness and
formality to modern ears which is
the exact opposite of what is intended.

either be food for it, or bring it for food to thee.
Thy conceit is nearer death than thy powers. For
my sake be comfortable; hold death awhile at the
arm's end. I will here be with thee presently, and   10
if I bring thee not something to eat, I will give thee
leave to die; but if thou diest before I come, thou
art a mocker of my labour. Well said! Thou lookst
cheerly, and I'll be with thee quickly. Yet thou
liest in the bleak air. Come, I will bear thee to some   15
shelter and thou shalt not die for lack of a dinner,
if there live any thing in this desert. Cheerly good
Adam.   *Exeunt.*

SCENE VII

[A meal set out.]

Enter DUKE SENIOR, [AMIENS] *and lords, like outlaws.*

Duke Sen. I think he be transform'd into a beast,
          For I can nowhere find him like a man.
First Lord. My lord, he is but even now gone hence.
          Here was he merry, hearing of a song.

---

14. cheerly] *F*; cheerily *Malone*².

Scene VII

Scene VII] *Scena Septima.* [Location] *Another part of the Forest. Johnson; not in F.*
SD *A Table set out. Rowe*; *A meal of fruit and wine set out under the tree; the Duke
and some of his lords reclining thereat. NCS*; *not in F. Amiens*] *Capell*; *not in F. and
lords*] *Rowe*; *and Lord | F*; *Lords, and Others. Capell.*

8. *conceit*] imagination.

9. *be comfortable*] take comfort,
colloquially 'cheer up'.

10. *presently*] immediately.

13. *Well said!*] equivalent to 'well
done'. Cf. *Tit.*, IV. iii. 63: 'Well said,
Lucius!', a comment on the shooting
of an arrow, not on anything that has
been said (H. Brooks).

17. *desert*] a lonely and uncultivated
but not necessarily an infertile place.
Cf. *Gent.*, V. iv. 2: 'This shadowy
desert, unfrequented woods'.

Scene VII

SD. Amiens and lords] If there were
only one lord, as in F, there would be
no need to distinguish him as *First
Lord*, the Duke would lack his usual
retinue, and the banquet would be
very ill attended. Presumably, at
some point in the transmission of the
text, copyist or printer expanded an
ambiguous abbreviation, *L.* or *Lo.* F
does not give Amiens an entrance by
name, nor assign the song to him, but
he must be there to sing it. *NCS* has

Duke Sen. If he, compact of jars, grow musical,   5
    We shall have shortly discord in the spheres.
    Go seek him, tell him I would speak with him.
First Lord. He saves my labour by his own approach.

Enter JAQUES.

Duke Sen. Why how now monsieur? What a life is this,
    That your poor friends must woo your company?   10
    What, you look merrily?
Jaques. A fool, a fool! I met a fool i' th' forest,
    A motley fool: a miserable world!

8. SD *Enter Jaques.*] *Dyce*; *F* (*after* 7); *Jaques is seen coming through the trees, a smile upon his face, and shortly behind him Amiens, who silently takes his seat next to the Duke at the meal when he comes up. NCS* (*after* 7).   13. a miserable] *F*; Ah miserable *conj. NCS* world] *F*; varlet *Hanmer*; ort *conj. Hunter*; word *conj. Becket*, *conj. Hulme*; —Well, —*conj. Jackson*.

him enter with Jaques, whose exit at the end of scene v was to 'seek the Duke'. Had he found him, he would have given him the information which in this scene the First Lord gives. The First Lord may, in fact, be Amiens, but if so it is the Duke who has sought him, not the Duke. It is a problem unlikely to trouble an audience.

5. *compact of jars*] composed of discords, forever in disagreement. Cf. the literal cacophonous music which accompanies Malevole in Marston's *Malcontent*, I. i. and ii.

6. *discord in the spheres*] The idea that microcosm and macrocosm, man and the universe, should be harmoniously ordered originated with the Greeks, was adopted enthusiastically by the Christian Middle Ages, and passed from them to the Renaissance. The Pythagorean philosophers taught that the celestial spheres as they circled the earth each emitted a musical note which together made up a perfect harmony, inaudible to the ears of imperfect mortals. See *Mer.*, v. i. 60–5, and Milton, *Nativity Hymn*, st. 13.

13. *motley*] See Intro., p. lv. Many qualify as fools without the fool's

distinctive dress, hence Jaques particularizes. Touchstone in motley is a certified half-wit.

a miserable world!] Jaques is shaking his head in mock concern over a world so well stocked with fools that they turn up in the most unexpected places and engage in philosophical meditations. Johnson interprets in a parallel but serious sense, saying it is 'A parenthetical exclamation frequent among melancholy men and natural to Jaques at the sight of a fool, or at the hearing of reflections on the fragility of life'. Far from feeding his melancholy, Touchstone's speech reduces Jaques to helpless laughter. Shakespeare's characters not infrequently apostrophize the world for its faults and injustices. Cf. II. iii. 14: 'O, what a world is this!'; *Oth.*, III. iii. 381; *Cor.*, IV. iv. 12. Marston, *The Malcontent*, I. viii. 53–4, combines an outcry against the world with the moralizing of fools: 'O world most vile, when thy loose vanities, / Taught by this fool, do make the fool seem wise!' Hulme notes (p. 208) that *world* was a possible spelling of *word*, and vice versa. Cf.

As I do live by food, I met a fool,
Who laid him down and bask'd him in the sun,   15
And rail'd on Lady Fortune in good terms,
In good set terms, and yet a motley fool.
'Good morrow, fool', quoth I. 'No, sir', quoth he,
'Call me not fool, till heaven hath sent me fortune'.
And then he drew a dial from his poke,   20
And looking on it, with lack-lustre eye,
Says, very wisely, 'It is ten o'clock.
Thus we may see', quoth he, 'how the world wags:
'Tis but an hour ago since it was nine,
And after one hour more 'twill be eleven;   25
And so from hour to hour, we ripe, and ripe,
And then from hour to hour, we rot, and rot,
And thereby hangs a tale.' When I did hear

H5, II. iii. 49: 'The world is, pitch and pay' (F, Q2). Jaques is then reflecting on the inadequacy of the term fool 'for such a one as Touchstone is and Jaques wishes to be'. Becket, who also conjectures 'word', prefers 'O wretched, that I should be under the necessity of calling any man a fool'. Tilley records a proverb that the world is full of fools (W896).

16. *Lady Fortune*] Fortune proverbially should favour fools. See Tilley (F600, F536, G220).

17. *In good set terms*] in the technical style of a dialectician. Touchstone has characteristically been displaying his learning.

20. *dial*] Halliwell[2] suggests either a portable sundial or a watch, making the owner appear a fashionably equipped courtier. That Touchstone should be so equipped is one of the things that amuses Jaques. Cf. Earle's character of 'An Idle Gallant', *Microcosmography* (1628): 'Though his life pass somewhat slidingly, yet he seems very careful of the time, for he is still drawing his watch out of his pocket, and spends part of his hours in numbering them' (ed. R. Bliss, p. 58). Hotson quotes a reference in 1611

to 'one houre dial commonly called a watch' (p. 52, note).

poke] A poke is a large bag. The fool's motley came to be called a cloak-bag, because it was a capacious kind of overall made of a material popular for cloak-bags. Thus Hotson (pp. 50–2) pictures Touchstone extracting his watch from among his voluminous garments. Cf. Feste, stowing away a gratuity with the words 'I did impeticos [empetticoat] thy gratillity', *Tw.N.*, II. iii. 25.

21. *lack-lustre*] with great solemnity, without a twinkle.

23. *wags*] goes its way, with a sense of the inevitability of time's passing. 'The world wags' and 'Let the world wag' were popular expressions. See Tilley (W874, 879).

26–8. *hour . . . ripe . . . rot . . . tale*] Kökeritz (pp. 58–9) indicates the bawdy significance of these words in collocation: *hour* = whore, *ripe* = search, *tale* = tail. It may extend to *dial*, which to an Elizabethan would have a possible phallic significance, and to *poke* = codpiece. It gives Jaques and the audience something to laugh at, but does not seem to have much relevance to his request for a motley

The motley fool thus moral on the time,
My lungs began to crow like chanticleer,   30
That fools should be so deep-contemplative;
And I did laugh, sans intermission,
An hour by his dial. O noble fool!
A worthy fool! Motley's the only wear.
Duke Sen. What fool is this?   35
Jaques. O worthy fool! One that hath been a courtier
And says, if ladies be but young and fair,
They have the gift to know it. And in his brain,
Which is as dry as the remainder biscuit
After a voyage, he hath strange places cramm'd   40
With observation, the which he vents
In mangled forms. O that I were a fool!
I am ambitious for a motley coat.

31. deep-contemplative] *Malone*; deepe contemplatiue *F*.   34–6. A worthy
. . . O worthy] *F*; O worthy . . . A worthy *NCS*, conj. Anon. ap. Camb.

suit. He had good reason to admire the skill with which Touchstone conceals indecencies under a mask of moral gravity. They have eluded critics for centuries.

29. *moral*] Either a verb=moralize or, as Schmidt thinks, an adjective. Commentators claim that Touchstone deliberately parodies Jaques's moral attitudinizing, but the pair have only just met. However appropriate, Touchstone's discourse is accidental, unless we are to suppose that he recognizes an old acquaintance who fails curiously to recognize him. It is not, however, accidental to Shakespeare's purpose in the play. The audience, who by this time do know something of Jaques, can enjoy it as parody.

30. *crow*] whoop with laughter.

chanticleer] the traditional name for a cock, from the story of Reynard the Fox. Cf. Chaucer, *The Nun's Priest's Tale.*

32. *sans*] in regular use for a time, meaning 'without', and pronounced as an English word. There is evidence that it was thought of as affected. Cf.

LLL, v. ii. 416: 'Sans sans, I pray you', and *Soliman and Perseda*, i. iii. 144–6: 'Saunce? What languidge is that? I think thou art a word-maker by thine occupation' (Kittredge). Jaques uses it again, to close his speech on the Seven Ages at l. 166 below. He has a very distinctive vocabulary and style.

34. *the only wear*] all the fashion, the only style worth wearing.

39. *dry*] A dry brain, in contemporary physiology, was slow to take an impression but sure to retain it (Wright).

biscuit] ship's biscuit, issued to sailors in lieu of fresh-baked bread. Cf. Jonson, *Every Man out of his Humour*: 'And (now and then) break a drie biscuit ieast', *Induction*, l. 165, and Marston, *The Malcontent*, i. vi. 16–17: 'called you . . . "dried biscuit"'.

40. *places*] (1) commonplaces or stock topics of rhetoric (Wright); (2) storage places (Johnson's *Dictionary*, quoting *AYL*). Rolfe translates 'odd corners'. Furness objects that you cannot *vent* or *mangle* odd corners, but the reference is to the observations

Duke Sen. Thou shalt have one.

Jaques.　　　　　　　　　　　It is my only suit,

　　Provided that you weed your better judgements　　45
　　Of all opinion that grows rank in them
　　That I am wise. I must have liberty
　　Withal, as large a charter as the wind,
　　To blow on whom I please, for so fools have;
　　And they that are most galled with my folly,　　50
　　They most must laugh. And why sir must they so?
　　The why is plain as way to parish church.
　　He that a fool doth very wisely hit
　　Doth very foolishly, although he smart,
　　Not to seem senseless of the bob. If not,　　55
　　The wiseman's folly is anatomiz'd
　　Even by the squand'ring glances of the fool.
　　Invest me in my motley. Give me leave
　　To speak my mind, and I will through and through
　　Cleanse the foul body of th'infected world,　　60
　　If they will patiently receive my medicine.

Duke Sen. Fie on thee! I can tell what thou wouldst do.

Jaques. What, for a counter, would I do but good?

Duke Sen. Most mischievous foul sin, in chiding sin.

　　For thou thyself hast been a libertine,　　65

---

55. Not to seem] *Theobald*; Seeme *F*.
Man's *Rowe*.

56. wiseman's] Wise-mans *F*; wise
Man's *Rowe*.

---

with which the odd corners were crammed. The second meaning perhaps comes from biscuit and its association with ships' stores.

44. *only suit*] (1) apparel; (2) petition.

48. *as large a charter*] John 3:8: 'The wind bloweth where it listeth.' Cf. *H5*, I. i. 48: 'The air, a charter'd libertine', and Marston, *The Malcontent*, I. iii. 2: 'He is as free as air; he blows over every man.'

52. *The why . . . church*] Kökeritz (p. 85) classes this with jingles. The way to church was well trodden in a century when attendance was compulsory.

55. *Not to*] Editors accept War-

burton's conjectural emendation here. The line in F is wanting both in metre and sense.

bob] a jest at someone's expense, a scoff.

If not] The meaning is plain though the syntax is not.

56. *anatomiz'd*] laid bare, dissected. Cf. I. i. 154.

57. *squand'ring*] random (*OED* a. 2, quoting *AYL*).

glances] innuendoes (*OED* sb. 1† 2. fig. a. 'a satirical allusion, a jest at (or upon) something').

63. *counter*] a round metal piece, of little or no value, used for reckoning or to adjust small change.

65. *hast been a libertine*] He has

As sensual as the brutish sting itself,
And all th'embossed sores and headed evils
That thou with licence of free foot hast caught
Wouldst thou disgorge into the general world.
Jaques. Why who cries out on pride,   70
    That can therein tax any private party?
    Doth it not flow as hugely as the sea,
    Till that the weary very means do ebb?

73. weary very means] wearie verie meanes *F*; very very means *Pope*; very
wearing means *conj. Collier*[1]; very means of wear *Collier*[2]; wearer's very means
Singer[2]; weary very mints *conj. NCS*; necessary means *conj. Tannenbaum, MLN
1929*.

consorted with vicious persons and
been a law to himself.

66. *brutish sting*] the urging of
animal passion. Cf. *Oth.*, I. iii. 361:
'our carnal stings, our unbitted lusts'.

67. *embossed sores*] purulent swell-
ings or scabs. A boss is a small
protuberance. Cf. *headed evils* and *Lr*,
II. iv. 222–3: 'A boil / A plague-sore,
an embossed carbuncle'.

68. *caught*] primarily in the sense of
'catching' an infection, whence *embossed sores* above, but cf. the burs
caught by the girls' petticoats when
they walk in untrodden paths
(I. iii. 13–15), as Jaques did when he
used the 'licence of free foot'.

70. *who cries out on pride*] The Duke
has voiced a common complaint
against the satirist, that anyone so
well informed about vice must himself
be vicious. Jaques defends himself
against quite another charge, that of
personal malice. Satire was under
attack in 1599. Shakespeare may have
written an expanded discussion, cut
in rehearsal, or as *NCS* would have it,
in revision. Alternatively, and more
probably, we may suppose that
Shakespeare was writing impression-
istically, to suggest in a short space a
more thorough exploration of the
subject than there is time for. He
makes it plain that the Duke used his
forest leisure to exercise his mind as
well as his body.

71. *tax*] Cf. l. 86 below and I. ii. 79
(taxation).

72–3. *Doth it . . . ebb*] Cf. *Tim.*,
II. ii. 141–3: 'I have / Prompted you
in the ebb of your estate / And your
great flow of debts.' The particular
effect of pride that Jaques is thinking
of is conspicuous display, which he
eventually narrows down to the city
woman's notorious extravagance in
dress. Doesn't everybody want to
make a show, he is saying, so that
everywhere the tide of luxury is
rising, until the basic means that
supply it are exhausted. There is
nothing surprising in the money
running out. What justifies the
emphatic *very* is that the gentlemen
were not only parting with their income but with their estates, the
source of their income, to keep up an
ostentatious life-style. Cf. IV. i. 21–2:
'I fear you have sold your own lands to
see other men's'; and the foolish Rod-
erigo's reply to Iago's insistent 'Put
money in thy purse', *Oth.* I. iii. 378:
'I'll sell all my land'; and *H8*
I. i. 83–4: 'O, many / Have broke
their backs with laying manors on
'em.' The laws of entail as then
administered made it all too easy to
part with land. See L. Stone, *The
Crisis of the Aristocracy 1588–1641*
(1965), p. 197. Stone imputes the
'generalized ostentation' to 'the fierce
competition for social status . . . in a

What woman in the city do I name,
When that I say the city-woman bears   75
The cost of princes on unworthy shoulders?
Who can come in and say that I mean her,
When such a one as she, such is her neighbour?
Or what is he of basest function,
That says his bravery is not on my cost,   80
Thinking that I mean him, but therein suits
His folly to the mettle of my speech?
There then! How then? What then? Let me see wherein
My tongue hath wrong'd him: if it do him right,
Then he hath wrong'd himself; if he be free,   85
Why then my taxing like a wild-goose flies
Unclaim'd of any man. But who comes here?

Enter ORLANDO [*with sword drawn.*]

Orl. Forbear, and eat no more.
Jaques. Why, I have eat none yet.

87. comes] *F2*; come *F*. SD *with sword drawn*] *Theobald*; *not in F*.   89. Why . . .
yet.] *This ed* (*prose*); *Steevens*³ (*verse*); *F* (*verse or prose*).

transitional period of uncertain
values' (p. 582). He amply documents
it and its consequences. *NCS*, emending *means* to 'mints' = places where
money is coined, depends on a
conjectural spelling 'ments'. Collier
is trying for a line that can be read
'means of wearing fine clothes'.
Singer thinks the final *-ie* of *verie* has
affected the end of *wearer's* so that it
reads *wearie*. Tannenbaum's *necessary* =
the means of purchasing their
necessaries. He conjectures *necesserie*
misread as *werie verie.*

76. *unworthy shoulders*] Costly clothes
on a princess would not be a fault.
Her shoulders are worthy. The city
woman has ideas above her station.
Jaques has moved rather abruptly
from the gentry to the citizenry,
sparing none.

80. *bravery*] fine clothes, improper
to his low employment. Cf. B. Rich,
The Honestie of the Age, 1614, p. 47:

'The pride of this age is growne to
that height, that we canne hardly
knowe a Prince from a pesant, by
the viewing of his apparell, and who
is able by the outward show, to
discerne betweene *Nobilitie* and *Seruili-
tie*?'

82. *mettle*] spirit.

83. *There then! . . . What then?*]
'There you are! what do you think
of that? (*NCS*).

84. *do him right*] speak truly of him,
do him justice.

85. *free*] innocent of offence. Cf.
Ham., ii. ii. 557: 'Make mad the
guilty and appal the free' and iii. ii.
236: 'We that have free souls'.

89. *Why . . . yet*] Most editors print
this as verse and find some difficulty
with *Why*. The line fills barely half
the width of the Folio column, so it
is impossible to tell whether verse or
prose is intended, but Jaques twice
more interrupts, at l. 91 and l. 101,

Orl. Nor shalt not till necessity be served.   90
Jaques. Of what kind should this cock come of?
Duke Sen. Art thou thus bolden'd man by thy distress?
    Or else a rude despiser of good manners,
    That in civility thou seem'st so empty?
Orl. You touch'd my vein at first: the thorny point   95
    Of bare distress hath ta'en from me the show
    Of smooth civility. Yet am I inland bred,
    And know some nurture. But forbear, I say,
    He dies that touches any of this fruit,
    Till I and my affairs are answered.   100
Jaques. And you will not be answered with reason, I must die.
Duke Sen. What would you have? Your gentleness shall force,
    More than your force move us to gentleness.
Orl. I almost die for food, and let me have it.
Duke Sen. Sit down and feed, and welcome to our table.   105
Orl. Speak you so gently? Pardon me, I pray you.
    I thought that all things had been savage here,
    And therefore put I on the countenance
    Of stern commandment. But whate'er you are
    That in this desert inaccessible   110
    Under the shade of melancholy boughs,
    Lose and neglect the creeping hours of time;
    If ever you have look'd on better days;
    If ever been where bells have knoll'd to church;
    If ever sat at any good man's feast;   115
    If ever from your eyelids wip'd a tear,

91. Of what] *F*; What *Johnson*; come of] *F*; come *Rowe*.   101. And ... die]
This ed (prose); And ... reason, / ... dye. / *F*; An ... not / ... die. / *conj.*
Capell; If ... not / ... die. *Pope (verse)*.   102–3. What ... shall force / ...
gentleness.] *As Pope*; What ... haue? / ... your force / ... gentlenesse. / *F*.
109. commandment] *Rowe*; command'ment *F*.

incontrovertibly in prose, despite the
verse setting in F at l. 101.
  94. *civility*] the conventions of
civilized living, something more than
polite manners.
  97. *inland bred*] not rustic and
awkward. Cf. III. ii. 337. 'Outlandish'
is still in use in an opposite sense.
  98. *nurture*] good upbringing.
  101. *reason*] with the favourite

Elizabethan quibble on 'raisin'.
  109. *commandment*] The apostrophe
in F is in deference to a form of the
word with four syllables.
  111. *melancholy*] dark and shadowy.
(*OED* 'expressing sadness', quoting
AYL. But does *AYL* express sadness
here?)
  114. *knoll'd*] a form of 'knelled'.

And know what 'tis to pity and be pitied,
Let gentleness my strong enforcement be;
In the which hope, I blush, and hide my sword.

Duke Sen. True is it that we have seen better days,   120
And have with holy bell been knoll'd to church,
And sat at good men's feasts, and wip'd our eyes
Of drops that sacred pity hath engender'd;
And therefore sit you down in gentleness,
And take upon command what help we have   125
That to your wanting may be minister'd.

Orl. Then but forbear your food a little while,
Whiles, like a doe, I go to find my fawn,
And give it food. There is an old poor man,
Who after me hath many a weary step   130
Limp'd in pure love; till he be first suffic'd,
Oppress'd with two weak evils, age and hunger,
I will not touch a bit.

Duke Sen.   Go find him out,
And we will nothing waste till you return.

Orl. I thank ye, and be blest for your good comfort.   135
                                                        [*Exit.*]

Duke Sen. Thou seest, we are not all alone unhappy:
This wide and universal theatre
Presents more woeful pageants than the scene
Wherein we play in.

Jaques.   All the world's a stage,

135. SD *Exit*] *Rowe*; *not in* F.   139. Wherein we play in.] *F*; Wherein we play. *Rowe*; Which we do play in. *Rann, conj Capell.* play in . . . All] *F*; play . . . Why, all *conj. Steevens*[3].

125. *upon command*] in answer to your command, at your will.

132. *weak evils*] bodily afflictions consequent upon or causing weakness.

138. *pageants*] shows. Cf. III. iv. 48.

139. *in*] Abbott 407.

All the world's a stage] The thought is a commonplace of long ancestry. See Tilley (W882), and T. W. Baldwin, *Shakespeare's Small Latine* (1944), I, pp. 652ff. with special reference to Palingenius's *Zodiacus Vitae* and J. Withals's *Little Dictionary*. The motto

of the Globe Theatre, which opened in the summer of 1599, was *Totus mundus agit histrionem*. Curtius derives it from John of Salisbury's *Policraticus*, 1159, where it appears as *quod fere totus mundus iuxta Petronium exerceat histrionem* (pp. 140–1). There had been a new edition of the *Policraticus* in 1595. Cf. *Mer. V.*, I. i. 77ff.; *Lr.*, IV. vi. 184; *Mac.*, v. v. 25. W. Maginn points out that 'all the characters in Jaques's sketch are well taken care of' and shrewdly deduces that 'such pictures

And all the men and women merely players.   140
They have their exits and their entrances,
And one man in his time plays many parts,
His acts being seven ages. At first the infant,
Mewling and puking in the nurse's arms.
Then, the whining school-boy with his satchel   145
And shining morning face, creeping like snail
Unwillingly to school. And then the lover,
Sighing like furnace, with a woeful ballad
Made to his mistress' eyebrow. Then, a soldier,
Full of strange oaths, and bearded like the pard,   150

145. Then] *F*; And then *Rowe*³; Then there's *conj. Anon. ap. Camb.*

of life do not proceed from a man very heavy at heart' (*Shakespeare Papers*, ed. Mackenzie (1856), pp. 50–1). J. Smith notes that Jaques's verse 'continues to demean itself elegantly even when describing in detail man's end' (*Scrutiny*, IX (1940) p. 25).

140. *merely players*] players and nothing else. There is not necessarily a derogatory sense.

143. *His acts being seven ages*] A commonplace. See Furness. E. E. Stoll, in 'Jaques and the antiquaries', *Modern Language Notes*, LIV (1939) pp. 79–85, argues that the division into *seven* ages was in fact uncommon, but can be found, in a way which parallels this speech, in *Batman uppon Bartolome* (1582), a translation of *De Proprietatibus Rerum* by Bartholomæus Anglicus.

145. *Then*] sometimes emended to *And then* to regularize the metre. Furness thinks the whole speech might be regarded as 'exquisitely metric prose, until . . . it glides into the solemn cadence that ends this strange, eventful history'. The lengthened pauses have the effect of a man stopping to consider what he will say next. Jaques is not giving a recitation, though he is giving a performance.

148. *Sighing like furnace*] Cf. *Cym.*, I. vi. 65–6: 'He furnaces / The thick

sighs from him'.
    ballad] The term is not complimentary.

149. *his mistress' eyebrow*] a scoffing exaggeration of the lover's poetical praise of his lady, combining the catalogue of physical beauties and the sonnets on trivial subjects. Cf. Nashe, *Lenten Stuffe*, 1599 (III, p. 176): 'the wantonner sort of them sing descant on their mistris gloue, her ring, her fanne, her looking glasse, her pantofle.' H. M. Richmond quotes from Marot's *Epistre liii*: 'Mais du sourcil la beauté bien chantée / A tellement nostre Court contentée' ('To His Mistress' Eyebrow', *Philological Quarterly*, XL (1961), pp. 157–8).

150. *bearded like the pard*] Beard could be applied to any form of facial hair, including whiskers. A leopard has no beard in the narrow sense. Elizabethans may have visualized it with something like a mane, recalling the lions passant gardant on the royal standard. These very familiar animals were sometimes blazoned as lions leopardé and were popularly known as leopards. Essex, the hero of Cadiz and the Islands Voyage, appears in portraits with a liberal supply of hair on head, lip and chin. Cf. Jonson, *Cynthia's Revels*, 1600, II. iii. 26–8: 'the grace of [your soldier's] face consis-

Jealous in honour, sudden, and quick in quarrel,
Seeking the bubble reputation
Even in the cannon's mouth. And then, the justice,
In fair round belly, with good capon. lin'd,
With eyes severe, and beard of formal cut,   155
Full of wise saws, and modern instances,
And so he plays his part. The sixth age shifts
Into the lean and slipper'd pantaloon,
With spectacles on nose, and pouch on side,
His youthful hose well sav'd, a world too wide   160
For his shrunk shank, and his big manly voice,
Turning again toward childish treble, pipes
And whistles in his sound. Last scene of all,
That ends this strange eventful history,
Is second childishness and mere oblivion,   165
Sans teeth, sans eyes, sans taste, sans everything.

151. sudden,] *F*; sudden *Rowe*; sudden; *conj. Hunter.*   162. treble, pipes]
treble, pipes, *Theobald*; trebble pipes, *F*.

teth much in a beard.' Apart from
whiskers or beard, a leopard was an
emblem of ferocity.

151. *sudden*] Hunter (p. 339)
argues for 'hasty' used absolutely, 'or
perhaps still more exactly *prompt in
executing a resolve*'. He punctuates with
a semi-colon. Halliwell[2] says 'It is
generally presumed that *sudden* is
here used in the sense of *passionate*,
and that otherwise it must be taken
as intentionally pleonastic.' F's comma would seem to be significant.
Steevens allows that *sudden* = 'violent'
is not necessarily synonymous with
quick in quarrel, but he does not keep
the comma. Cf. *3H6*: 'He's sudden,
if a thing comes in his head'; *Mac.*,
IV. iii. 59; *Oth.*, II. i. 266. The speech
is carefully punctuated except for the
misplaced comma after *pipes*.

154. *capon*] J. W. Hales, in *Essays
and Notes on Shakespeare* (1892), shows
that *capons* = cocks bred for the table
were a common present to a justice to
engage his good will. Cf. J. Taylor,
The Water-Cormorant:

But when he's blind in Iustice,
     'tis a doubt
But Turkies tallons scratcht his
     eyes halfe out,
Or capons clawes, but 'tis a
     heavy case,
That fowles should flye so in a
     Iustice face.

Kittredge denies that any satire is
intended in this mild imputation of a
love of good living to successful men
of late middle age. The speech, he
says, 'insists, not upon the vices of
mankind, but upon the futility of
man's career'.

156. *modern instances*] trite examples.
Hunter (p. 341) prefers 'cases recently
decided, judgments lately given'.

157. *shifts*] the technical term for a
change of scene in the theatre.

158. *pantaloon*] the stock Old Man of
Italian comedy.

163. *his*] its. Abbott 228.

164. *history*] In keeping with the extended metaphor, *NCS* interprets
'chronicle play'. It was usual to

Enter ORLANDO *with* ADAM.

Duke Sen. Welcome. Set down your venerable burden,
    And let him feed.
Orl. I thank you most for him.
Adam.   So had you need,
    I scarce can speak to thank you for myself.   170
Duke Sen. Welcome, fall to. I will not trouble you
    As yet to question you about your fortunes.
    Give us some music, and good cousin, sing.
[*Amiens sings.*]

        Blow, blow, thou winter wind,
        Thou art not so unkind   175
            As man's ingratitude.
        Thy tooth is not so keen,
        Because thou art not seen,
            Although thy breath be rude.
        Heigh-ho, sing heigh-ho, unto the green holly   180
        Most friendship is feigning, most loving mere folly.
        Then heigh-ho, the holly,
            This life is most jolly.

        Freeze, freeze, thou bitter sky,
        That dost not bite so nigh   185

167–8. Welcome . . . burden, / . . . feed.] *As Rowe*[3] *(verse)*; *F (prose)*.   173.
SD *Amiens sings.*] *Johnson*; *Song F.*   174–6. *As Pope*; *Blow . . . winde,* / . . .
ingratitude / *F.*   177–8] *As Pope*; *one line F.*   182. *Then*] *Rowe*; *The F.*
184–5. *As Pope*; *one line F.*

complete the comparison of man's life
to a stage play by calling it either a
comedy or a tragedy. Jaques, when he
calls it a history, takes a characteristically eccentric stance on what had
become a subject of humanist debate.

    168. The second half of this line is
presumably filled with business about
settling the old man. Alternatively,
Orlando could complete the line and
Adam's speech begin with a half line.

    175. unkind] (1) cruel; (2) contrary
to nature.

    177. Thy tooth . . . keen] Cf. Seneca,
Hippolytus, II, 492–3: *haud illum niger* /
edax livor dente degeneri petit, 'Him
venomous spite assails not with bite of
baseborn tooth' (Loeb ed., l. 357).

    178. Because . . . seen] The wind,
without visible substance, cannot be
conceived of as a fellow creature
guilty of deliberate malice. Johnson
explains 'thou art an enemy that does
not brave us with thy presence'.

    180. holly] The evergreen holly was
venerated and thought to have some
connection with the word 'holy'. Cf.
the carol, 'The holly and the ivy'.

As benefits forgot.
Though thou the waters warp,
Thy sting is not so sharp,
    As friend remember'd not.
Heigh-ho, sing heigh-ho, unto the green holly,   190
Most friendship is feigning, most loving mere folly.
Then heigh-ho the holly,
    This life is most jolly.

Duke Sen. If that you were the good Sir Rowland's son,
As you have whisper'd faithfully you were,   195
And as mine eye doth his effigies witness
Most truly limn'd and living in your face,
Be truly welcome hither. I am the duke
That lov'd your father. The residue of your fortune,
Go to my cave and tell me. Good old man,   200
Thou art right welcome as thy master is.
Support him by the arm. Give me your hand
And let me all your fortunes understand.   *Exeunt.*

187–8. *As Pope; one line F.*   201. master] *F2; masters F.*

187. warp] 'To warp is to turn, and to turn is to change. We say milk turns or curdles' (Johnson). The word is commonly used of wood, twisted as it contracts. Here it refers to another forceful alteration, water turned to ice. Frozen water is preferable to frozen faces. Cf. *Lr*, III. vi. 52–3: 'And here's another, whose warp'd looks proclaim / What store her heart is made on.'

196. *effigies*] likeness. The word keeps the Latin stress, on the second syllable. See Abbott 490.

197. *limn'd*] painted in colours.

ACT III

SCENE I

Enter DUKE, *lords and* OLIVER.

Duke F. Not see him since? Sir, sir, that cannot be.
But were I not the better part made mercy,
I should not seek an absent argument
Of my revenge, thou present. But look to it:
Find out thy brother whereso'er he is;   5
Seek him with candle: bring him dead or living
Within this twelvmonth, or turn thou no more
To seek a living in our territory.
Thy lands and all things that thou dost call thine,
Worth seizure, do we seize into our hands,   10
Till thou canst quit thee by thy brother's mouth
Of what we think against thee.

Oli. O that your Highness knew my heart in this!
I never lov'd my brother in my life.

Duke F. More villain thou. Well, push him out of doors, 15
And let my officers of such a nature
Make an extent upon his house and lands.
Do this expediently, and turn him going.   *Exeunt.*

ACT III

Scene 1

ACT III. Scene 1] *Actus Tertius. Scena Prima. F.* [Location] *the Palace. Rowe; not in F. Duke] F; Duke junior. Capell; Duke Frederick. Malone.*

3. *argument*] subject.

6. *Seek him with candle*] Luke 15:8.

7. *turn*] return.

11. *quit*] acquit.

17. *Make an extent*] 'A legal phrase, from the words of a writ *extendi facias* whereby the sheriff is directed to cause certain lands to be appraised to their full extended value, before he delivers them to the person entitled under a recognisance, etc. in order that it may be certainly known how soon the debt will be paid' (Malone). Furness observes that Shakespeare is not being very precise in the matter of Oliver's expropriation, but adds that 'the use of a legal term or so would be all-sufficient to create the required impression'.

18. *expediently*] expeditiously.

turn him going] send him packing.

60

SCENE II

Enter ORLANDO [*with a paper.*]

Orl. Hang there my verse, in witness of my love,
    And thou thrice-crowned queen of night, survey
    With thy chaste eye, from thy pale sphere above,
    Thy huntress' name, that my full life doth sway.
    O Rosalind, these trees shall be my books,   5
    And in their barks my thoughts I'll character,
    That every eye which in this forest looks,
    Shall see thy virtue witness'd everywhere.
    Run, run Orlando, carve on every tree
    The fair, the chaste, and unexpressive she.   *Exit.* 10

Enter CORIN *and* TOUCHSTONE.

Corin. And how like you this shepherd's life, Master
    Touchstone?
Touch. Truly shepherd, in respect of itself, it is a good
    life; but in respect that it is a shepherd's life, it is
    naught. In respect that it is solitary, I like it very 15

Scene II] *Scena Secunda.* F. [Location] *The Forest. Rowe; not in F.*   SD *with a paper.*] *Capell; with a paper, which he hangs on a tree Dyce; not in F.*   1. SD *fixing it to a Tree.*] *Capell; not in F.*

1–10. See Intro., pp. xxxi–xxxii for a parallel in Greene's *Orlando Furioso*, and a discussion of whether the scene opens by moonlight.

2. *thrice-crowned queen*] *diva triformis* (Ovid, *Metam.*, VII, 177); *Hecate triformis* (Seneca, *Hippolytus*, 411). The moon goddess was Cynthia, Phoebe or Luna in the heavens, Diana on earth, Lucina and Hecate in the underworld. Cf. *MND*, v. i. 372–3: 'And we fairies, that do run / By the triple Hecate's team'.

4. *Thy huntress*] Rosalind, as a maiden, came under the protection of Diana. Cf. *Ado*, v. iii. 12–13; *All's W.*, I. iii. 106–8.

sway] control, an astrological term.

Cf. *Tw.N.*, II. v. 99: 'M. O. A. I. doth sway my life.' There is an analogy between the moon's influence over earthly things and Rosalind's over Orlando.

6. *character*] inscribe.

10. *unexpressive*] inexpressible. Cf. Milton, *Lycidas*, l. 176 and *Nativity Hymn*, l. 116.

13–22.] This whole speech is a piece of high fooling. It sounds sage and philosophical but it is nonsense. Cf. ll. 39–43. Touchstone's demand for an *instance* and his rebuke of *shallow* both derive from the art of formal disputation.

15. *naught*] Bad, worthless, the original meaning of 'naughty'.

well; but in respect that it is private, it is a very
vile life. Now in respect it is in the fields, it pleaseth
me well; but in respect it is not in the court, it is
tedious. As it is a spare life, look you, it fits my
humour well; but as there is no more plenty in it,   20
it goes much against my stomach. Hast any
philosophy in thee, shepherd?

Corin. No more but that I know the more one sickens the
worse at ease he is; and that he that wants money,
means, and content is without three good friends;   25
that the property of rain is to wet and fire to burn;
that good pasture makes fat sheep; and that a great
cause of the night is lack of the sun; that he that
hath learned no wit by nature nor art may complain
of good breeding or comes of a very dull kindred.   30

Touch. Such a one is a natural philosopher. Wast ever in
court, shepherd?

Corin. No truly.

Touch. Then thou art damned.

Corin. Nay, I hope.   35

Touch. Truly thou art damned, like an ill-roasted egg,
all on one side.

Corin. For not being at court? Your reason.

Touch. Why, if thou never wast at court, thou never
saw'st good manners; if thou never saw'st good   40
manners, then thy manners must be wicked, and

31–2. Such . . . shepherd?] *As Pope (prose)*; Such . . . Philosopher: / . . .
Shepheard? / *F*.   35. hope.] *F*; hope— *Rowe*.

25. *means*] gainful employment.

29–30. *complain of good breeding*]
complain of [lack of] good breeding.
Cf. II. iv. 73: 'faints for [lack of]
succour'.

31. *a natural philosopher*] playing on
physical scientist and natural fool.
The reference is not to Corin but to
the ninny he has just described, who
has 'no wit by nature nor art'.

35. *I hope*] Some editors assume that
Corin is interrupted in the middle of a
sentence. An Elizabethan would find

no difficulty in accepting his statement as complete. We are com-
manded neither to despair of salvation
nor to be too certain of heaven, but
to hope. Corin replies very properly.
Sisson interprets 'I hope not'.

36. *like an ill-roasted egg*] 'being but
half-bred, as the egg . . . but half
roasted' (Rann). Eggs were roasted
in the ashes of wood fires, and had to
be turned frequently.

41. *manners*] (1) polite behaviour;
(2) moral character.

wickedness is sin, and sin is damnation. Thou art in
a parlous state, shepherd.

Corin. Not a whit, Touchstone. Those that are good
manners at the court are as ridiculous in the country   45
as the behaviour of the country is most mockable at
the court. You told me you salute not at the court,
but you kiss your hands: that courtesy would be
uncleanly if courtiers were shepherds.

Touch. Instance, briefly; come, instance.   50

Corin. Why we are still handling our ewes, and their fells
you know are greasy.

Touch. Why, do not your courtier's hands sweat? And is
not the grease of a mutton as wholesome as the
sweat of a man? Shallow, shallow. A better instance   55
I say. Come.

Corin. Besides, our hands are hard.

Touch. Your lips will feel them the sooner. Shallow again.
A more sounder instance, come.

Corin. And they are often tarred over with the surgery of   60
our sheep; and would you have us kiss tar? The
courtier's hands are perfumed with civet.

Touch. Most shallow man! Thou worms-meat in respect
of a good piece of flesh indeed! Learn of the wise
and perpend. Civet is of a baser birth than tar, the   65
very uncleanly flux of a cat. Mend the instance,
shepherd.

Corin. You have too courtly a wit for me, I'll rest.

Touch. Wilt thou rest damned? God help thee, shallow

44. Touchstone] *F*; Mr. Touchstone *Capell*.   63. shallow man!] *Theobald*;
shallow man: *F*; shallow, Man: *Rowe*.

43. *parlous*] perilous.

47–8. *salute . . . hands*] Do not greet
one another without kissing hands.
If *but* expresses an alternative, Corin
may be contrasting a hearty kiss on
cheek or lips with a courtly kissing of
hands only, either one's own (cf.
Malvolio, at III. iii. 31–2) or another's.

51. *still*] constantly.

fells] fleeces.

63. *Thou worms-meat*] a proverbial
expression to denote the worthless-
ness of mortal man. See Whiting
(W675).

65. *perpend*] consider. Schmidt notes
this as a word used only by Polonius,
Pistol and Touchstone, all epideictic
speakers.

66. *cat*] The civet cat, of which the
musky secretions from an anal gland
were much used in perfumes.

man! God make incision in thee, thou art raw!   70
Corin. Sir, I am a true labourer: I earn that I eat, get that
I wear; owe no man hate, envy no man's happiness;
glad of other men's good, content with my harm;
and the greatest of my pride is to see my ewes graze
and my lambs suck.   75
Touch. That is another simple sin in you, to bring the
ewes and the rams together, and to offer to get your
living by the copulation of cattle; to be bawd to a
bell-wether, and to betray a she-lamb of a twelve-
month to a crooked-pated old cuckoldly ram, out of   80
all reasonable match. If thou beest not damned for
this, the devil himself will have no shepherds. I
cannot see else how thou shouldst 'scape.
Corin. Here comes young Master Ganymede, my new
mistress's brother.   85

Enter ROSALIND [*with a paper, reading.*]

73. good,] *F2*; good *F*.   85. SD *with a paper, reading.*] *Capell; with a Paper.
Rowe; Rosalind, unwitting of their presence, comes up, sees Orlando's paper on the tree
and, plucking it down, begins to read it NCS; not in F.*

70. *make incision . . . raw*] To be *raw*
is to be inexperienced or unseasoned.
Make incision, which seems to have had
a general meaning of driving something into a thick head, here has been
interpreted (1) to score and salt meat
for roasting (Babcock in *Modern
Language Notes*, XLIV (1929), pp.
41–2); (2) to graft a cultivated scion
on a wild stock, properly written
insition (*NCS*); (3) to let blood
(Wright). Both roasting and grafting
were running in Shakespeare's head.
There is no need to seek an interpretation which depends on the use of the
precise word *incision*. Touchstone is
still speaking grandiloquently. Cf.
Pistol, *2H4*, II. iv. 210–11: 'shall we
have incision? shall we imbrue?' A
possible connection with blood-letting
may lie in an imaginary surgical
operation to cure a dull mind.
Steevens quotes from Heath's *Revisal*

of Shakespeare's Text (1765), p. 147 a
proverbial phrase, 'to be cut for the
simples', which Collier would link
with l. 76 below, 'another simple sin
in you'. Cf. the modern 'wants his
head examining'. The roast/raw
opposition is the most obvious today.
    71. *get*] acquire by one's own
labour. Cf. II. v. 37–8: 'Seeking the
food he eats, / And pleas'd with what
he gets'.
    76–81. Cf. *The Maydes Metamorpho-
sis*, II. ii. 21–3: '*Io.* I am Page to a
Courtier. *Mop.* And I a Boy to a
Shepheard. *Fris.* Thou art the
Apple-squier [pimp] to an Eawe'
(Bond, III).
    79. *bell-wether*] the leader of the
flock.
    80. *cuckoldly*] on account of his
horns.
    85. SD *with a paper*] Most editors
assume that Rosalind comes in, like

Ros.   *From the east to western Inde,*
                No jewel is like Rosalind.
                Her worth being mounted on the wind,
                Through all the world bears Rosalind.
                All the pictures fairest lin'd   90
                Are but black to Rosalind.
                Let no face be kept in mind
                But the fair of Rosalind.

Touch. I'll rhyme you so, eight years together; dinners
    and suppers and sleeping-hours excepted. It is the   95
    right butter-women's rank to market.

Ros. Out fool!

Touch. For a taste.

                If a hart do lack a hind,
                Let him seek out Rosalind.   100
                If the cat will after kind,
                So be sure will Rosalind.
                Winter'd garments must be lin'd,

92. face] *F*; fair *Grant White²*, *conj. Walker.*   93. fair of] *F*; most fair *F3*; Face of *Rowe³*.   96. women's] *F*; woman's *Johnson.* rank] *F*; rate *Hanmer.*   103. *Winter'd*] Wintred *F*; Winter *F3*.

Celia at l. 121 below, with a paper of verses in her hand. It is curious (though not unprecedented, cf. Richard III's oration before Bosworth) that F should omit a stage direction at one place that it finds necessary at another. J. P. Kemble, followed by *NCS*, makes Rosalind take down a paper Orlando has just hung up.

87. Rosalind] For the pronunciation, see Intro., pp. lxvi–lxvii.

90. lin'd] delineated with lines, pictured.

92. face] Walker (I, 327) would read *fair*, from a possible spelling *fare*.

93. fair] beauty, Cf. *Err.*, II. i. 98: 'My decayed fair' and *MND*, I. i. 182: 'Demetrius loves your fair.'

96. *right*] regular, typical. Cf. l. 269 below.

butter-women's rank to market] The couplets remind Touchstone of

country women riding to market one after another at a heavy jog-trot. *Rank, OED* sb. i† c, 'movement in line or file', a rare usage, quoting *AYL*.

101. after kind] proverbially 'cat will after kind', i.e. will act according to her nature, with various extensions, such as 'will catch mice', 'will eat cream', and here 'will seek to mate'. Touchstone plays upon the strong sexual connotations of *kind*. See *OED* sb. 3†c, 'To do the act of kind' = 'to perform the sexual act'. His extempore verses are a series of indecent equivocations. Tarlton and Armin were famous for such performances.

103. Winter'd garments] Grant White quotes from *A Knack to Know a Knave* (c. 1590) 'wint'red oxen, fodder'd in their stalls'. This seems to mean 'oxen as they are in winter' and applies equally well to garments. *NCS*

> So must slender Rosalind.
> They that reap must sheaf and bind,   105
> Then to cart with Rosalind.
> Sweetest nut hath sourest rind,
> Such a nut is Rosalind.
> He that sweetest rose will find
> Must find love's prick, and Rosalind.   110

This is the very false gallop of verses; why do you infect yourself with them?

Ros. Peace you dull fool! I found them on a tree.

Touch. Truly the tree yields bad fruit.

Ros. I'll graff it with you, and then I shall graff it with   115
a medlar. Then it will be the earliest fruit i' th' country; for you'll be rotten ere you be half ripe, and that's the right virtue of the medlar.

Touch. You have said; but whether wisely or no, let the forest judge.   120

Ros. Peace! Here comes my sister, reading. Stand aside.

Enter CELIA *with a writing.*

120. forest] F; Forester *Warburton.*   121. Peace! . . . aside.] *As F (prose)*; Peace! / . . . aside. / *Capell.* SD Enter *Celia*] *Keightley*; F (*after 120*). SD *reads*] *Dyce, Grant White; not in F.*

has 'exposed to winter'. Sisson prefers 'used in winter', 'for use in winter'.

lin'd] with a play on canine copulation.

106. to cart] (1) as corn in harvest; (2) as a whore.

111. *false gallop*] a canter. Cf. Nashe, *Strange Newes*, 1592 (I, p. 278): 'I would trot a false gallop through the rest of his ragged Verses, but that if I should retort his rime dogrell aright, I must make my verses (as he doth his) run hobling like a Brewers Cart vpon the stones, and obserue no length in their feete; which were . . . to infect my vaine with his imitation.' *NCS* relates 'Brewers Cart' to 'butterwomen's rank to market', l. 96 above. Intro., p. xxxii.

115. *graff*] graft, from sb. *graff* = scion. The *t* is an accretion.

you] (1) yew; (2) personal pronoun.

116. *medlar*] (1) a fruit; (2) a meddler. See Tilley, 'Fools will be meddling' (F546).

117. *rotten . . . ripe*] A medlar is not fit for eating (*ripe*) until it is rotten (in a very soft condition). Touchstone will be *rotten* (dead and decomposing) before his mind ever matures (is ripe). See Tilley 'Soon ripe, soon rotten' (R133) and 'Medlars are never good till they be rotten' (M863).

119–20. *let the forest judge*] Warburton's reading 'forester' for *forest* does little to clarify this general appeal to the environment. H. Jenkins points to the propriety of a character's acknowledging that the forest has its own scale of values (*Shakespeare Survey 8*, p. 51).

Celia [*reads*] *Why should this desert be,*
          For it is unpeopled? No.
          Tongues I'll hang on every tree,
               That shall civil sayings show.   125
          Some, how brief the life of man
          Runs his erring pilgrimage,
          That the stretching of a span
          Buckles in his sum of age.
          Some of violated vows,   130
               'Twixt the souls of friend and friend.
          But upon the fairest boughs,
               Or at every sentence end,
          Will I Rosalinda write,
               Teaching all that read to know   135
          The quintessence of every sprite
          Heaven would in little show.
          Therefore Heaven Nature charg'd
          That one body should be fill'd
          With all graces wide-enlarg'd.   140

122. *desert*] *Desert F; a Desart Rowe;* desert silent *Steevens²,* conj. *Tyrwhitt.*
122-3. *be, . . . unpeopled?*] *F; be? . . . unpeopled. Rowe;* be? . . . unpeopl'd?
Capell; be . . . unpeopled? *Steevens¹.*

122-3. Few editors favour the F
punctuation here, but it satisfactorily
expresses Orlando's meaning. The
forest need not be a desert because
(*for*) it is unpeopled. He does not
propose to people it but to civilize it,
by giving tongues to the trees.

125. civil sayings] sober, serious
reflections, such as follow. Once
'civility' is introduced the forest is no
longer an uncultivated place.

127. erring] wandering.

128. span] Psalm 39:6 in the
Prayer Book version, 'Thou hast made
my days as it were a span long.'

136. quintessence] Stressed on the
first and third syllables. See Abbott
492. A highly refined essence or
extract (*OED* sb. 2). There is no
occasion to go further and invoke a
philosophical 'fifth essence'.

137. in little] contracted into small

space, i.e. into one woman. To paint
in little was used of miniature painting.

140. wide-enlarg'd] spread widely
through a number of women, to be
distilled (*extracted*) and brought together in Rosalind. The wantonness
of Helen is twice dismissed, in *not her
heart* and again in *Atalanta's better part.*
Tollet notes that Pliny has compared
'two pictures of ladie *Atalanta* and
queene *Helena . . .* for beautie incomparable, and yet a man may
discerne the one of them to be a
maiden by her modest and chast
countenance' (*Natural History* XXV,
iii, p. 525). Few if any of Shakespeare's audience would pick up the
reference and know that he was saying
Rosalind was as beautiful as Helen
but more chaste, yet it exactly fits a
context where Atalanta's swiftness of
foot, by which she outran her suitors

Nature presently distill'd
Helen's cheek, but not her heart,
Cleopatra's majesty,
Atalanta's better part,
Sad Lucretia's modesty.   145
Thus Rosalind of many parts
By heavenly synod was devis'd,
Of many faces, eyes, and hearts,
To have the touches dearest priz'd.
Heaven would that she these gifts should have,   150
And I to live and die her slave.

Ros. O most gentle Jupiter, what tedious homily of love
have you wearied your parishioners withal, and
never cried, 'Have patience good people!'

Celia. How now? Back-friends! Shepherd, go off a little.   155
Go with him sirrah.

Touch. Come shepherd, let us make an honourable re-

142. her] *Rowe*; his *F.*   152. Jupiter,] *F3*; *Iupiter F*; Juniper! *Warburton*;
pulpiter! *Camb. conj. Spedding.*   155. How now? Back-friends!] *Theobald*;
How now backe friends: *F*; How now! back friends? *Capell*; how now! back
friends; *Malone²*. How now? back, friends.— *Collier.*

and exacted their lives as a penalty, is
incongruous. In Pliny, XXV, xi, p.
534, we read how Zeuxis painted a
picture of Juno, choosing from the
maidens of the city 'five of the fairest
to take out as from severall patterns,
whatsoever hee liked best in any of
them; and of all the lovely parts of
those five, to make one bodie of incomparable beautie'. This passage
haunts Elizabethan literature.

147. synod] Cf. *Cor.*, v. ii. 65–6:
'The glorious gods sit in hourly synod
about thy particular prosperity.'

149. touches] traits. Cf. v. iii. 27.

152. *Jupiter*] Cf. II. iv. 1, where
Rosalind swears by Jupiter. Though
F does not here use the italic customary for proper names, the practice
was not invariable, e.g. at III. iii. 6
Ovid rates italic and at l. 8 Jove is in
roman. Warburton's emendation depends on a popular saying, a 'Juniper

lecture'=a sharp or unpleasing one.
Spedding's ingenious 'pulpiter' is
arrived at from the context, but all
the context basically requires is an
exclamatory oath. *Gentle* is used for its
plosive and alliterative force.

155. *Back-friends*] a word once in
common use for false friends. *OED*
reports it as late as 1827. Celia uses it
here because it is a literal description
of Rosalind, Touchstone and Corin,
at her back. Cf. *Err.*, IV. ii. 37, where
a sergeant making an arrest is
described as 'a back-friend, a shoulder
clapper'. Mason says 'Celia means
only to desire that the shepherd and
clown should retire.' Editors who
follow him, punctuating 'Back,
friends', imply that she is confining
her order to Corin and Touchstone,
since she does not dismiss Rosalind,
to whom neither the manner nor the
words of the address are quite
suitable.

treat, though not with bag and baggage, yet with
scrip and scrippage.   *Exit [with Corin.]*

Celia. Didst thou hear these verses?   160

Ros. O yes, I heard them all, and more too, for some of
them had in them more feet than the verses would
bear.

Celia. That's no matter: the feet might bear the verses.

Ros. Ay, but the feet were lame, and could not bear   165
themselves without the verse, and therefore stood
lamely in the verse.

Celia. But didst thou hear without wondering how thy
name should be hanged and carved upon these
trees?   170

Ros. I was seven of the nine days out of the wonder
before you came; for look here what I found on a
palm-tree. I was never so berhymed since Pythagoras' time that I was an Irish rat, which I can
hardly remember.   175

Celia. Trow you who hath done this?

Ros. Is it a man?

159. SD [*with Corin*]]. *Cor. and Clowne. Rowe.*

159. *scrip and scrippage*] *retreat*, used
in connection with *baggage*, indicates
an army that withdraws honourably,
not in rout. Touchstone points to all
the baggage he and the shepherd have
about them, the usual shepherd's
scrip = bag, and the pouch which was
part of a fool's equipment. Scrippage
is presumably a nonce-word. On the
stage he sometimes snatches the copies
of verses from the girls, to represent
scrip[t]. *NCS* suggests that *bag and
baggage* is 'an unmannerly reference'
to the two girls.

173. *palm-tree*] There is no recorded
instance of the country name *palm*,
for willow, being used in the form
palm-tree. The improbable flora and
fauna of Arden derive from Greek and
Roman poetry, by way of the Middle
Ages, and can be matched in Sidney's
Arcadia. (See Curtius, p. 185.) *NCS*
claims that Rosalind requires palm to

celebrate her victory over Orlando.
E. A. Armstrong, in *Shakespeare's
Imagination* (1946), pp. 111–12 and
footnote, sees a reminiscence of Eden
in paradisal Arden.

173–4. *Pythagoras*] who believed in
the transmigration of souls. Shakespeare's probable source is Ovid,
Metam., XV, 158ff.

174. *an Irish rat*] In ancient Ireland,
a poet could destroy his enemies by
satirical and cursing verses. See R. C.
Elliott, *The Power of Satire* (1960), pp.
35–7. It seems to have been a joke in
sixteenth-century England that the
Irish rid themselves of rats by incan-
tation. Cf. Jonson, *Poetaster*: 'rhime
'em to death, as they do Irish rats,
'An Apologeticall Dialogue', l. 163;
Sidney, *Defence of Poetry*, 'not to be
rhymed to death, as is said to be done
in Ireland' (ed. J. van Dorsten (1973),
p. 121).

Celia. And a chain, that you once wore, about his neck.
Change you colour?

Ros. I prithee who?   180

Celia. O Lord, Lord! It is a hard matter for friends to
meet; but mountains may be remov'd with earth-
quakes, and so encounter.

Ros. Nay, but who is it?

Celia. Is it possible?   185

Ros. Nay, I prithee now, with most petitionary
vehemence, tell me who it is.

Celia. O wonderful, wonderful! And most wonderful
wonderful! And yet again wonderful! And after
that out of all whooping.   190

Ros. Good my complexion! Dost thou think though I
am caparisoned like a man I have a doublet and
hose in my disposition? One inch of delay more is
a South Sea of discovery. I prithee tell me who is it
quickly, and speak apace. I would thou couldst   195
stammer, that thou mightst pour this concealed

181–3. *friends . . . encounter*] proverbially 'friends may meet, but
mountains never greet.' Tilley
(F738). Ray says it means that 'two
haughty persons will never agree
together' (p. 110), but there are times
when it seems to mean simply 'You
are not pinned down. You are mobile,
aren't you?' Cf. Lyly, *Mother Bombie*,
v. iii. 229–30: 'then wee foure met,
which argues we were no mountaines'; Francis Davison, *A Poetical
Rhapsody* (1602): 'Though mountaines
meet not, Louers may'; and J. Taylor,
Taylors Pennilesse Pilgrimage: 'I found
the Proverbe true, that men have
more priviledge than mountaines in
meeting.'

185. *Is it possible?*] . . . *that you
don't know?*

190. *out of all whooping*] past all
power of exclamation.

191. Good my complexion!] One
of Rosalind's 'pretty oaths that are
not dangerous'. Since *complexion* often
meant a person's whole make-up or

temperament, the exclamation seems
directly relevant to *disposition* in the
next sentence.

194. *A South Sea of discovery*] As long
and frustrating as a voyage to the
South Seas. The paramount image is
of *one inch* stretched out to extreme
lengths by the hearer's impatience,
testing endurance to the uttermost.
The phrase has puzzled commentators. *Discovery* may mean simply and
neutrally *something revealed*, as in stage
usage, when an actor is *discovered*. It
also means a systematic exploration,
especially geographical, as in Ralegh's
Discovery of Guiana (1595), and in
collocation with *South Sea*, this sense
seems to be invoked here. To the
tedium of a protracted voyage is
added the deferred hope of an El
Dorado at the end of it. Cf. *Wiv.* 1.
iii. 64–5: 'She is a region in Guiana,
all gold.' Of course Rosalind knows
that Celia has seen Orlando but she
can hardly believe her luck and wants
assurance.

man out of thy mouth, as wine comes out of a
narrow-mouthed bottle; either too much at once
or none at all. I prithee take the cork out of thy
mouth, that I may drink thy tidings.   200

Celia. So you may put a man in your belly.

Ros. Is he of God's making? What manner of man? Is
his head worth a hat? Or his chin worth a beard?

Celia. Nay, he hath but a little beard.

Ros. Why God will send more, if the man will be   205
thankful. Let me stay the growth of his beard, if
thou delay me not the knowledge of his chin.

Celia. It is young Orlando, that tripped up the wrestler's
heels and your heart, both in an instant.

Ros. Nay, but the devil take mocking. Speak sad brow   210
and true maid.

Celia. I' faith, coz, 'tis he.

Ros. Orlando?

Celia. Orlando.

Ros. Alas the day, what shall I do with my doublet and   215
hose? What did he when thou saw'st him? What
said he? How looked he? Wherein went he?
What makes he here? Did he ask for me? Where
remains he? How parted he with thee? And when
shalt thou see him again? Answer me in one word.   220

Celia. You must borrow me Gargantua's mouth first.
'Tis a word too great for any mouth of this age's
size. To say ay and no to these particulars is more
than to answer in a catechism.

---

202. *of God's making*] Wright
explains '. . . or his tailor's?' but
Kittredge says it is 'merely a proverbial phrase for "a normal human
creature" '. Cf. Viola's comment on
Olivia's face, 'Excellently done, if
God did all', *Tw.N.*, I. v. 221.

206. *stay*] wait for.

210–11. *Speak sad brow and true
maid*] in all seriousness and sincerity.
Cf. *H5*, v. ii. 148–9: 'I speak to thee
plain soldier'; *Tw.N.*, I. v. 221: 'He
speaks nothing but madman.'

217. *Wherein went he?*] How was he

dressed?

218. *What makes he?*] What is he
doing? As at I. i. 29.

221. *Gargantua's mouth*] Rabelais'
giant, Gargantua, was known in
England in chapbooks. There had
been no translation of the original
work. This would not have prevented
Shakespeare, who knew the language,
from reading it. P. Reyher, *Essai sur les
idées de Shakespeare* (1947), pp. 111–16,
quotes a number of references to it
made by English authors of the
1590s.

Ros. But doth he know that I am in this forest, and in   225
      man's apparel? Looks he as freshly as he did the
      day he wrestled?

Celia. It is as easy to count atomies as to resolve the pro-
      positions of a lover. But take a taste of my finding
      him, and relish it with good observance. I found   230
      him under a tree like a dropped acorn.

Ros. It may well be called Jove's tree, when it drops
      such fruit.

Celia. Give me audience, good madam.

Ros. Proceed.   235

Celia. There lay he stretched along like a wounded
      knight.

Ros. Though it be pity to see such a sight, it well be-
      comes the ground.

Celia. Cry holla to the tongue, I prithee; it curvets un-   240
      seasonably. He was furnished like a hunter.

Ros. O ominous! he comes to kill my heart!

Celia. I would sing my song without a burden. Thou
      bringest me out of tune.

Ros. Do you not know I am a woman? When I think, I   245
      must speak. Sweet, say on.

Celia. You bring me out. Soft! comes he not here?

Enter ORLANDO *and* JAQUES.

233. such] *Capell*; forth *F*; forth such *F2*.   239. the] *F*; thy *Rowe*.   247.
SD *Enter Orlando and Jaques.*] *Camb.*; *F* (*after 246*); *Halliwell*[2] (*after 248*); *Sisson*
(*after out 247*).

228. *atomies*] atoms, motes.

230. *relish it*] add a pleasing flavour,
carrying on the metaphor of taste. Cf.
III. v. 69: 'I'll sauce her with bitter
words.'

observance] attention.

232. *Jove's tree*] the oak. See Virgil,
Georgics, III, 332.

233 *such*] 'forth' in F is probably a
misreading of *such* in the manuscript,
with long *s* mistaken for *f* and *c* for *t*.
Sisson supposes that the compositor
who added *such* in F2 failed to see that
he could then discard *forth*.

238–9. *well becomes the ground*] need

mean no more than that the ground
was improved by Orlando's lying on
it, but there is probably also a
reference to the background of an
embroidery or a picture.

240. *Cry holla*] an exclamation to
check a horse, from which *curvets*
follows naturally. *OED* quotes *AYL*.

242. *heart*] with an obvious play on
'hart'.

243. *burden*] probably the recurring,
sometimes nonsensical refrain which
punctuates a ballad. It is not likely
here to be 'bourdon'=sustained base.

Ros. 'Tis he. Slink by and note him.

Jaques. I thank you for your company, but good faith, I
    had as lief have been myself alone.   250

Orl. And so had I: but yet for fashion sake I thank you
    too, for your society.

Jaques. God buy you: let's meet as little as we can.

Orl. I do desire we may be better strangers.

Jaques. I pray you mar no more trees with writing love- 255
    songs in their barks.

Orl. I pray you mar no more of my verses with reading
    them ill-favouredly.

Jaques. Rosalind is your love's name?

Orl. Yes, just.   260

Jaques. I do not like her name.

Orl. There was no thought of pleasing you when she
    was christened.

Jaques. What stature is she of?

Orl. Just as high as my heart.   265

Jaques. You are full of pretty answers. Have you not
    been acquainted with goldsmiths' wives, and
    conned them out of rings?

Orl. Not so; but I answer you right painted cloth, from

249–50. I thank . . . alone.] *As F (prose)*; I thanke . . . faith / . . . alone. /
Keightley, conj. Walker (verse).   251–2. And . . . society.] *As Pope (prose)*; And
. . . sake / . . . societie. / *F (verse).*   253. God buy] *F*; God b'w' *Rowe*; God
be wi' *Capell*; God be with *Steevens*; Good bye *Collier*; God b'wi' *Dyce, Grant
White.*   257. more] *F2*; moe *F.*

249–52. These lines can stand
perfectly well as prose, and occur in a
wholly prose context. It is chance that
a personal pronoun begins l. 250 in F
with a capital. There is nothing about
the printing of l. 249 to show whether
verse or prose is intended. It completely fills the width of the column.
The accidental capital at l. 250 may
have encouraged the compositor to
misdivide at ll. 251–2.

253. *God buy you*] God be with you,
now 'good-bye'.

260. *just*] precisely.

268. *conned*] learned by heart.

rings] frequently engraved with

commonplace sentiments or 'love-
posies'. Cf. *Mer.V.*, v. i. 147–50 and
Every Man in his Humour, II. ii. 34–41.
There are specimens in E. Arber's
English Garner, I, p. 611–19, from a
manuscript source, and in *Wits
Recreations* (1640) under 'Fancies and
Fantasticks'.

269. *right*] in the regular style of. Cf.
l. 96 above.

painted cloth] used for cheap hang-
ings in place of tapestry, with pictures
and moralistic inscriptions. It answers
'posies out of rings' because it employs
similar clichés. Orlando has been
called tritely sentimental. He retorts

whence you have studied your questions.   270

Jaques. You have a nimble wit; I think 'twas made of
   Atalanta's heels. Will you sit down with me and
   we two will rail against our mistress the world and
   all our misery?

Orl. I will chide no breather in the world but myself,   275
   against whom I know most faults.

Jaques. The worst fault you have is to be in love.

Orl. 'Tis a fault I will not change for your best virtue.
   I am weary of you.

Jaques. By my troth, I was seeking for a fool when I   280
   found you.

Orl. He is drowned in the brook. Look but in and you
   shall see him.

Jaques. There I shall see mine own figure.

Orl. Which I take to be either a fool, or a cipher.   285

Jaques. I'll tarry no longer with you. Farewell good
   Signior Love.

Orl. I am glad of your departure. Adieu good Monsieur
   Melancholy.   [*Exit Jaques.*]

Ros. [*aside to Celia*] I will speak to him like a saucy   290
   lackey and under that habit play the knave with
   him.—Do you hear, forester?

Orl. Very well. What would you?

Ros. I pray you, what is't o'clock?

---

289. SD *Exit Jaques.*] *Capell; Rowe (after 287); not in F.*   290. SD *aside to
Celia*] *Capell; not in F.*

---

that Jaques's didactic gravity is
equally trite. Neil quotes J. Taylor,
Certain Travels, 1651: 'As upon my
bed I musing lay, / The chamber
hanged with painted cloth, I found /
Myself with "Sentences" beleaguered
round'. In *No Whipping, nor Tripping*,
Taylor gives examples of what is
written on the painted cloth.

   272. *Atalanta's heels*] Cf. l. 140, note.
This time the reference is to Atalanta's swiftness of foot.

   275. *breather*] living being.

   285. *a cipher*] a figure nought. The
audience, expected to follow some of

the very quick exchanges in this play,
has this joke spelled out at length. It
may have been a point at which
simpler auditors enjoyed a good
laugh. It seems unduly severe to
suggest that this is Shakespeare
telling us what value to put on
Jaques. We must not even think that
it convicts him of being slow on the
uptake, though he is so used to being
the banterer that he is not quick to
recognize himself as somebody else's
target. He lacks the modesty of
Orlando, who sees in himself 'most
faults'.

Orl. You should ask me what time o' day; there's no   295
    clock in the forest.

Ros. Then there is no true lover in the forest, else sigh-
    ing every minute and groaning every hour would
    detect the lazy foot of Time, as well as a clock.

Orl. And why not the swift foot of Time? Had not that   300
    been as proper?

Ros. By no means sir. Time travels in divers paces with
    divers persons. I'll tell you who Time ambles
    withal, who Time trots withal, who Time gallops
    withal, and who he stands still withal.   305

Orl. I prithee, who doth he trot withal?

Ros. Marry he trots hard with a young maid, between
    the contract of her marriage and the day it is
    solemnized. If the interim be but a se'nnight,
    Time's pace is so hard that it seems the length of   310
    seven year.

Orl. Who ambles Time withal?

Ros. With a priest that lacks Latin, and a rich man that
    hath not the gout, for the one sleeps easily because
    he cannot study, and the other lives merrily be-   315
    cause he feels no pain; the one lacking the burden
    of lean and wasteful learning; the other knowing
    no burden of heavy tedious penury. These Time
    ambles withal.

Orl. Who doth he gallop withal?   320

Ros. With a thief to the gallows; for though he go as
    softly as foot can fall, he thinks himself too soon
    there.

Orl. Who stays it still withal?

Ros. With lawyers in the vacation; for they sleep be-   325
    tween term and term, and then they perceive not
    how Time moves.

307. *trots hard*] Hard trotting is
uncomfortable for the rider. The girl
waiting for her wedding day finds the
time hard to bear. Cf. *Rom.*, III. ii. 1:
'Gallop apace, you fiery-footed
steeds.'

311. *seven year*] 'Year belongs to a
class of nouns that in Anglo-Saxon

have the nominative and accusative
plural identical in form with the
singular' (Kittredge). Cf. 'fathom' at
IV. i. 196.

317. *wasteful*] causing one to waste
away, a consequence of hard study
and low living.

322. *softly*] slowly.

Orl. Where dwell you pretty youth?

Ros. With this shepherdess my sister; here in the skirts
    of the forest, like fringe upon a petticoat.   330

Orl. Are you native of this place?

Ros. As the cony that you see dwell where she is kindled.

Orl. Your accent is something finer than you could
    purchase in so removed a dwelling.

Ros. I have been told so of many. But indeed, an old   335
    religious uncle of mine taught me to speak, who
    was in his youth an inland man, one that knew
    courtship too well, for there he fell in love. I have
    heard him read many lectures against it, and I
    thank God I am not a woman, to be touched with   340
    so many giddy offences as he hath generally taxed
    their whole sex withal.

Orl. Can you remember any of the principal evils that
    he laid to the charge of women?

Ros. There were none principal: they were all like one   345
    another as half-pence are, every one fault seeming
    monstrous, till his fellow-fault came to match it.

Orl. I prithee recount some of them.

Ros. No; I will not cast away my physic but on those
    that are sick. There is a man haunts the forest that   350
    abuses our young plants with carving 'Rosalind'
    on their barks; hangs odes upon hawthorns and
    elegies on brambles; all, forsooth, deifying the
    name of Rosalind. If I could meet that fancy-
    monger, I would give him some good counsel, for   355
    he seems to have the quotidian of love upon him.

353. deifying] *F2*; defying *F*.

332. *kindled*] used of the littering of
conies = rabbits. *OED* v. 2, quoting
AYL.

334. *purchase*] acquire.

removed] remote.

337. *an inland man*] brought up in
civility. Cf. II. vii. 97.

courtship] (1) courtly manners; (2)
wooing.

340. *touched*] tainted.

346. *half-pence*] Silver halfpence,

not coined under Elizabeth between
1561 and 1582, thereafter must have
stood out among the very various
small coins and counters in circulation
(C. Oman, *Coinage of England*, 1931,
p. 287).

354–5. *fancy-monger*] dealer in love.

356. *quotidian*] an ague or malarial
attack accompanied by continuous
shivering, as distinct from a tertian

Orl. I am he that is so love-shaked. I pray you tell me
your remedy.

Ros. There is none of my uncle's marks upon you. He
taught me how to know a man in love; in which   360
cage of rushes I am sure you are not prisoner.

Orl. What were his marks?

Ros. A lean cheek, which you have not; a blue eye and
sunken, which you have not; an unquestionable
spirit, which you have not; a beard neglected,   365
which you have not—but I pardon you for that,
for simply your having in beard is a younger
brother's revenue. Then your hose should be un-
gartered, your bonnet unbanded, your sleeve un-
buttoned, your shoe untied, and everything about   370
you demonstrating a careless desolation. But you
are no such man: you are rather point-device in
your accoutrements, as loving yourself than seeming the lover of any other.

Orl. Fair youth, I would I could make thee believe I   375
love.

Ros. Me believe it! You may as soon make her that you
love believe it, which I warrant she is apter to do
than to confess she does. That is one of the points
in the which women still give the lie to their con-   380
sciences. But in good sooth, are you he that hangs
the verses on the trees, wherein Rosalind is so
admired?

Orl. I swear to thee youth, by the white hand of Rosalind, I am that he, that unfortunate he.   385

367. in] *F*; no *F2*.

or a quartan ague, where the fits were
intermittent.

357. *love-shaked*] in a fever of love.

361. *cage of rushes*] Instanced as a
slight impediment to a strong man.
Rings plaited from rushes were exchanged by country sweethearts. Cf.
All's W., II. ii. 21 : 'fit . . . as Tib's rush
for Tom's forefinger'; Chapman, *The
Gentleman Usher*, II. ii. 77: 'Rushes

make true-loue knots; Rushes make
rings.'

363. *a blue eye*] shadowed by sleep-
lessness.

364-5. *an unquestionable spirit*] irri-
table when spoken to, or else 'a mind
indifferent' (Johnson). To question =
to converse with.

372. *point-device*] neat and trim, in
perfect order.

380. *still*] always, constantly.

Ros. But are you so much in love as your rhymes speak?

Orl. Neither rhyme nor reason can express how much.

Ros. Love is merely a madness, and I tell you, deserves
as well a dark house and a whip as madmen do;
and the reason why they are not so punished and   390
cured is that the lunacy is so ordinary that the
whippers are in love too. Yet I profess curing it by
counsel.

Orl. Did you ever cure any so?

Ros. Yes, one, and in this manner. He was to imagine   395
me his love, his mistress; and I set him every day
to woo me. At which time would I, being but a
moonish youth, grieve, be effeminate, changeable,
longing and liking, proud, fantastical, apish,
shallow, inconstant, full of tears, full of smiles, for   400
every passion something and for no passion truly
anything, as boys and women are for the most part
cattle of this colour; would now like him, now
loathe him; then entertain him, then forswear
him; now weep for him, then spit at him; that I   405
drave my suitor from his mad humour of love to a
living humour of madness, which was, to forswear
the full stream of the world and to live in a nook
merely monastic. And thus I cured him, and this
way will I take upon me to wash your liver as clean   410
as a sound sheep's heart, that there shall not be one
spot of love in't.

Orl. I would not be cured, youth.

Ros. I would cure you, if you would but call me Rosa-

407. living] *F*; loving *Collier, conj. Johnson.*   410. clean] cleane *F*; cleare *F2.*

388. *merely*] purely. Cf. 'merely
monastic', l. 409 below.

389. *a dark house and a whip*] the
contemporary way of dealing with the
violence of the insane.

398. *moonish*] changeable. See
Intro., pp. lix–lxiii for a possible
relation to Lyly's *Woman in the Moon.*

404. *entertain*] receive courteously.

406–7. *from his mad humour of love to
a living humour of madness*] from being

metaphorically mad to being
clinically mad. Cf. *Oth.,* III. iii. 413:
'Give me a living reason she's dis-
loyal' which Whiter (p. 51) takes to
mean 'give me a *direct, absolute* and
unequivocal proof'. He goes on to
interpret *a living humour of madness* as 'a
confirmed, absolute, and *direct* state of
madness'.

410. *liver*] the seat of the passions in
the old physiology.

lind and come every day to my cote and woo me.   415

Orl. Now by the faith of my love, I will. Tell me where
it is.

Ros. Go with me to it, and I'll show it you; and by the
way, you shall tell me where in the forest you live.
Will you go?   420

Orl. With all my heart, good youth.

Ros. Nay, you must call me Rosalind. Come sister, will
you go?   *Exeunt.*

SCENE III

Enter TOUCHSTONE, AUDREY *and* JAQUES [*behind.*]

Touch. Come apace good Audrey. I will fetch up your
goats, Audrey. And how Audrey, am I the man
yet? Doth my simple feature content you?

Aud. Your features? Lord warrant us! What features?

Touch. I am here with thee and thy goats, as the most   5
capricious poet, honest Ovid, was among the Goths.

Jaques. [*aside*] O knowledge ill-inhabited, worse than
Jove in a thatched house!

Scene III

Scene III] *Scæna Tertia.* F. [Location] *Another part of the forest. Dyce; not in* F.
SD *behind*] *Dyce, Grant White; watching them Johnson; at a Distance, observing them.*
Capell; not in F.   4. What features?] F; what's feature? *conj. Farmer.*   7. SD
aside] *Johnson; not in* F.

3. *feature*] a general term for how a
person is made, not confined to the
face. Audrey fails to understand the
word, perhaps, as Steevens conjectures, confusing it with 'faitors' =
cheats and villains. See Kökeritz, pp.
106 and 175 for contemporary
pronunciation.

6. *capricious ... Goths*] Both the first
and last words play on *goats. Capricious*
= goatish and hence lascivious, is the
antithesis of *honest* = chaste. As author
of the *Ars Amatoria* and lover of Julia,
Ovid had no high reputation for
chastity. This may account in part for
his exile among the Getae. He complained that in their barbarous
country his verses were not under-

stood. 'A hearer rouses zeal, excellence
increases with praise, and renown
possesses a mighty spur. In this place
who is there to whom I can read my
compositions?' (*Ex Ponto*, IV. ii. 15–38,
trs. A. L. Wheeler. See also *Tristia*,
V. xii. 53–4; III. xiv. 39–40; IV. i. 89–
90.) Touchstone reflects on these
sentiments at ll. 9–12 below. Jaques
comments in ll. 7–8 on the incongruity of a well-read fool. Cf. Nashe,
Pierce Pennilesse, 1592: '*Ouid* might as
well haue read his verses to the *Getes*
that vnderstood him not' (I. p. 180).

7. *ill-inhabited*] badly lodged. *Inhabited* = 'made to inhabit' (Abbott
294).

8. *Jove in a thatched house*] As related

Touch. When a man's verses cannot be understood, nor
a man's good wit seconded with the forward child,   10
understanding, it strikes a man more dead than a
great reckoning in a little room. Truly, I would the
gods had made thee poetical.

Aud. I do not know what 'poetical' is. Is it honest in deed
and word? Is it a true thing?   15

Touch. No truly; for the truest poetry is the most feigning,
and lovers are given to poetry; and what they swear
in poetry may be said as lovers they do feign.

Aud. Do you wish then that the gods had made me
poetical?   20

Touch. I do truly. For thou swear'st to me thou art
honest. Now if thou wert a poet, I might have some
hope thou didst feign.

Aud. Would you not have me honest?

Touch. No truly, unless thou wert hard-favoured; for   25
honesty coupled to beauty is to have honey a sauce
to sugar.

18. may] *F*; it may *Collier²*, *conj. Mason.*

by Ovid, *Metam.*, VIII, 626ff., Jove
and Mercury in disguise were turned
from all doors until a poor couple
called Philemon and Baucis took
them under their roof, *stipulis et canna
tecta palustri*, and displayed exemplary
courtesy. It was a favourite instance
of the simple life being the good life.
Cf. *Ado*, II. i. 82–4: '*Don Pedro.* My
visor is Philemon's roof; within the
house is Jove. *Hero.* Why, then, your
visor should be thatch'd.' Hulme
shows that the collocation of *Jove* and
thatched house is likely to be indecent
(p. 150).

11. *strikes a man . . . dead*] inhibits
life and action, damps all enthusiasm.
Cf. strikes dumb. See Intro., pp.
xxxiii–xxxiv, for a possible reference
to the death of Marlowe.

11–12. *a great reckoning in a little
room*] *reckoning* = bill or account and
room = chamber or space. 'The entertainment was mean and the bill

extravagant' (Warburton). 'An ex-
tensive reckoning to be written out in
a very small space' (Hunter). Warburton explains, 'the silence that falls
on a merry company when a jest falls
flat is like the silence when they are
confronted with a big bill.' Hunter
stresses lack of scope. Touchstone
could have impressed an intelligent
and educated audience, but he is
confined to Audrey and her goats. He
is not lamenting the failure of any
particular joke. All his learned jokes
will fall flat in unlettered Arden.

14. *honest*] chaste. Cf. *honest Ovid* at
l. 6 above.

16. *feigning*] This touches on the
many contemporary arguments as
to whether poets are liars. See Tilley
(P28); Sidney's *Defence of Poetry*, ed.
J. van Dorsten (1973), pp. 101–3;
and Marston's retort to a lady who
discounted his compliments, because
he was a poet. ''Tis true, said he, for

Jaques. [aside] A material fool!

Aud. Well, I am not fair, and therefore I pray the gods
    make me honest.   30

Touch. Truly, and to cast away honesty upon a foul slut
    were to put good meat into an unclean dish.

Aud. I am not a slut, though I thank the gods I am foul.

Touch. Well, praised be the gods for thy foulness; slut-
    tishness may come hereafter. But be it as it may be,   35
    I will marry thee; and to that end I have been with
    Sir Oliver Martext, the vicar of the next village,
    who hath promised to meet me in this place of the
    forest and to couple us.

Jaques. [aside] I would fain see this meeting.   40

Aud. Well, the gods give us joy!

Touch. Amen. A man may, if he were of a fearful heart,

---

28. SD *aside] Johnson; not in* F.   40. SD *aside] Johnson; not in* F.

poets feigne and lye, and so did I
when I commended your beauty, for
you are exceeding foul' (Mann-
ingham's *Diary*, 21 November 1602).

28. *material]* 'A fool with matter in
him; a fool stocked with notions'
(Johnson). Hotson (p. 127) suggests
'dull or shallow-witted' from Florio's
gloss upon *materiale*, but Jaques is
admiring Touchstone's cleverness.

29. *pray the gods]* Touchstone's
references to Ovid and poetry keep
the conversation within an area where
the term *gods* is appropriate and
Audrey follows suit. Thus no one can
complain of the name of God being
invoked in an unsuitable context.

32. *good meat into an unclean dish]* See
Tilley (M834).

33. *I thank the gods I am foul]* My
face is as God made it. Cf. IV. i. 34–5,
'almost chide God for making you
that countenance you are'; *Ado*, III.
iii. 16–18: 'for your favour, sir, why,
give God thanks, and make no boast
of it'; *Tw.N.*, I. v. 221: 'Excellently
done, if God did all'. The thought
is proverbial. See Tilley (G188).
Foul = plain looking, opposed to 'fair'.
Cf. fair and foul weather, fair and foul

play, etc. Audrey says she can't help
her face, she was born that way, but
she does keep herself clean and tidy.

37. *Sir Oliver Martext] Sir* =
Dominus, the title proper to a BA of a
university. It ultimately gave way to
Master and came to be used of a priest
who had not graduated. Since Touchstone calls him *vicar* we must assume
that Sir Oliver has been ordained.
His name suggests to some editors
that he is a puritan preacher, recalling
the notorious Marprelate tracts of the
late eighties, though Martext would
suit any comic parson. His conduct of
the ceremony might be interpreted as
a defiance of the Catholic concept of
marriage as a sacrament. Here, as
elsewhere, Jaques is conservative. His
outbursts are almost all in favour of
the good old days. The nostalgic
element in pastoralism is one of the
things that recommends it to him.
Elizabethan country clergy were
notoriously ignorant and slack, the
Reformation requiring more men
trained in the new theology than were
instantly available, and there were
many jibes at their expense. See
Appendix B on irregular marriages.

stagger in this attempt; for here we have no temple
but the wood, no assembly but horn-beasts. But
what though? Courage! As horns are odious, they   45
are necessary. It is said, many a man knows no end
of his goods. Right. Many a man has good horns
and knows no end of them. Well, that is the
dowry of his wife, 'tis none of his own getting.
Horns? Even so. Poor men alone? No, no. The   50
noblest deer hath them as huge as the rascal. Is the
single man therefore blessed? No. As a walled town
is more worthier than a village, so is the forehead of
a married man more honourable than the bare
brow of a bachelor; and by how much defence is   55
better than no skill, by so much is a horn more
precious than to want. Here comes Sir Oliver.

Enter SIR OLIVER MARTEXT.

Sir Oliver Martext, you are well met. Will you dispatch us here under this tree or shall we go with you
to your chapel?   60
Sir O. Is there none here to give the woman?
Touch. I will not take her on gift of any man.

50. Horns? Even so. Poor men alone?] *Grant White*[2]; hornes, euen so poore
men alone: *F*; Hornes? even so—poor Men alone— *Rowe*; Horns? even so—
poor men alone?— *Theobald*; Horns! never for poor men alone? *Singer*[2];
Horns? ever to poor men alone? *Dyce*; [are] horns given to poor men alone?
Grant White after Collier MS; Horns. Even so poor men alone. *Sisson*.   57. SD
Enter Sir Oliver Martext.] *Dyce, Grant White; F (after* want *at* 57.)

44. *horn-beasts*] alluding to the
cuckold's horns.

46. *necessary*] inevitable.

46–7. *no end of his goods*] A proverbial indication that a man is well-off.
Tilley (E122).

50. *Horns? . . . alone?*] *NCS* finds
Theobald's punctuation 'only a make-
shift' but it is good comic sense and
supplies good material for an actor.

51. *rascal*] 'the hunters terme giuen
to a young deere, leane and out of
season' (Puttenham, *Arte of Poesie*,

1589, ed. Arber, p. 191). Cf. 'The
Bucks and lusty Stags amongst the
Rascalls strew'd / As sometimes
gallant spirits amongst the multitude',
(Drayton, *Polyolbion*, XIII, 91–2) a
description of the Warwickshire
Forest of Arden, and *The Maydes
Metamorphosis*, I. i. 338ff.

55. *defence*] Generally read as a
reference to fencing, but reflecting
also on the defensive walls which make
a town nobler than a village. Such
fortifications included a type known
as a 'horn-work'.

Sir O. Truly she must be given, or the marriage is not
    lawful.

Jaques [*advancing*]. Proceed, proceed. I'll give her.   65

Touch. Good even, good Master What-ye-call't. How do
    you sir? You are very well met. God 'ild you for
    your last company. I am very glad to see you. Even
    a toy in hand here sir. Nay, pray be covered.

Jaques. Will you be married, Motley?   70

Touch. As the ox hath his bow sir, the horse his curb, and
    the falcon her bells, so man hath his desires, and as
    pigeons bill, so wedlock would be nibbling.

Jaques. And will you, being a man of your breeding, be
    married under a bush like a beggar? Get you to   75
    church, and have a good priest that can tell you
    what marriage is. This fellow will but join you to-
    gether as they join wainscot; then one of you will
    prove a shrunk panel, and like green timber, warp,
    warp.   80

Touch. [*aside*]. I am not in the mind but I were better
    to be married of him than of another, for he is not
    like to marry me well; and not being well married,
    it will be a good excuse for me hereafter to leave my
    wife.   85

Jaques. Go thou with me, and let me counsel thee.

Touch. Come sweet Audrey,
    We must be married or we must live in bawdry.

---

65. SD *advancing*] *Malone*[1]; *discovering himself. Johnson; not in F.*   81. SD *aside*]
Singer; not in F. the mind but] *Capell*; the minde, but *F*; the mind; but *Sisson.*
86. Go . . . thee.] *As Pope (prose)*; Goe . . . mee, / . . . thee. / *F.*   87. *Touch.*]
F3; Ol. F.   87–8. Come . . . bawdry.] *As F. (verse)*; *Pope (prose)*.

66. *Master What-ye-call't*] This is the
only place in the play where the name
of Jaques is equated with jakes = a
privy. See Intro., p. lxviii.

67. *God 'ild you*] God yield = reward
you.

69. *toy*] trifle.

be covered] Jaques has removed his
hat out of respect for the priest and
the ceremony.

71. *bow*] yoke. *Bow, curb* and *bells*
are all means of controlling and

domesticating an animal. Cf. Kyd's
Spanish Tragedy, II. i. 3–4 (ed. Boas,
1901): 'In time the sauage Bull sus-
taines the yoake, / In time all haggard
Hawkes will stoope to lure' and *Ado*,
I. i. 225–32 where Benedick declines to
imitate the savage bull.

79. *panel*] Hulme suggests a play on
parnel = a harlot (p. 105).

warp] (1) to shrink (as wood); (2)
to stray (as a sinner).

81. *I am not in the mind but*] I do not

Farewell good Master Oliver. Not—
><center>*O sweet Oliver,*</center>   90
> *O brave Oliver,*
> *Leave me not behind thee:*
but—

> *Wind away,*
><center>*Be gone, I say,*</center>   95
> *I will not to wedding with thee.*
> [*Exeunt Jaques, Touchstone and Audrey.*]

Sir O. 'Tis no matter. Ne'er a fantastical knave of them
all shall flout me out of my calling.   *Exit.*

SCENE IV

Enter ROSALIND *and* CELIA.

Ros. Never talk to me, I will weep.
Celia. Do I prithee, but yet have the grace to consider
that tears do not become a man.

89–90. *As Malone; Not O sweet Oliver | Capell (verse); prose F.*   90–1. *As Capell; prose italicized Warburton; prose F.*   92. *behind thee] F*; behi' thee *Steevens³, conj. Farmer;* behind thee, pr'ythee! *Keightley.*   93–4. *As Malone; But wind away | Capell (verse); prose F.*   96. *with thee] F*; wi' thee *Steevens³, conj. Farmer.*   96. *Exeunt Jaques, Touchstone and Audrey] Exeunt Jaques, Clown and Audrey. Capell; not in F.*   98. SD *Exit.] Capell; Exeunt F.*

Scene IV

Scene IV] *Scæna Quarta. F.* [Location] *a Cottage in the Forest. Theobald; not in F.*

think otherwise than that=I am inclined to think that. F has one of its habitual commas before *but*, which may not have any special significance. Sisson makes the comma a semi-colon and has Touchstone say that he 'is not inclined to marriage now, but if he is driven to it an invalid marriage is best'. It would appear that the marriage would not have been invalid, though perhaps irregular (see Appendix B).

90. O sweet Oliver] A popular song and catchphrase of the day. The text was entered in SR August 1584. It was sung to 'Pescod time', otherwise known as 'Hunts up' and 'Sweet

Oliver'. See W. Chappell, *Old English Popular Music* ed. H. E. Wooldridge (1893), I, pp. 86–90 and Sternfeld, p. 114 note. The way in which Feste triumphs over Malvolio in a snatch of popular song is strikingly similar. Cf. *Tw.N.*, IV. ii. 116ff. F does not set Touchstone's lines as verse. They were perhaps said, not sung. See Intro., p. liv. Warburton, followed by Johnson, italicizes *O Sweet Oliver . . . behind thee* as a manifest quotation, and Johnson in a footnote sets *Wind away . . . with thee* as verse, recognizing it as a parody.

94. Wind] cognate with 'wend'=to go on one's way.

Ros. But have I not cause to weep?

Celia. As good cause as one would desire, therefore weep.   5

Ros. His very hair is of the dissembling colour.

Celia. Something browner than Judas's. Marry his kisses
are Judas's own children.

Ros. I'faith his hair is of a good colour.

Celia. An excellent colour. Your chestnut was ever the   10
only colour.

Ros. And his kissing is as full of sanctity as the touch of
holy bread.

Celia. He hath bought a pair of cast lips of Diana. A nun
of winter's sisterhood kisses not more religiously, the   15
very ice of chastity is in them.

Ros. But why did he swear he would come this morning
and comes not?

Celia. Nay certainly there is no truth in him.

Ros. Do you think so?   20

Celia. Yes, I think he is not a pick-purse nor a horse-
stealer, but for his verity in love, I do think him as
concave as a covered goblet or a worm-eaten nut.

Ros. Not true in love?

Celia. Yes, when he is in, but I think he is not in.   25

Ros. You have heard him swear downright he was.

5–13. *As Pope* (*prose*); As . . . desire, / . . . weepe. / . . . haire / . . . colour. /
. . . Iudasses: / . . . children. / . . . colour. / . . . colour: / . . . colour: / sancti-
tie, / . . . bread. / *F*.   13. bread] *F*; Beard *Theobald, conj. Warburton.*   14.
cast *F*; chast *F2*; chaste *Rowe.*

5–13. The compositor was spreading prose copy by setting it as verse.
See note at II. vi.

6. *the dissembling colour*] Judas's hair
was commonly painted red. Singer
quotes Marston, *The Insatiate Coun-
tess*: 'I ever thought by his red head
he would prove a Judas.' Orlando's
dark auburn matches the hair of the
young man to whom Shakespeare's
sonnets were addressed, if the un-
conventional comparison with mar-
joram buds in Sonnet 99 is literal.

10. *Your chestnut*] Abbott 221.

13. *holy bread*] bread blessed after

the Eucharist and distributed to the
congregation, French *pain bénit*. After
the Reformation the term was used
for the wafer. *OED* quotes *AYL*. The
earlier and widespread meaning is
presumably intended here, as the
less offensive. Warburton's 'holy
beard' = 'the kiss of a holy saint or
hermit' shows that by his time the
term did appear improper in the
context.

14. *cast*] cast off, as in 'cast off
clothing' (*Theobald*).

23. *covered*] The domed lid of a
covered goblet turned it into a hollow
sphere.

Celia. 'Was' is not 'is'; besides, the oath of a lover is no
    stronger than the word of a tapster. They are both
    the confirmer of false reckonings. He attends here in
    the forest on the Duke your father.   30
Ros. I met the Duke yesterday and had much question
    with him. He asked me of what parentage I was: I
    told him of as good as he, so he laughed and let me
    go. But what talk we of fathers, when there is such a
    man as Orlando?   35
Celia. O that's a brave man! He writes brave verses,
    speaks brave words, swears brave oaths, and breaks
    them bravely, quite traverse, athwart the heart of
    his lover, as a puisny tilter that spurs his horse but
    on one side breaks his staff like a noble goose. But   40
    all's brave that youth mounts and folly guides. Who
    comes here?

Enter CORIN.

Corin. Mistress and master, you have oft enquir'd
    After the shepherd that complain'd of love,
    Who you saw sitting by me on the turf   45
    Praising the proud disdainful shepherdess
    That was his mistress.
Celia.   Well, and what of him?
Corin. If you will see a pageant truly play'd

27. a lover] *F2*; Louer *F.*   29. confirmer *F*; confirmers *Pope.*   39. puisny]
F; puny *Capell.*   40. noble goose] *F*; notable goose *Singer²*; noble joust *conj.*
Becket; noble goofe *conj. NCS.*

31. *question*] conversation. Cf. v. iv.
160, and 'unquestionable' at III. ii.
364.
    38. *quite traverse*] To strike an
opponent in a tournament athwart,
snapping the lance in half, and not
directly on his shield, splintering it
lengthways, was considered disgrace-
ful (Wright).
    39. *puisny*] petty, inferior (*OED* a.
and sb. †3, quoting *AYL*).
    40. *a noble goose*] *NCS* suggests
'goofe'=a clumsy fellow, the *f* having

been misread as long *s*. See *OED*
'goff' and Supplement 'goof' (slang).
    48. *pageant*] show. Cf. *MND*, III. ii.
114, where Puck offers to display
Lysander pleading with Helena as a
'fond pageant'. Lodge makes Corydon, comically unable to supply the
sentimental analysis that Aliena demands of him, offer to 'bring Montanus and her down, that you may
both see their persons, and note their
passions; and then where the blame
is, there let it rest' (p. 111).

Between the pale complexion of true love
And the red glow of scorn and proud disdain,   50
Go hence a little, and I shall conduct you
If you will mark it.

Ros.   O come, let us remove.
The sight of lovers feedeth those in love.
Bring us to this sight, and you shall say
I'll prove a busy actor in their play.   *Exeunt.*   55

SCENE V

Enter SILVIUS *and* PHEBE.

Sil. Sweet Phebe do not scorn me, do not Phebe.
Say that you love me not, but say not so
In bitterness. The common executioner,
Whose heart th'accustom'd sight of death makes hard,
Falls not the axe upon the humbled neck   5
But first begs pardon. Will you sterner be
Than he that dies and lives by bloody drops?

Enter ROSALIND, CELIA *and* CORIN [*behind*].

Phebe. I would not be thy executioner;
I fly thee, for I would not injure thee.
Thou tell'st me there is murder in mine eye: 10
'Tis pretty, sure, and very probable,
That eyes, that are the frail'st and softest things,

54. Bring us to] *F*; Bring us but to *Pope*; Come, bring us to *Capell*; Bring us unto *Malone*; Bring us to see *Dyce²*, conj. *Jervis*.

Scene v

Scene v] *Scena Quinta. F.* [Location] *another part of the Forest. Theobald; not in F.*
7. SD *and Corin behind*] *Collier; at a Distance, Corin leading them. Capell; and Corin F.*
11. pretty, sure,] *Theobald*; pretty sure, *F*.

55. Cf. *MND*, III. i. 70–1: What, a play toward! I'll be an auditor; / An actor too perhaps, if I see cause.

Scene v

6. *first begs pardon*] the common practice.

7. *dies and lives*] There are comparable instances of this reversal of the normal word order. See Arrowsmith, *Notes and Queries*, VII (1853), p. 542.

Who shut their coward gates on atomies,
Should be call'd tyrants, butchers, murderers.
Now I do frown on thee with all my heart, 15
And if mine eyes can wound, now let them kill thee.
Now counterfeit to swoon: why now fall down,
Or if thou canst not, O for shame, for shame,
Lie not, to say mine eyes are murderers.
Now show the wound mine eye hath made in thee. 20
Scratch thee but with a pin, and there remains
Some scar of it; lean upon a rush,
The cicatrice and capable impressure
Thy palm some moment keeps; but now mine eyes,
Which I have darted at thee, hurt thee not, 25
Nor, I am sure, there is no force in eyes
That can do hurt.

Sil.   O dear Phebe,
If ever, as that ever may be near,
You meet in some fresh cheek the power of fancy,
Then shall you know the wounds invisible 30
That love's keen arrows make.

Phebe.   But till that time
Come not thou near me; and when that time comes,
Afflict me with thy mocks, pity me not,
As till that time I shall not pity thee.

Ros. [*advancing*] And why I pray you? Who might be your
    mother, 35
That you insult, exult, and all at once,
Over the wretched? What though you have no beauty—

22. lean] *F*; Leane but *F2*.   35. SD *advancing*] *Capell* (*after* you); *not in F*.
37. What though] What though? *Singer*; What! though *Keightley*. have no]
Rowe; hau no *F*; ha no *F2*; have *Theobald*; have some *Hanmer*; have mo *Malone*;
have more *Steevens³*.

13. *atomies*] as before at III. ii. 228.

23. *cicatrice*] the only instance of
this word being used for something
other than a scar (*OED* 1. b. quoting
AYL).

capable] a curious usage. It does not
mean that the impress can receive
but that it can be received. Schmidt
glosses it 'impressible'.

34–5. *your mother*] who should have
contributed the feminine virtues of
gentleness and compassion to her
make-up.

36. *all at once*] all in a breath
(Steevens).

37. *have no beauty*] A sarcasm. F's
hau has made commentators suspect
corruption in this line and they suggest

As by my faith I see no more in you
Than without candle may go dark to bed—
Must you be therefore proud and pitiless?   40
Why what means this? Why do you look on me?
I see no more in you than in the ordinary
Of Nature's sale-work. 'Od's my little life,
I think she means to tangle my eyes too!
No faith proud mistress, hope not after it.   45
'Tis not your inky brows, your black silk hair,
Your bugle eyeballs, nor your cheek of cream
That can entame my spirits to your worship.
You foolish shepherd, wherefore do you follow her
Like foggy South puffing with wind and rain?   50
You are a thousand times a properer man
Than she a woman. 'Tis such fools as you
That makes the world full of ill-favour'd children.
'Tis not her glass but you that flatters her,
And out of you she sees herself more proper   55
Than any of her lineaments can show her.
But mistress, know yourself. Down on your knees
And thank heaven, fasting, for a good man's love;
For I must tell you friendly in your ear,

emendations. Furness points to the illogic of *therefore* applied to *no beauty*, but Rosalind is inverting logic, as in her description of *black silk hair* and *bugle eyeballs*, which she offers as praise, in defiance of the fact that dark colouring was not admired. One must assume that Phebe's hair was not unequivocally black, in view of her outraged exclamation at ll. 130–1. There must have been euphemisms available to the nut-brown maidens. Lodge's Phoebe has hair as white as wool (p. 50).

39. *without candle . . . bed*] Phebe can't hope to be bedded if there is light enough to see her by. Cf. 'When candles be out all cats be gray', and 'Joan's as good as my lady in the dark'. Tilley (C50 and J57). In *Strange Newes*, 1592 (I, p. 273) Nashe says that, from Jacob's mistaking Leah for Rachel, 'I learne to buy my wife candle to goe to bed withall, and admit her not by darke, but by light.'

43. *sale-work*] Ready-made goods. 'What nature makes for general sale and not according to order or pattern' (Wright).

'Od's] May God save.

47. *bugle*] a tube-shaped glass bead, usually black (*OED*).

48. *entame*] 'bring into a state of tameness' (Abbott).

50. *foggy South*] the south-west wind. Cf. *Rom.*, I. iv. 103: 'dew-dropping south' and *Cym.*, IV. ii. 349: 'spongy south'.

51. *properer*] more handsome. Cf. ll. 55 and 115 below.

52. *such fools as you*] who marry plain girls.

Sell when you can, you are not for all markets.   60
Cry the man mercy, love him, take his offer;
Foul is most foul, being foul to be a scoffer.
So take her to thee shepherd. Fare you well.
Phebe. Sweet youth, I pray you chide a year together.
I had rather hear you chide than this man woo.   65
Ros. [*to Phebe*] He's fallen in love with your foulness, [*to
Silvius*] and she'll fall in love with my anger. If it be
so, as fast as she answers thee with frowning looks,
I'll sauce her with bitter words. [*To Phebe*] Why
look you so upon me?   70
Phebe. For no ill will I bear you.
Ros. I pray you do not fall in love with me,
For I am falser than vows made in wine.
Besides, I like you not. If you will know my house,
'Tis at the tuft of olives here hard by.   75
Will you go sister? Shepherd, ply her hard.
Come sister. Shepherdess, look on him better
And be not proud; though all the world could see,
None could be so abus'd in sight as he.
Come, to our flock.   80

Exeunt [*Rosalind, Celia and Corin*].

Phebe. Dead shepherd, now I find thy saw of might,
'Who ever lov'd that lov'd not at first sight?'

62. being foul] *F*; being found *Warburton*.   66–70. He's . . . me?] *As Pope*
(*prose*); He's . . . shee'll / . . . fast / . . . sauce / . . . me? / *F*; He's . . . she'll /
. . . so, / . . . looks, / . . . words / . . . me? / *Keightley*.   66. SD *to Phebe*] *NCS*;
aside *Johnson*; *not in F. to Silvius*] *Singer²*; *conj. Collier*; *not in F.* your] *F*; her
Hanmer.   67. she'll] *F*; you'll *Keightley*.   69. SD *To Phebe*] *Singer²*.   80.
SD *Exeunt Rosalind, Celia and Corin.*] *Theobald; Exit. F.*

62. *Foul . . . scoffer*] It is bad enough
to be ill-favoured. Why make it
worse by being ill-natured as well?

66. Sisson objects to the direct
address adopted by *NCS* and prefers
Johnson's *aside*, yet the passage is cast
very much in the form of personal
address. Mason (p. 86) says that if
Rosalind speaks aside, Silvius will not
understand what follows, and that
she is throughout addressing Silvius.

78–9. *though all the world . . . as he*]
'Though all mankind could look on

you, none could be so *deceived* as to
think you beautiful but he' (Johnson).

81. *Dead shepherd*] From Marlowe's
Hero and Leander, I, 176. Marlowe
died 1 June 1593. His poem was
printed in 1598. There is evidence
that Shakespeare knew it before that
in manuscript. See J. Bakeless, *The
Tragical History of Christopher Marlowe*
(1942), II, chapter 16. There are
echoes in *MND*. When Phebe calls
Marlowe a shepherd she is speaking
in her pastoral character. *NCS* notes

Sil. Sweet Phebe!

Phebe.   Hah? What say'st thou, Silvius?

Sil. Sweet Phebe pity me.

Phebe. Why I am sorry for thee gentle Silvius.   85

Sil. Wherever sorrow is, relief would be.
 If you do sorrow at my grief in love,
 By giving love, your sorrow and my grief
 Were both extermined.

Phebe. Thou hast my love. Is not that neighbourly?   90

Sil. I would have you.

Phebe.   Why that were covetousness.
 Silvius, the time was that I hated thee;
 And yet it is not that I bear thee love,
 But since that thou canst talk of love so well,
 Thy company, which erst was irksome to me,   95
 I will endure; and I'll employ thee too.
 But do not look for further recompense
 Than thine own gladness that thou art employ'd.

Sil. So holy and so perfect is my love,
 And I in such a poverty of grace,   100
 That I shall think it a most plenteous crop
 To glean the broken ears after the man
 That the main harvest reaps. Loose now and then
 A scatter'd smile, and that I'll live upon.

Phebe. Know'st thou the youth that spoke to me erewhile?

Sil. Not very well, but I have met him oft,   106
 And he hath bought the cottage and the bounds
 That the old carlot once was master of.

83. Phebe!] *Rowe*³; Phebe. *F*; Phebe,— *Capell.* 88. love,] *Rowe*; love *F.*
89. Extermined] *Camb.*; extermin'd *F.* 108. carlot] *Steevens*²; Carlot *F*; Carlot *Steevens*¹.

that Nashe, in *Summer's Last Will*, 1600, played *c.* 1592, l. 1172, introduces a quotation from Sidney in a very similar way, 'Well sung a shepheard (that now sleepes in skies)' (III, p. 271).

saw] wise saying.

83. *Hah*] Not an arresting ha! but the vague and questioning interjection with which someone emerges from a daydream when he hears his own name, possibly 'Eh?', more likely 'Mmh?'. There is no reason therefore to punctuate 'Sweet Phebe—'. Silvius has said all he had to say.

90. *neighbourly*] a biblical reference, picked up by 'covetousness' at l. 91 and 'poverty of grace' at l. 100. Silvius wants more than the love we must all give our neighbour.

108. *carlot*] '*peasant*, from *carl* or *churl*; probably a word of Shakes-

Phebe. Think not I love him, though I ask for him.
    'Tis but a peevish boy—yet he talks well—   110
    But what care I for words? Yet words do well
    When he that speaks them pleases those that hear.
    It is a pretty youth—not very pretty—
    But sure he's proud, and yet his pride becomes him.
    He'll make a proper man. The best thing in him   115
    Is his complexion; and faster than his tongue
    Did make offence, his eye did heal it up.
    He is not very tall, yet for his years he's tall.
    His leg is but so so; and yet 'tis well.
    There was a pretty redness in his lip,   120
    A little riper and more lusty red
    Than that mix'd in his cheek; 'twas just the difference
    Betwixt the constant red and mingled damask.
    There be some women Silvius, had they mark'd him
    In parcels as I did, would have gone near   125
    To fall in love with him: but for my part
    I love him not, nor hate him not; and yet
    I have more cause to hate him than to love him.
    For what had he to do to chide at me?
    He said mine eyes were black, and my hair black,   130
    And now I am remember'd, scorn'd at me.
    I marvel why I answer'd not again.
    But that's all one. Omittance is no quittance.
    I'll write to him a very taunting letter,
    And thou shalt bear it, wilt thou Silvius?   135
Sil. Phebe, with all my heart.
Phebe.   I'll write it straight.

---

118. very] *not in Hanmer.*   128. I have] *F2*; Haue *F*; Have much *conj. Staunton.*

peare's own coinage' (Douce). Cf.
II. iv. 78. F prints in italic as though
it were a proper name; understan-
dably, since it has a pastoral ring. Cf.
Spenser's Thenot and Perigot. *OED*
quotes this as its only instance.
  110. *peevish*] silly.
  123. *mingled damask*] cf. Sonnet 130,
'Roses damask'd, red and white'.

Damask = Damascus silk.
  125. *In parcels*] in particular items.
  128. *I have*] The F reading might
stand. The speech is deliberately
broken, to express Phebe's emotional
disturbance.
  129. *what had he to do*] what business
had he?
  131. *I am remember'd*] I remember.

The matter's in my head, and in my heart.
I will be bitter with him and passing short.
Go with me Silvius.   *Exeunt.*

138. and] *not in Capell.*

ACT IV

SCENE I

Enter ROSALIND, CELIA *and* JAQUES.

Jaques. I prithee, pretty youth, let me be better acquainted with thee.

Ros. They say you are a melancholy fellow.

Jaques. I am so. I do love it better than laughing.

Ros. Those that are in extremity of either are abomin-   5
able fellows, and betray themselves to every modern
censure, worse than drunkards.

Jaques. Why, 'tis good to be sad and say nothing.

Ros. Why then 'tis good to be a post.

Jaques. I have neither the scholar's melancholy, which is   10
emulation; nor the musician's, which is fantastical;
nor the courtier's, which is proud; nor the soldier's,
which is ambitious; nor the lawyer's, which is
politic; nor the lady's, which is nice; nor the lover's,
which is all these; but it is a melancholy of mine   15
own, compounded of many simples, extracted from

ACT IV

Scene 1

ACT IV. Scene 1] *Actus Quartus. Scena Prima F.* [Location] *the Forest. Rowe; not in F. Rosalind*] *Rowe; Rosalind and* / *F.*   1. be better] *F2*; better *F.*   5–6. abominable] *F* (abhominable).

5–6. *abominable*] The F spelling reflects a false etymology from 'unfit for a man' = beastly.

6. *modern*] trite. They make themselves an obvious target for reproach.

8. *sad*] grave. Cf. III. ii. 210–11: 'Sad brow and true maid'.

11. *emulation*] a consequence of professional jealousy.

fantastical] a manifestation of artistic temperament.

14. *politic*] calculated.

14. *nice*] an affected refinement.

16. *simples*] ingredients.

many objects, and indeed the sundry contemplation
of my travels, in which my often rumination wraps
me in a most humorous sadness.

Ros. A traveller! By my faith, you have great reason to   20
be sad. I fear you have sold your own lands to see
other men's. Then to have seen much and to have
nothing is to have rich eyes and poor hands.

Jaques. Yes, I have gained my experience.

Enter ORLANDO.

Ros. And your experience makes you sad. I had rather   25
have a fool to make me merry than experience to
make me sad, and to travel for it too!

Orl. Good day and happiness, dear Rosalind.

Jaques. Nay then God buy you, and you talk in blank
verse!   30

Ros. Farewell Monsieur Traveller. Look you lisp, and
wear strange suits; disable all the benefits of your
own country; be out of love with your nativity, and
almost chide God for making you that countenance
you are; or I will scarce think you have swam in a   35
gondola. [*Exit Jaques.*] Why how now Orlando,
where have you been all this while? You a lover!
And you serve me such another trick, never come
in my sight more.

17–18. contemplation of my] *F*; contemplations of *F3*.   18. in which my] *F2*;
in which by *F*; and which, by *conj. Malone*¹; which by *Malone*²; which, by
Collier.   19. in] *F*; is *Steevens*³.   29. buy *F*; (*see III. i. 253*).   36. SD *Exit
Jaques.*] *Dyce*; *F2* (*after 29*); *not in F.*

19. *humorous*] whimsical.

24. SD. Enter Orlando] See Intro.,
p. xiv.

31. *lisp*] affect a foreign accent.
There is no evidence that Jaques is
guilty of any of these faults, though he
does boast of his travels. It is a stock
diatribe, such as he might himself
have voiced had occasion offered. Cf.
John, I. i. 189ff.: 'Now your traveller
. . . My picked man of countries'.

Rosalind's determination to delay
Jaques and appear deep in talk with
him is directed at Orlando, because
he has arrived late. F does not mark
the place at which Jaques leaves the
stage. Later folios put it after *blank
verse*, in consequence of the adieux
exchanged then, without observing
that Rosalind must have an audience
for her anatomy of the returned
traveller.

32. *disable*] disparage. Cf. v. iv. 75.

Orl. My fair Rosalind, I come within an hour of my   40
   promise.

Ros. Break an hour's promise in love! He that will
   divide a minute into a thousand parts, and break
   but a part of the thousand part of a minute in the
   affairs of love, it may be said of him that Cupid   45
   hath clapped him o' th' shoulder, but I'll warrant
   him heart-whole.

Orl. Pardon me dear Rosalind.

Ros. Nay, and you be so tardy, come no more in my
   sight. I had as lief be wooed of a snail.   50

Orl. Of a snail?

Ros. Ay, of a snail. For though he comes slowly, he
   carries his house on his head; a better jointure I
   think than you make a woman. Besides, he brings
   his destiny with him.   55

Orl. What's that?

Ros. Why horns—which such as you are fain to be
   beholding to your wives for: but he comes armed
   in his fortune, and prevents the slander of his wife.

Orl. Virtue is no horn-maker; and my Rosalind is vir-   60
   tuous.

Ros. And I am your Rosalind.

Celia. It pleases him to call you so: but he hath a Rosalind of a better leer than you.

---

57. horns—] *This ed*; hornes: *F*.   58. beholding] *F*; beholden *Pope*.

44. *thousand part*] *OED* quotes this usage as late as 1680. 'Thousandth' is not found before the sixteenth century.

46. *clapped him o' th' shoulder*] (1) a light tap on the shoulder with which we attract someone's attention, and which can be ignored, or (2) an encouraging slap, a usage common in Shakespeare, or (3) as Schmidt and others interpret, the action of an officer making an arrest. Cf. *Cym.*, v. iii. 77–8: 'yield me to the veriest hind that shall / Once touch my shoulder'; *Err.*, iv. ii. 37: 'shoulder-clapper' = sergeant. The first two are equivalent to 'You might think him a little in

love, but he's not even that, he' not in love at all'. The last, perhaps too seriously for the context, represents a man deeply in thrall to love, Cupid's prisoner.

57. *horns*—] The punctuation of F suggests a decided pause.

58–9. *armed in his fortune*] already provided with the cuckold's horns.

59. *prevents*] anticipates.

64. *leer*] cheek, complexion, or general appearance. Hulme adds two further meanings (1) a brownish colour, used of the coats of cattle, hence 'not so sunburnt'; (2) flank or loin (pp. 121–2).

Ros. Come, woo me, woo me; for now I am in a holiday 65
humour and like enough to consent. What would
you say to me now, and I were your very very
Rosalind?

Orl. I would kiss before I spoke.

Ros. Nay, you were better speak first, and when you 70
were gravelled for lack of matter, you might take
occasion to kiss. Very good orators when they are
out, they will spit, and for lovers lacking—God
warr'nt us!—matter, the cleanliest shift is to kiss.

Orl. How if the kiss be denied? 75

Ros. Then she puts you to entreaty, and there begins new
matter.

Orl. Who could be out, being before his beloved
mistress?

Ros. Marry that should you, if I were your mistress, or 80
I should think my honesty ranker than my wit.

Orl. What, of my suit?

Ros. Not out of your apparel, and yet out of your suit.
Am not I your Rosalind?

74. warr'nt us] *conj. Anon. (ap. Camb.)*; warne *F.*   83-4. Not . . . Rosalind?]
As Pope; Not . . . suite: / . . . Rosalind? / *F.*

71. *gravelled*] at a loss, colloquially
'stuck'. Cf. Lyly, *Sapho and Phao*, 1584,
I. iv. 34-7: 'It is good sporte to see
them want matter: for then they fall
to good manners . . . wearing our
hands out with courtly kissings, when
their wits faile in courtly discourses'
(Brooks). Nashe, *Summer's Last Will*,
played *c.* 1592 III, p. 236: 'Actors . . .
cleare your throats . . . ere you enter,
that you may take no occasion to spit
or to cough, when you are *non plus*'
(Kittredge). Burton, *Anatomy of Melancholy* 1632 p. 511: '. . . and when he
hath pumped his wittes dry, and can
say no more, kissing and colling are
never out of season' (Halliwell[2]).

74. *warr'nt*] F 'warn' is a widespread
dialect pronunciation of 'warrant'
(Onions). *NCS* says Shakespeare's
usual spelling is 'warnt' or 'warnd'.
Lovers should never lack words in one

another's company, so Rosalind prays
God to spare them from such a
disaster.

81. *ranker*] Shakespeare generally
uses *rank* in a bad sense, of coarse
weeds strong tastes, or smells. If
Rosalind's wit is stronger than her
modesty=bashfulness, she will be
clever enough and bold enough to
keep a young man in his place (*ou of
his suit*). For Grant White[2] *ranker*=
sharper set, 'as we say that a scythe or
a plane is rank'. There seems to be a
shadowy jest somewhere in the background about being clever enough
and shameless enough to get a young
man out of his clothes. The transition
to 'Am not I your Rosalind?' begins
a new line in F, although the previous
line consists of the single word *suit*,
suggesting a cut.

Orl. I take some joy to say you are, because I would be   85
　　talking of her.

Ros. Well, in her person, I say I will not have you.

Orl. Then in mine own person, I die.

Ros. No, faith, die by attorney. The poor world is almost
　　six thousand years old, and in all this time there   90
　　was not any man died in his own person, videlicet,
　　in a love-cause. Troilus had his brains dashed out
　　with a Grecian club, yet he did what he could to
　　die before, and he is one of the patterns of love.
　　Leander, he would have lived many a fair year   95
　　though Hero had turned nun, if it had not been for
　　a hot mid summer night; for, good youth, he went
　　but forth to wash him in the Hellespont, and being
　　taken with the cramp, was drowned, and the fool-
　　ish chroniclers of that age found it was Hero of   100
　　Sestos. But these are all lies: men have died from
　　time to time and worms have eaten them, but not
　　for love.

Orl. I would not have my right Rosalind of this mind,
　　for I protest her frown might kill me.   105

Ros. By this hand, it will not kill a fly. But come, now I
　　will be your Rosalind in a more coming-on dis-
　　position; and ask me what you will, I will grant it.

Orl. Then love me Rosalind.

Ros. Yes faith will I, Fridays and Saturdays and all.   110

Orl. And wilt thou have me?

Ros. Ay, and twenty such.

Orl. What sayest thou?

Ros. Are you not good?

Orl. I hope so.   115

Ros. Why then, can one desire too much of a good

100. chroniclers] chronoclers *F*; coroners *Hanmer*. was Hero] *F*; was,—Hero /
Theobald; Hero *Hanmer*.

92–5. *Troilus . . . Leander*] a bur-
lesque account of these two patterns
of love. Lodge has 'As constant as
Troylus as loving as Leander' (p. 12).
Cf. *Ado*, v. ii. 27–9: 'Leander the
good swimmer, Troilus the first

employer of panders, and a whole
bookful of these quondam carpet-
mongers'. Nashe burlesques the story
of Hero and Leander at some length
in *Lenten Stuffe*, 1599.

   thing? Come sister, you shall be the priest and
marry us. Give me your hand Orlando. What do
you say sister?

Orl. Pray thee marry us.　　　　　　　　　　　　　120

Celia. I cannot say the words.

Ros. You must begin, 'Will you Orlando—'

Celia. Go to. Will you Orlando have to wife this
   Rosalind?

Orl. I will.　　　　　　　　　　　　　　　　　125

Ros. Ay, but when?

Orl. Why now, as fast as she can marry us.

Ros. Then you must say 'I take thee Rosalind for wife.'

Orl. I take thee Rosalind for wife.

Ros. I might ask you for your commission; but I do take　130
   thee Orlando for my husband. There's a girl goes
before the priest, and certainly a woman's thought
runs before her actions.

Orl. So do all thoughts, they are winged.

Ros. Now tell me how long you would have her, after　135
   you have possessed her?

Orl. For ever, and a day.

Ros. Say a day, without the ever. No, no, Orlando,
men are April when they woo, December when
they wed. Maids are May when they are maids,　140
but the sky changes when they are wives. I will be
more jealous of thee than a Barbary cock-pigeon

---

122. Orlando—] *As Pope*; Orlando. *F.*　　130. commission; but] *As Pope*;
Commission, / But *F.* but I] *F*; but, I *Capell*; but,—I *Malone.*

130. *ask you for your commission*] Ask
what authority you have to take me.
Orlando is taking the real Rosalind,
and she is willing, but he does not
know it. He has not spoken to her in
her own person of love and marriage.
Rosalind is on the point of asking
'Who told you you could have her?
Did she?' Hence the force of the
following *but*. For a consideration of
the validity of the proceedings which
between a man and a woman were as
binding as any other form of marriage
see Appendix B.

131–2. *a girl goes before the priest*] She
has given the answer before the priest
put the question.

142. *Barbary cock-pigeon*] Ever since
Pliny (*Natural History*, X, xxxiv,
p. 90) it had been a commonplace to
contrast the meekness of the hen-
pigeon with the jealousy of the cock.
The situation may be thought to be
exacerbated by the oriental (not
African) origin of the Barbary Dove.
This domestic descendant of *strepo-
pelia decaocto*, the Ring-Necked Dove,

over his hen, more clamorous than a parrot against
rain, more new-fangled than an ape, more giddy in
my desires than a monkey. I will weep for nothing,   145
like Diana in the fountain, and I will do that when
you are disposed to be merry. I will laugh like a
hyen, and that when thou art inclined to sleep.

Orl. But will my Rosalind do so?

Ros. By my life, she will do as I do.   150

Orl. O but she is wise.

Ros. Or else she could not have the wit to do this. The
wiser, the waywarder. Make the doors upon a
woman's wit, and it will out at the casement; shut
that, and 'twill out at the keyhole; stop that, 'twill   155
fly with the smoke out at the chimney.

Orl. A man that had a wife with such a wit, he might
say, 'Wit, whither wilt?'

Ros. Nay, you might keep that check for it, till you met
your wife's wit going to your neighbour's bed.   160

Orl. And what wit could wit have to excuse that?

Ros. Marry to say she came to seek you there. You
shall never take her without her answer, unless you
take her without her tongue. O that woman that
cannot make her fault her husband's occasion, let   165
her never nurse her child herself, for she will breed
it like a fool.

Orl. For these two hours Rosalind, I will leave thee.

Ros. Alas, dear love, I cannot lack thee two hours.

Orl. I must attend the Duke at dinner. By two o'clock   170
I will be with thee again.

Ros. Ay, go your ways, go your ways. I knew what you
would prove. My friends told me as much, and I

was introduced into Europe from
Asia by the Turks.

143-4. *against rain*] when rain
threatens.

144. *new-fangled*] fond of novelty.

146. *Diana in the fountain*] the tearful
heroine of Montemayor's *Diana*. See
Intro., p. lviii. Attempts to identify a
weeping fountain-figure to explain
the allusion have not met with success.

148. *hyen*] hyena.

153. *Make*] make fast=shut.

158. *Wit, whither wilt*] A catchword
of the day, used to check a chatterer
or to curb one's own tongue. Cf. I. ii.
53-4, 'How now Wit, whither wander
you?'

165. *her husband's occasion*] 'A handle
against her husband' (*NCS*).

thought no less. That flattering tongue of yours
won me. 'Tis but one cast away, and so, come   175
death! Two o'clock is your hour?

Orl. Ay, sweet Rosalind.

Ros. By my troth, and in good earnest, and so God mend
me, and by all pretty oaths that are not dangerous,
if you break one jot of your promise, or come one   180
minute behind your hour, I will think you the most
pathetical break-promise, and the most hollow
lover, and the most unworthy of her you call
Rosalind, that may be chosen out of the gross band
of the unfaithful: therefore beware my censure and   185
keep your promise.

Orl. With no less religion than if thou wert indeed my
Rosalind. So adieu.

Ros. Well, Time is the old justice that examines all such
offenders, and let Time try. Adieu.   190

Exit [Orlando.]

Celia. You have simply misused our sex in your love-
prate. We must have your doublet and hose
plucked over your head, and show the world what
the bird hath done to her own nest.

Ros. O coz, coz, coz, my pretty little coz, that thou didst   195
know how many fathom deep I am in love! But it
cannot be sounded. My affection hath an unknown bottom, like the Bay of Portugal.

---

190. SD *Exit Orlando.*] *Rowe; Exit.* F.

179. *not dangerous*] The Elizabethans
took swearing seriously and there was
a strong religious objection to it. In
1605 an act was passed against
blasphemy on the stage. Ladies
tended to mince their oaths. Cf. *1H4*,
III. i. 247ff.

182. *pathetical*] shocking (*Schmidt*),
pitiable, miserable (Onions). Used
intensitively, the word can refer to
any kind of strong feeling.

189. *old justice*] Cf. *Troil.*, IV. v.
225–6: 'That old common arbitrator,
Time, / Will one day end it.'

193–4. *what the bird . . . nest*] Cf.

Rosalynde: '"And I pray you", quoth
Aliena, "if your robes were off, what
mettle are you made that you are so
satirical against women? Is it not a
foul bird defiles his own nest?"' (p.
37).

196. *fathom*] See note at III. ii. 311.

198. *the Bay of Portugal*] A letter
from Ralegh supplies the only other
known instance of this placename,
which Wright (1877) said was still
used by sailors for the sea off the coast
of Portugal from Oporto to the
headland of Cintra. (E. Edwards,
Life of Ralegh, II, p. 56.) The water
there is in fact very deep.

Celia. Or rather bottomless, that as fast as you pour
affection in, it runs out.   200
Ros. No. That same wicked bastard of Venus, that was
begot of thought, conceived of spleen and born of
madness, that blind rascally boy that abuses everyone's eyes because his own are out, let him be judge
how deep I am in love. I'll tell thee Aliena, I can-   205
not be out of the sight of Orlando. I'll go find a
shadow and sigh till he come.
Celia. And I'll sleep.   *Exeunt.*

SCENE II

Enter JAQUES *and lords,* [*like*] *foresters.*

Jaques. Which is he that killed the deer?
First Lord. Sir, it was I.

200. in, it] *F3*; in, in *F.*

Scene II] *Scena Secunda. F.* [Location] *Another part of the forest. Malone. and lords,*
like foresters.] Collier; *and Lords, Forresters. F. Lords, and Foresters. Rowe; and Others,*
Foresters. Capell; and Lords, in the habit of Foresters. Steevens³.   2. *First Lord*] *1 Lord.*
Malone. Lord. F; 1. F. | Capell; A Lord. Camb.

201. *bastard of Venus*] Cupid was the
son of Venus by Mercury, not by her
husband Vulcan.
202. *spleen*] 'A sudden impulse of
passion, whether of love or hatred'
(Wright).
207. *a shadow*] a shady place.
Pastoral, being of Mediterranean
origin, puts a high value on shade.

Scene II

This scene, as Johnson observes, is
to fill the two hours before Rosalind
can declare Orlando a promise-
breaker. Hunting scenes were popular
with Elizabethan audiences. See
Tit., II. ii; *Shr.* I. i; *LLL,* IV. i; *MND,*
IV. i; *Wiv.,* v. v. There are hunting
scenes in Munday's *Robert Earl of
Huntington,* in Greene's *James IV,* and
in several of Lyly's plays. Foresters
and huntsmen had long been employed in the kind of alfresco enter-
tainments which were devised for
Queen Elizabeth's progresses. It was
in this way that the English pastoral
became allied with singing huntsmen,
sounding horns, and trophies of the
chase, all quite improper to the
Golden Age. (See A. H. Thorndike,
'The pastoral element in the English
drama before 1605' *Modern Language
Notes,* XIV (1899), pp. 228–46.)
SD. Enter . . . lords, like foresters]
There is doubt whether the F direction requires lords dressed as foresters,
or lords with foresters in attendance,
though it would be hard to say just
who the latter might be. The distinction, on the modern stage at any
rate, is a fine one. Without the support
of the Second Lord, the First Lord,
who admits to killing the deer, would
have to sing himself home. The

Jaques. Let's present him to the Duke like a Roman con-
    queror; and it would do well to set the deer's horns
    upon his head for a branch of victory. Have you no   5
    song, forester, for this purpose?
Second Lord. Yes sir.
Jaques. Sing it. 'Tis no matter how it be in tune, so it
    make noise enough.
[*Given a note, they sing*].

>   *What shall he have that kill'd the deer?*   10
>   *His leather skin and horns to wear.*
>   *Then sing him home. The rest shall bear*
>   *This burden.*

7. *Second Lord*] 2. *Lord. Malone; Lord. F; For. Rowe; 2. F.* | *Capell; Amiens NCS.*
9. SD *Given . . . they sing*]. Musicke, Song. *F.*   12–13. *Then . . . bear* | *This
burden.* |] *Then . . . bear—* | *This burthen.* | *Halliwell²; one line F; Then . . . home;
—take Thou no Scorn* | SD *The rest . . . Burthen. Theobald; Then . . . home;—Take
thou no Scorn Capell;* SD *Then . . . burden. Singer; not in Knight;* SD *They . . .
burden. Grant White;* SD *Then . . . home. Jaq.* The . . . burden. *conj. Malone²,
conj. E. Brennecke (Musical Times, 1952); Jaq.* Then . . . burden. *conj. P. Seng
(Shakespeare Quarterly, 1959).*

Second Lord is addressed as *forester*
because that is the role he is playing.
The exiled lords are, as is to be expected, dressed in a way suited to their
woodland life. Twice before, their
entrance has been accompanied with
direction as to their costume, at II. i
'. . . two or three lords like foresters'
and at II. vii '. . . lords, like outlaws'.
As a theatrical term *like* = dressed as.

3–4. *present him . . . conqueror*] Cf. Sir
T. Elyot, *The Governour,* 1531: 'to
them which in this hunting [of the red
deer], do showe moste prowesse and
actyuytie, a garlande or some other
lyke token to be gyuen, in signe of
victorie, and with a ioyfull maner to
be brought in the presence of him
that is chiefe in the company; there
to receiue condigne prayse for their
good endeuour' (Everyman ed.,
pp. 82–3).

9. SD. E. Brennecke, in *The
Musical Times,* XCIII, 1952, p. 247,
says that F's *Musicke* 'is simply a
prompter's signal to a lutenist, on or
off stage, to sound a chord in order to

give the proper pitch for the "Song"
that follows'. Jaques's demand for
noise enough implies choral singing,
though this may have been confined
to the *burden.* All depends on how the
word *burden* is interpreted. See note on
ll. 12–13 below. Capell divides the
song between two solo voices, with
chorus at ll. 14, 15 and ll. 18, 19.
Staunton thought *Then sing him home*
was the burden and should perhaps
be repeated after each couplet. See
Intro., p. xxv for the earliest known
setting.

What shall he have] Cf. *Rosalynde*:
'What news, forester? hast thou
wounded some deer, and lost him
in the fall? Care not man for so
small a loss; thy fees was but the skin,
the shoulder, and the horns' (p. 67).

12–13. Then . . . burden] Many
editors, beginning with Theobald,
have considered this line, or the latter
part of it, to be a stage direction which
has accidentally been incorporated in
the song. It has also been thought to
be interjected dialogue. The fact that

Take thou no scorn to wear the horn,
It was a crest ere thou wast born.   15
Thy father's father wore it,
And thy father bore it.
The horn, the horn, the lusty horn,
Is not a thing to laugh to scorn.   *Exeunt.*

SCENE III

Enter ROSALIND *and* CELIA.

Ros. How say you now, is it not past two o'clock? And here much Orlando!
Celia. I warrant you, with pure love and troubled brain, he hath ta'en his bow and arrows, and is gone forth to sleep. Look who comes here.   5

14. *Take . . . horn*] F; *To wear the horn, the horn,* Theobald; *to wear the horn, the lusty horn.* Capell.   18. SD *All.* Malone; SD *Burthen.* Grant White[2].   19. SD *Exeunt*] F; *They bear off the deer, singing.* Grant White[1].

bear and *wear* and probably *deer* are rhyme-words argues strongly for F. Those who print *The rest . . . burden* in the margin have been put to considerable shifts to rearrange the text which remains to them, and have in fact rewritten l. 14. *NCS* quotes a parallel from *The Tempest*, I. ii. 379–80: 'Foot it featly here and there, / And, sweet sprites, the burden bear', which nobody has taken as a stage direction to sprites to sing. The chorus appears to begin at *Take thou no scorn,* and we must suppose the song familiar to the singers, but F's direction *Musicke* may

imply that it was sung in unison throughout. Amiens, and the singing-boys at v. iii, are experts and do not need a note. *Burden*=(1) a refrain; (2) the horns that the cuckold must carry. It was for some time a stage practice, alluded to by Dyce, to carry on the body of a slaughtered deer in this scene, yet another *burden.* The text seems to call rather for antlers, in the style of the Abbots Bromley horn-dance, and they would be easier to keep in store and to handle (see C. J. Sharpe, *The Sword Dances of England,* 1951).

Scene III

Scene III.] *Scæna Tertia,* F. [Location] *The Forest.* Steevens[3]; not in F.   1–2. And . . . Orlando!] F; I wonder much *Orlando* is not here. *Pope*; and how much *Orlando* comes? *Capell*; and here's much Orlando! Steevens[1]; and here's no Orlando. conj. Ritson.   1–5. How . . . here.] *As* Steevens (*prose*); How . . . aclock? / . . . Orlando. / . . . brain, / . . . forth / . . . heere. / F; 1–2 (*verse*) 3–5. (*prose*) Pope.   4. forth] F; forth-Capell.   5. SD *Enter Silvius*] Pope; F (*after* brain *at* 3); Sisson (*after* sleep *at* 5).

4–5. *ta'en his bow . . . to sleep*] A catchphrase. Cf. Nashe, *Lenten Stuffe,* 1599: 'I would not be snibd . . . that

therefore I prayse Yarmouth so rantantingly because I neuer elsewhere bayted my horse, or tooke my

Enter SILVIUS.

Sil. My errand is to you, fair youth.
My gentle Phebe did bid me give you this.
I know not the contents, but as I guess
By the stern brow and waspish action
Which she did use as she was writing of it,   10
It bears an angry tenour. Pardon me.
I am but as a guiltless messenger.

Ros. Patience herself would startle at this letter,
And play the swaggerer. Bear this, bear all.
She says I am not fair, that I lack manners.   15
She calls me proud, and that she could not love me,
Were man as rare as phoenix. 'Od's my will,
Her love is not the hare that I do hunt;
Why writes she so to me? Well shepherd, well,
This is a letter of your own device.   20

Sil. No, I protest, I know not the contents,
Phebe did write it.

Ros.   Come, come, you are a fool,
And turn'd into the extremity of love.
I saw her hand. She has a leathern hand,
A freestone-colour'd hand. I verily did think   25
That her old gloves were on, but 'twas her hands.
She has a hussif's hand. But that's no matter.
I say she never did invent this letter.
This is a man's invention, and his hand.

Sil. Sure it is hers.   30

Ros. Why, 'tis a boisterous and a cruel style,
A style for challengers. Why, she defies me,
Like Turk to Christian. Women's gentle brain

---

7. did] F; *not in* F2.   27. hussif's] huswife's *Singer*[1]; huswiues F.

bowe and arrowes and went to bed'
(III, p. 167). McKerrow quotes
Greene's *Menaphon*, 1589, 'amongst
these swaines there was such melodie,
that Menaphon tooke his bow and
arrowes and went to bedde.'

17. *phoenix*] of which there is only
one living at a time. Cf. Lyly,
Euphues and his England, 1580, II, p.

86: 'For as there is but one *Phoenix* in
the world, so is there but one tree in
Arabia, where-in she buyldeth.'

'*Od's my will*] As God is my will.
23. *turn'd into*] brought into
(Wright).
25. *freestone*] a greyish yellow sand-
stone. Rosalind, as usual, is slandering
Phebe's beauty.

Could not drop forth such giant-rude invention,
Such Ethiop words, blacker in their effect   35
Than in their countenance. Will you hear the letter?

Sil. So please you, for I never heard it yet;
Yet heard too much of Phebe's cruelty.

Ros. She Phebes me. Mark how the tyrant writes.

[*Reads.*] *Art thou god to shepherd turn'd,*   40
           That a maiden's heart hath burn'd?

Can a woman rail thus?

Sil. Call you this railing?

Ros. [*Reads.*] *Why, thy godhead laid apart,*
                  Warr'st thou with a woman's heart?   45

Did you ever hear such railing?

           Whiles the eye of man did woo me,
           That could do no vengeance to me.

Meaning me a beast.

           If the scorn of your bright eyne   50
           Have power to raise such love in mine,
           Alack, in me, what strange effect
           Would they work in mild aspect?
           Whiles you chid me, I did love;
           How then might your prayers move?   55
           He that brings this love to thee
           Little knows this love in me;
           And by him seal up thy mind,
           Whether that thy youth and kind
           Will the faithful offer take   60

---

34. giant-rude] *Capell*; giant rude *F*.   40. SD *Reads*] *Rowe*; Read. *F*.   44.
SD *Reads*] *Rowe*; Read *F*.

48. vengeance] mischief.

49. *me a beast*] Men had had no
success, and Rosalind deliberately
ignores Phebe's flattering 'Art thou
god?' Elizabethans were very sure
they were more than beasts.

50. eyne] an old plural of eye.

53. aspect] with an accent on the
last syllable. It is an astrological term,
used of the way one planet is situated
towards another (*OED* v. Obs. 3) and
agrees with the image of eyes as stars.

58. seal up thy mind] (1) make up
your mind; (2) write me your decision
in a sealed letter. Silvius, who carries
the letter, has not been permitted to
read it (ll. 8 and 21) and Phebe is
loud in her resentment when Rosalind
shows it to him (v. ii. 76–7). It is
Phebe's nature to be sly and to
manipulate others. Lodge deals less
harshly with Silvius and Phebe in the
matter of the letter, Intro., p. xli.

59. kind] nature.

> *Of me and all that I can make,*
> *Or else by him my love deny,*
> *And then I'll study how to die.*

Sil. Call you this chiding?

Celia. Alas poor shepherd!   65

Ros. Do you pity him? No, he deserves no pity. Wilt
thou love such a woman? What, to make thee an
instrument and play false strains upon thee? Not to
be endured! Well, go your way to her, for I see love
hath made thee a tame snake, and say this to her: 70
that if she love me, I charge her to love thee. If
she will not, I will never have her, unless thou entreat for her. If you be a true lover, hence, and not a
word; for here comes more company.   *Exit Silvius.*

Enter OLIVER.

Oli. Good morrow, fair ones. Pray you, if you know,   75
Where in the purlieus of this forest stands
A sheep-cote fenc'd about with olive-trees?

Celia. West of this place, down in the neighbour bottom.
The rank of osiers by the murmuring stream
Left on your right hand, brings you to the place.   80
But at this hour the house doth keep itself,
There's none within.

Oli. If that an eye may profit by a tongue,
Then should I know you by description,
Such garments and such years. 'The boy is fair,   85
Of female favour, and bestows himself

86. and] *F*; but *conj. Lettsom.*

67-8. *make thee . . . upon thee*] cf.
Ham., III. ii. 354ff.

70. *a tame snake*] a wretched or
miserable fellow (Cotgrave). Colloquially 'a creep'.

75. *fair ones*] the epithet is appropriate to either sex. Cf. l. 15 above,
where Rosalind, as Ganymede, affects
indignation at Phebe's letter. 'She
says I am not fair.'

78. *bottom*] a low-lying place, a
hollow. J. Wright's *Dialect Dictionary*

gives many instances of local usage. It
survives in placenames, and personal
names derived from placenames, e.g.
Broadbottom in Yorkshire, Rams-
bottom in Lancashire.

80. *Left*] passed. 'If you leave the
rank of osiers on your right hand.'

86. *favour*] appearance. Cf. ill-
favouredly at I. ii. 38.

bestows himself] comports himself
(Schmidt). Rosalind's appearance
has been adequately described above.

Like a ripe sister. The woman low,
And browner than her brother.' Are not you
The owner of the house I did enquire for?

Celia. It is no boast, being ask'd, to say we are.   90

Oli. Orlando doth commend him to you both,
And to that youth he calls his Rosalind
He sends this bloody napkin. Are you he?

Ros. I am. What must we understand by this?

Oli. Some of my shame, if you will know of me   95
What man I am, and how, and why, and where
This handkerchief was stain'd.

Celia.   I pray you tell it.

Oli. When last the young Orlando parted from you,
He left a promise to return again
Within an hour; and pacing through the forest,   100
Chewing the food of sweet and bitter fancy,
Lo what befell! He threw his eye aside,
And mark what object did present itself.
Under an old oak, whose boughs were moss'd with age
And high top bald with dry antiquity,   105
A wretched ragged man, o'ergrown with hair,
Lay sleeping on his back. About his neck
A green and gilded snake had wreath'd itself,
Who with her head, nimble in threats, approach'd
The opening of his mouth. But suddenly   110
Seeing Orlando, it unlink'd itself,

87. ripe sister] *F*; right forester *Hudson, conj. Lettsom*; ripe forester *NCS, conj. Gould*. The] *F*; But the *F2*.   97. handkerchief] *F* (handkercher), *Rowe*. 103. itself.] it self. *Theobald*; it selfe *F*.   104. old] *F*; *not in Pope*.   105. bald with] *F*; bald, of *Hanmer*. antiquity,] *Rann*; antiquity: *F*.

87. *a ripe sister*] Many critics cannot accept this description, which Furness declares 'almost unintelligible'. Lettsom suggests that *sister* is a misreading of 'foster' = forester, and emends *ripe* to 'right'. *NCS* favours 'forester' and keeps *ripe* = 'obviously expert and well-equipped'. A *ripe sister* = a girl who has just reached womanhood. In Jonson's *To Penshurst*, 'ripe daughters' = girls of marriageable age (VIII, p. 95, l. 54). If Oliver has

been told that Celia's brother looks for all the world like her elder sister, it is no more than the truth.

88. *browner*] the reference must be to her hair. Rosalind's skin was smirched with umber.

93. *napkin*] handkerchief.

101. *fancy*] love-thoughts.

104. *Under an old oak*] The line is metrical if the vowel in the second syllable of *under* or in *an* is elided.

And with indented glides did slip away
Into a bush, under which bush's shade
A lioness, with udders all drawn dry,
Lay couching head on ground, with catlike watch   115
When that the sleeping man should stir; for 'tis
The royal disposition of that beast
To prey on nothing that doth seem as dead.
This seen, Orlando did approach the man,
And found it was his brother, his elder brother.   120

Celia. O I have heard him speak of that same brother,
And he did render him the most unnatural
That liv'd amongst men.

Oli.   And well he might so do,
For well I know he was unnatural.

Ros. But to Orlando. Did he leave him there,   125
Food to the suck'd and hungry lioness?

Oli. Twice did he turn his back, and purpos'd so.
But kindness, nobler ever than revenge,
And nature, stronger than his just occasion,
Made him give battle to the lioness,   130
Who quickly fell before him; in which hurtling
From miserable slumber I awak'd.

Celia. Are you his brother?

Ros.   Was't you he rescu'd?

Celia. Was't you that did so oft contrive to kill him?

Oli. 'Twas I. But 'tis not I. I do not shame   135
To tell you what I was, since my conversion
So sweetly tastes, being the thing I am.

Ros. But for the bloody napkin.

Oli.   By and by.
When from the first to last betwixt us two

---

123. amongst] *F*; 'mongst *Rowe*[3].   133. Was't] *F*; Was it *Theobald*[2]. rescu'd]
F; rescued *Knight*.   134. Was't] *F*; Was it *Theobald*[2].

118. *To . . . dead*] Cf. *Rosalynde*:
'seeing he lay still without any
motion, he left to touch him, for that
lions hate to prey on dead carcases'
(p. 94), and Holland's *Pliny*, VIII,
p. 201: 'The Lion alone of all wild
beasts is gentle to those that humble
themselues vnto him, and will not
touch any such vpon their submission
but spareth what creature soeuer lieth
prostrate before him.'

Tears our recountments had most kindly bath'd—   140
As how I came into that desert place—
In brief, he led me to the gentle Duke,
Who gave me fresh array and entertainment,
Committing me unto my brother's love,
Who led me instantly unto his cave,   145
There stripp'd himself, and here upon his arm
The lioness had torn some flesh away,
Which all this while had bled; and now he fainted,
And cried in fainting upon Rosalind.
Brief, I recover'd him, bound up his wound,   150
And after some small space, being strong at heart,
He sent me hither, stranger as I am,
To tell this story, that you might excuse
His broken promise, and to give this napkin,
Dy'd in his blood, unto the shepherd youth   155
That he in sport doth call his Rosalind.

                                    [*Rosalind faints.*]

Celia. Why how now Ganymede! Sweet Ganymede!
Oli. Many will swoon when they do look on blood.
Celia. There is more in it. Cousin Ganymede!
Oli. Look, he recovers.   160
Ros. I would I were at home.
Celia. We'll lead you thither. I pray you, will you take
    him by the arm?

---

140. bath'd—] *Alexander*; bath'd, F.   141. As how] F; As, how *Steevens*³.
place—] *Alexander*; place. F.   142. In] *F2*; I F.   155. his] *F2*; this F.
156. SD *Rosalind faints.*] *Pope; not in F.*   159. more in it.] F; no more in it *F3*;
no more in't *Pope.* Cousin Ganymede!] *Rowe*; Cosen *Ganimed.* F; —cousin—
Ganymed! Johnson; —Cousin!—Ganymede! *Collier.*   160-3. Look . . . arm?]
This ed (prose); Look . . . recouers. / . . . home. / . . . thither: / . . . arme. / F;
Look . . . home. / . . . thither. / . . . arm. / *Steevens*³; Look . . . recovers. / . . .
thither. / . . . arm. / *Malone*².

---

140. *recountments*] recitals. *OED*
quotes *AYL* as its only instance.

141. *As*] Such as, qualifying *recountments.* Capell and Malone think
a line or more has been lost here.

150. *recover'd*] restored.

159. *Cousin Ganymede*] One would
expect 'brother'. Johnson, accustomed to dramatic 'discoveries' made

in this way, supposes that Celia says
cousin inadvertently, and then corrects
herself. Nothing, however, is made of
it. *Cousin*, which could be very loosely
used, as a term of affection, appears
from the text to go unremarked. See
I. ii. I note.

160-8. From the entry of Oliver the
scene has been in verse. After

Oli. Be of good cheer, youth. You a man! You lack a
     man's heart.   165

Ros. I do so, I confess it. Ah, sirrah, a body would think
     this was well counterfeited. I pray you tell your
     brother how well I counterfeited. Heigh-ho!

Oli. This was not counterfeit, there is too great testi-
     mony in your complexion that it was a passion of   170
     earnest.

Ros. Counterfeit, I assure you.

Oli. Well then, take a good heart, and counterfeit to be
     a man.

Ros. So I do. But i' faith, I should have been a woman   175
     by right.

Celia. Come, you look paler and paler. Pray you draw
     homewards. Good sir, go with us.

Oli. That will I. For I must bear answer back how you
     excuse my brother, Rosalind.   180

Ros. I shall devise something. But I pray you commend
     my counterfeiting to him. Will you go?   *Exeunt.*

161. I would] *F*; Would *Pope*.   164–6. Be . . . it.] *As Pope (prose)*; Be . . .
man? / . . . heart. / . . . it: / *F*.   179–80. That . . . Rosalind.] *This ed
(prose)*; That . . . backe / . . . *Rosalind.* / *F*.

Rosalind's swoon, at l. 160, it changes
into what can very well be set consistently as prose, despite the occasional verse setting in F, occurring
at ll. 160–3, which is possible, at ll.
164–6, which is not, and at ll. 179–80,
which is again possible, but can stand
as normal prose and is in a prose
context. *NCS* claims to 'follow the F.

lining here exactly, which shows an
interesting mixture of prose and
verse'. An edition which indents the
latter half of a supposed blank-verse
line, when it is given to a new
speaker, cannot follow F exactly. All
half lines in F begin at the margin, a
practice from which Steevens was the
first to deviate, in 1793.

ACT V

SCENE I

Enter TOUCHSTONE *and* AUDREY.

Touch. We shall find a time, Audrey. Patience gentle
    Audrey.

Aud. Faith the priest was good enough, for all the old
    gentleman's saying.

Touch. A most wicked Sir Oliver, Audrey, a most vile   5
    Martext. But Audrey, there is a youth here in the
    forest lays claim to you.

Aud. Ay, I know who 'tis. He hath no interest in me in
    the world. Here comes the man you mean.

Enter WILLIAM.

Touch. It is meat and drink to me to see a clown. By my   10
    troth, we that have good wits have much to answer
    for: we shall be flouting: we cannot hold.

Wil. Good ev'n Audrey.

Aud. God ye good ev'n William.

Wil. And good ev'n to you sir.   15

Touch. Good ev'n gentle friend. Cover thy head, cover
    thy head. Nay prithee be covered. How old are
    you friend?

Wil. Five and twenty sir.

ACT V

Scene I

Act V. Scene I] *Actus Quintus. Scena Prima. F.* [Location] *the Forest. Rowe; not in
F.*   9. SD *Enter William.*] *F; Dyce, Grant White (after 12); Sisson (after* world
at *9).*

3–4. *old gentleman*] provoked by the   Audrey.
manner and appearance of Jaques,   12. *flouting*] exchanging scoffs. 'We
and the youth and inexperience of   must have our joke' (Wright).

112

Touch. A ripe age. Is thy name William?   20
Wil. William, sir.
Touch. A fair name. Was't born i' th' forest here?
Wil. Ay sir, I thank God.
Touch. 'Thank God.' A good answer. Art rich?
Wil. Faith sir, so so.   25
Touch. 'So so' is good, very good, very excellent good.
  And yet it is not, it is but so so. Art thou wise?
Wil. Ay sir, I have a pretty wit.
Touch. Why, thou sayest well. I do now remember a say-
  ing: 'The fool doth think he is wise, but the wise-   30
  man knows himself to be a fool'. The heathen
  philosopher, when he had a desire to eat a grape,
  would open his lips when he put it into his mouth,
  meaning thereby that grapes were made to eat and
  lips to open. You do love this maid?   35
Wil. I do sir.
Touch. Give me your hand. Art thou learned?
Wil. No sir.
Touch. Then learn this of me. To have is to have: for it is
  a figure in rhetoric that drink, being poured out   40
  of a cup into a glass, by filling the one doth empty
  the other. For all your writers do consent that *ipse*
  is he. Now you are not *ipse*, for I am he.
Wil. Which he sir?
Touch. He sir that must marry this woman. Therefore   45
  you clown, abandon—which is in the vulgar leave

24. *As Pope (prose);* Thanke . . . answer: / Art rich? / *F.*   27. *As Pope (prose)*;
and . . . so, so: / Art thou wise? / *F.*   30–1. wiseman] *F*; Wise Man *Rowe.*
36. sir] *F2*; sit *F.*

30–1. *The fool . . . fool*] See Tilley
(M425).

32. *eat a grape*] Cf. *Rosalynde*:
'Phoebe is no lettuce for your lips and
her grapes hangs so high, that gaze at
them you may, but touch them you
cannot' (p. 121). Here Audrey seems
to be the grape, with some accom-
panying business, perhaps at the
expense of William's open-mouthed
astonishment. Cf. Tilley (W617)
quoting from Giovanni Torriano: 'A

woman at a window is like grapes on
the highway', i.e. everyone will reach
for her.

42–3. ipse *is he*] Cf. Lyly's *Euphues*,
where '*Ipse*, hee' is used of a successful
suitor (Bond, II, p. 247 and his Intro.
p. 126).

45–56. *Therefore . . . ways*] 'Touchstone puts his protasis into the form of
a construe, which he puts together as
a translation, and then varies his
conclusion therefrom "copiously", as

—the society—which in the boorish is company—
of this female—which in the common is woman.
Which together is, abandon the society of this female, or clown thou perishest; or to thy better   50
understanding, diest; or, to wit, I kill thee, make
thee away, translate thy life into death, thy liberty
into bondage. I will deal in poison with thee, or in
bastinado, or in steel. I will bandy with thee in
faction; I will o'er-run thee with policy; I will kill   55
thee a hundred and fifty ways. Therefore tremble
and depart.

Aud. Do, good William.

Wil. God rest you merry, sir.   *Exit.*

Enter CORIN.

Cor. Our master and mistress seeks you. Come away,   60
away.

Touch. Trip Audrey, trip Audrey. I attend, I attend.   *Exeunt.*

SCENE II

Enter ORLANDO *and* OLIVER.

Orl. Is't possible, that on so little acquaintance you
should like her? That but seeing, you should love

55. policy] F (police), F2.   60. *seeks*] F; seek Rowe.   62. *As* Pope (*prose*);
Trip . . . attend, / I attend. / F.

Scene II

Scene II] *Scœna Secunda.* F. [Location] *The same.* Capell; *not in* F.

any grammarian was supposed to be
able to do—a very learned performance indeed!' T. W. Baldwin,
Shakespere's Small Latine, I, p. 715.
Baldwin's own learned analysis of
Touchstone's performance continues
to p. 718.

48. *this female—which in the common
is woman*] Cf. Sidney, *The Lady of May,*
ll. 30–1: 'a certain she-creature,
which we shepherds call a woman'
(*Miscellaneous Prose,* ed. K. Duncan-
Jones, 1973).

54. *bastinado*] a cudgelling. Cf.

Jonson, *Every Man in his Humour,* I. v.
100ff.: '*Mat.* He brags he will gi' me
the *bastinado,* as I heare. *Bob.* How! He
the bastinado! how came he by that
word, trow? *Mat.* Nay, indeed, he
said cudgell me; I termed it so, for my
more grace. *Bob.* That may bee: For I
was sure, it was none of his word.'
Touchstone is characteristically
speaking for his 'more grace'. *bandy*]
contend.

55. *policy*] stratagems.

59. *rest you*] keep you.

60. *seeks*] Abbott 336.

her? And loving woo? And wooing, she should
grant? And will you persever to enjoy her?

Oli. Neither call the giddiness of it in question, the   5
poverty of her, the small acquaintance, my sudden
wooing, nor her sudden consenting. But say with
me, I love Aliena; say with her that she loves me;
consent with both, that we may enjoy each other. It
shall be to your good; for my father's house and all   10
the revenue that was old Sir Rowland's will I estate
upon you, and here live and die a shepherd.

Orl. You have my consent. Let your wedding be tomorrow. Thither will I invite the Duke and all's
contented followers. Go you and prepare Aliena;   15
for look you, here comes my Rosalind.

Enter ROSALIND.

Ros. God save you brother.

Oli. And you fair sister.   [*Exit.*]

Ros. O my dear Orlando, how it grieves me to see thee
wear thy heart in a scarf!   20

Orl. It is my arm.

Ros. I thought thy heart had been wounded with the
claws of a lion.

Orl. Wounded it is, but with the eyes of a lady.

Ros. Did your brother tell you how I counterfeited to   25
swoon, when he showed me your handkerchief?

Orl. Ay, and greater wonders than that.

Ros. O, I know where you are. Nay, 'tis true. There was
never anything so sudden, but the fight of two rams,

---

7. her] *Rowe; not in* F.   13–16. You . . . Rosalind.] *As Pope (prose)*; You . . .
consent. / . . . I / . . . followers: / . . . looke you, / . . . Rosalinde. / F.   14.
all's] F; all his *Pope.*   16. Enter Rosalind.] *Dyce, Grant White;* F *(after 12)*;
Collier (after followers *at 15*); *Rosalind is seen coming in the distance. NCS (after 12).*
18. Oli.] Ol. F; Orl. F3. SD Exit] *Capell; Halliwell*[2] *(after 16)*; *not in* F.   26.
swoon] F *(sound), Rowe*[3]; swound *F4.*   handkerchief] F *(handkercher), F4.*

Location] Dyce suggests 'Before a
cottage' here and at v. iv.

4. *persever*] accented on the second
syllable.

18. *fair sister*] Oliver is joining in
Orlando's make-believe, which he
knows about already. See IV. iii. 156
and 180.

and Caesar's thrasonical brag of I came, saw, and   30
overcame. For your brother and my sister no
sooner met, but they looked; no sooner looked, but
they loved; no sooner loved, but they sighed; no
sooner sighed, but they asked one another the
reason; no sooner knew the reason, but they sought   35
the remedy. And in these degrees have they made a
pair of stairs to marriage, which they will climb incontinent, or else be incontinent before marriage.
They are in the very wrath of love, and they will together. Clubs cannot part them.   40

Orl. They shall be married tomorrow, and I will bid the
Duke to the nuptial. But O, how bitter a thing it
is to look into happiness through another man's
eyes! By so much the more shall I tomorrow be
at the height of heart-heaviness, by how much I   45
shall think my brother happy in having what he
wishes for.

Ros. Why then tomorrow I cannot serve your turn for
Rosalind?

Orl. I can live no longer by thinking.   50

Ros. I will weary you then no longer with idle talking.
Know of me then—for now I speak to some purpose—that I know you are a gentleman of good
conceit. I speak not this that you should bear a good

31. overcame] *F2*; overcome *F*.

30. *thrasonical*] an epithet not
uncommon in Elizabethan English,
from Thraso, the boaster, in Terence's
Eunuch. Other references to Caesar's
boast are *LLL*, IV. i. 65ff.; *2H4* IV. iii.
40–1; *Cym.* III. i. 23–4.

36–7. *a pair of stairs*] a flight of
stairs, reflecting on *degrees*=steps.
Kökeritz sees a pun on 'stares', going
back to 'looked' (p. 147).

37–8. *incontinent*] immediately, with
a double meaning.

40. *Clubs*] The cry that is said to
have roused the London apprentices
when there was occasion for them to
keep order in the streets was 'Clubs!

Clubs!' (Malone and Dyce). Cf. *Tit.*,
II. i. 37 and *H8*, v. iv. 47ff. *NCS*
declares the style of this speech to be
flat, repetitive, and so unlike the rest
of the play that it is doubtfully
authentic. The peculiar tone may be
accounted for by noting that Rosalind
at this point is weaving a web. Her
words lack the ring of conviction because they are in fact a pack of lies.
They leave Orlando fascinated and
bewildered.

53–4. *of good conceit*] intelligent, and
therefore likely to make a sensible
distinction between black and white
magic, and to approve Rosalind's
plan.

opinion of my knowledge, insomuch I say I know   55
you are; neither do I labour for a greater esteem
than may in some little measure draw a belief from
you to do yourself good, and not to grace me. Believe then, if you please, that I can do strange
things. I have since I was three year old conversed   60
with a magician, most profound in his art and yet
not damnable. If you do love Rosalind so near the
heart as your gesture cries it out, when your brother
marries Aliena, shall you marry her. I know into
what straits of fortune she is driven, and it is not   65
impossible to me, if it appear not inconvenient to
you, to set her before your eyes tomorrow, human
as she is, and without any danger.
Orl. Speak'st thou in sober meanings?
Ros. By my life I do, which I tender dearly, though I   70
say I am a magician. Therefore put you in your
best array, bid your friends; for if you will be
married tomorrow, you shall; and to Rosalind if
you will. Look, here comes a lover of mine, and a
lover of hers.   75

Enter SILVIUS *and* PHEBE.

Phebe. Youth, you have done me much ungentleness,
    To show the letter that I writ to you.
Ros. I care not if I have. It is my study
    To seem despiteful and ungentle to you.
    You are there follow'd by a faithful shepherd,   80
    Look upon him, love him. He worships you.
Phebe. Good shepherd, tell this youth what 'tis to love.
Sil. It is to be all made of sighs and tears,
    And so am I for Phebe.

56. you] *F*; what you *Rowe.*   69. meanings] *F*; meaning *Dyce*[2], *conj. Walker.*
75. SD *Enter Silvius and Phebe.*] *Capell; F (after* will *at 74).*

66. *not inconvenient*] not altogether
wrong to be practising magic.
    67–8. *human as she is*] no phantom.
Cf. the spirit of Helen, conjured up by
black magic in Marlowe's *Dr Faustus.*
    70. *tender dearly*] value highly. There

were severe legal penalties under
Elizabeth for the practice of witch-
craft.
    81. *Look upon him*] Abbott, 483,
notes the inevitability of the special
stress on *him.*

Phebe. And I for Ganymede.   85
Orl. And I for Rosalind.
Ros. And I for no woman.
Sil. It is to be all made of faith and service,
     And so am I for Phebe.
Phebe. And I for Ganymede.   90
Orl. And I for Rosalind.
Ros. And I for no woman.
Sil. It is to be all made of fantasy,
     All made of passion and all made of wishes,
     All adoration, duty and observance,   95
     All humbleness, all patience and impatience,
     All purity, all trial, all observance;
     And so am I for Phebe.
Phebe. And so am I for Ganymede.
Orl. And so am I for Rosalind.   100
Ros. And so am I for no woman.
Phebe [*To Ros.*] If this be so, why blame you me to love
     you?
Sil. [*To Phebe.*] If this be so, why blame you me to love
     you?   105
Orl. If this be so, why blame you me to love you?
Ros. Who do you speak to 'Why blame you me to love
     you?'?
Orl. To her that is not here, nor doth not hear.
Ros. Pray you no more of this, 'tis like the howling of 110
     Irish wolves against the moon. [*To Sil.*] I will
     help you if I can. [*To Phebe*] I would love you if I

95. observance] obedience *Collier*². 97. observance] *F*; obedience, *conj.*
Malone; obeisance *Singer*¹, *conj. Ritson*; perseverance *conj. Heath*; endurance
*Singer*², *conj. Harness*. 102. SD *Pope* (*and at 104, 113, 115, 117*); *not in F.*
107. Who . . . to] *Rowe*; Why . . . too *F.* 111. SD *to Sil.*] *Capell; to Orl.* |
Johnson; not in F. 112. SD *Johnson* (*and at 119, 120*); *not in F.*

95. *observance*] respect. It seems to
be by a copyist's slip that the same
word is repeated in l. 97.

111. *Irish wolves*] *NCS* suspects a
reference to the Irish rebellion of 1598
and to Elizabeth as the moon. Dogs
or wolves howling at full moon were
a proverbial image of ineffective

clamour. See Tilley (M119, 123). Cf.
Rosalynde: 'I tell thee, Montanus, in
courting Phoebe, thou barkest with
the wolves of Syria against the moon'
(p. 139), and Lyly, *Euphues and His
England*, 1580: 'as lykely to obtain thy
wish, as the Wolfe is to catch the
Moone' (Bond, II, p. 90).

could. Tomorrow meet me all together. [*To Phebe*]
I will marry you, if ever I marry woman, and I'll
be married tomorrow. [*To Orl.*] I will satisfy you, 115
if ever I satisfied man, and you shall be married
tomorrow. [*To Sil.*] I will content you, if what
pleases you contents you, and you shall be married
tomorrow. [*To Orl.*] As you love Rosalind meet.
[*To Sil.*] As you love Phebe meet. And as I love no 120
woman, I'll meet. So fare you well. I have left you
commands.

Sil. I'll not fail, if I live.
Phebe. Nor I.
Orl. Nor I.   125

                                                     Exeunt.

SCENE III

Enter TOUCHSTONE *and* AUDREY.

Touch. Tomorrow is the joyful day, Audrey. Tomorrow
    will we be married.
Aud. I do desire it with all my heart; and I hope it is no
    dishonest desire, to desire to be a woman of the
    world. Here come two of the banished Duke's pages.   5

Enter two pages.

First Page. Well met honest gentleman.
Touch. By my troth well met. Come, sit, sit, and a song.
Sec. Page. We are for you. Sit i' th' middle.

---

116. satisfied] F; satisfy *Dyce²*, *conj. Douce.*   123–5. *As* F; *Steevens³* (*verse, one line*).

Scene III] *Scæna Tertia.* F. [Location] *The same. Capell; not in* F.

4. *dishonest*] immodest.

4–5. *a woman of the world*] To go to the world = to get married, to reject the cloister. Audrey has conscientious scruples about worldliness. Commentators seem happy, with no more evidence than this play, to gloss her phrase as equivalent to 'a married

woman', but it is tempting to think that she has stumbled on an impropriety. If 'woman of the world' can mean 'loose woman', then to desire to be one is no 'honest' desire.

8. *Sit i' th' middle*] Echoing a popular saying, 'Hey diddle diddle, fool in the middle' (Furness, quoting Dingelstedt, *Wie es euch gefäut* (1865)).

First Page. Shall we clap into't roundly, without hawking
    or spitting or saying we are hoarse, which are the   10
    only prologues to a bad voice?
Sec. Page. I' faith, i' faith, and both in a tune like two
    gipsies on a horse.
[*They sing*].

> *It was a lover and his lass,*
> > *With a hey and a ho and a hey nonino,*   15
> *That o'er the green corn-field did pass,*
> > *In spring-time, the only pretty ring-time,*
> *When birds do sing, hey ding a ding, ding,*
> *Sweet lovers love the spring.*

17. *In*] Knight; *In the* F. only] F; *not in* Rowe³. *ring*] Rann, conj. Steevens²; *rang* F; *Spring* Rowe; *rank* Johnson; *range* conj. Whiter.

9. *clap into't roundly*] Begin promptly and without fuss. Sternfeld (p. 56) discerns the professional pride of the chorister, who does not have to make the amateur's excuses. The boys give a virtuoso performance, unaccompanied.

10–11. *the only prologues*] Cf. II. vii. 44: 'my only suit', and III. iv. 10–11: 'the only colour'. *Only*= habitual, in regular use.

12–13. *two gipsies on a horse*] on the same horse, one behind the other, perhaps with reference to a song in canon. The words are set for a single voice in Thomas Morley's *First Book of Ayres*, 1600. A copy of words and music in Adv. MS. 5.2.14, f.18 (National Library of Scotland), apparently derives from Morley. These two texts preserve the correct order of the stanzas and, apart from repetitions called for by the music, show the following variants when collated with F:

15. and a hoe] F; with a hoe M, *Adv.* and a hey nonino] F, M; with a hey nonneno *Adv. 16* field] F, *Adv*; fields M. *17.* In the] F; in M, *Adv.* rang] F; ring M, *Adv.* folks] F; fools M, *Adv.* would] F, M; did *Adv. 32.* And . . . time] F; Then prettie lovers take the tyme M, *Adv.*

F prints the first and last stanzas of the song as one, and that one the first. A scribe, preparing a manuscript for the printer, might have gone to the trouble to get the complete song where the prompt book carried only the first and last stanzas. We must then further suppose that either he, or more probably the printer confused by an insertion, failed to see how the extra stanzas should be arranged. E. Brennecke doubts whether more than two stanzas would have been sung on the stage, since the song holds up the action (*TLS*, 12 January 1933). The whole scene is outside the action of the play and a song well rendered, as we are promised this one will be, is a pleasure to hear. Touchstone's scoffing relieves the feelings of those who find it tedious. Its proliferation of nonsense words plainly invites his criticism. Tieck (*Uebersitzt von Schlegel*, 1826) calls it 'this utterly silly ditty'. It is a loving parody and presumably reflects the taste of the pages who sing it.

17. *ring-time*] taken to be a reference to the exchange of wedding rings and/or the chiming of wedding bells. It may also refer to ring dances. A carol was a song which accompanied a ring

> Between the acres of the rye,   20
> > With a hey and a ho and a hey nonino,
> These pretty country-folks would lie,
> > In spring-time, the only pretty ring-time,
> When birds do sing, hey ding a ding, ding,
> Sweet lovers love the spring.   25
>
> This carol they began that hour,
> > With a hey and a ho and a hey nonino,
> How that a life was but a flower,
> > In spring-time, the only pretty ring-time,
> When birds do sing, hey ding a ding, ding,   30
> Sweet lovers love the spring.
>
> And therefore take the present time,
> > With a hey and a ho and a hey nonino,
> For love is crowned with the prime,
> > In spring-time, the only pretty ring-time,   35
> When birds do sing, hey ding a ding, ding,
> Sweet lovers love the spring.

Touch. Truly young gentlemen, though there was no great matter in the ditty, yet the note was very untuneable.   40

First Page. You are deceived sir. We kept time, we lost not our time.

Touch. By my troth yes. I count it but time lost to hear such a foolish song. God buy you, and God mend your voices. Come Audrey.   *Exeunt.*   45

28. a life] *F*; our life *Hanmer*; life *Steevens²*.   32–7. As *Johnson*; *F* (after 19).
40. untuneable] *F*; untimeable *Theobald*.   44. buy you] *F* (see III. i. 253).

dance. Cf. Nashe, *Summer's Last Will*, 1600, played *c.* 1592: 'Spring, the sweete spring . . . then maydes daunce in a ring' (ll. 161–2).

20. acres] unploughed balks in an open field (W. Ridgeway, *The Academy*, October 1883).

34. prime] (1) spring time; (2) at its best.

39–40. *the note was very untuneable*] 'I think it sounded very disagreeable',

said with no implication that the boys sang out of tune. Cf. *MND*, I. i. 184: 'More tuneable than lark to shepherd's ear', where tuneable = melodious. The singers defend their *time*, giving a lead-in to Touchstone's jest about time lost. Cf. Dekker, *Penny-Wise Pound Foolish*, 1631, sig. D-Dv: 'All Discords before are here put into time' (not, as one might expect, *tune*); *R2*, v. v. 42–3: 'how

SCENE IV

Enter Duke Senior, Amiens, Jaques, Orlando,
Oliver [*and*] Celia.

Duke Sen. Dost thou believe, Orlando, that the boy
    Can do all this that he hath promised?
Orl. I sometimes do believe, and sometimes do not,
    As those that fear they hope, and know they fear.

Enter Rosalind, Silvius *and* Phoebe.

Ros. Patience once more, whiles our compact is urg'd.   5
    You say, if I bring in your Rosalind,
    You will bestow her on Orlando here?
Duke Sen. That would I, had I kingdoms to give with her.
Ros. And you say you will have her, when I bring her?
Orl. That would I, were I of all kingdoms king.   10
Ros. You say you'll marry me, if I be willing?
Phebe. That will I, should I die the hour after.
Ros. But if you do refuse to marry me,
    You'll give yourself to this most faithful shepherd?
Phebe. So is the bargain.   15
Ros. You say that you'll have Phebe if she will?
Sil. Though to have her and death were both one thing.
Ros. I have promis'd to make all this matter even.

---

sour sweet music is, / When time is broke'; *Wiv.*, I. iii. 25: 'like an unskilful singer; he kept not time.';

Tw.N., III. iii. 89: 'We did keep time, sir, in our catches.'

Scene IV

Scene IV] *Scena Quarta.* F. [Location] *another Part of the Forest. Theobald; not in F.*
18. I have] *F;* I've *Pope.* all] *F; not in Sisson.*

Location] Dyce suggests 'Before a Cottage'.

4. *fear they hope*] are afraid of wishful thinking. 'They fear that they only hope the best, but they know they fear the worst' (Sisson). Many emendations have been suggested in the past.

5. *compact*] accented on the last syllable.

urg'd] laid down, plainly stated.

18. *make all this matter even*] set this situation to rights. The expression *to*

make even = to straighten out irregularities, to balance accounts, is used again at l. 25 and yet a third time by Hymen at l. 108. Halliwell[2] quotes two instances of the phrase 'to make even with Heaven', in Cartwright's *The Goblins*, 1646, and *The Ordinary*, 1651. Cf. *Meas.*, III. i. 40–1: 'yet death we fear, / That makes these odds all even'.

18–25. The passage wavers uncertainly between prose and blank

Keep you your word, O Duke, to give your daughter,
You yours, Orlando, to receive his daughter; 20
Keep you your word Phebe, that you'll marry me,
Or else refusing me to wed this shepherd.
Keep your word Silvius, that you'll marry her
If she refuse me; and from hence I go
To makes these doubts all even. 25

Exeunt Rosalind and Celia.

Duke Sen. I do remember in this shepherd boy
Some lively touches of my daughter's favour.
Orl. My lord, the first time that I ever saw him,
Methought he was a brother to your daughter.
But my good lord, this boy is forest-born, 30
And hath been tutored in the rudiments
Of many desperate studies, by his uncle,
Whom he reports to be a great magician,
Obscured in the circle of this forest.
Jaques. There is sure another flood toward, and these 35
couples are coming to the ark. Here comes a pair
of very strange beasts, which in all tongues are
called fools.

Enter TOUCHSTONE *and* AUDREY.

Touch. Salutation and greeting to you all.
Jaques. Good my lord, bid him welcome. This is the mot- 40
ley-minded gentleman that I have so often met in
the forest. He hath been a courtier he swears.
Touch. If any man doubt that, let him put me to my purgation. I have trod a measure, I have flattered a

---

21. you your] *F*; your *Rowe*³. 37. very strange] *F*; unclean *Hanmer*. 38.
SD *Enter . . . Audrey*] *Dyce*; *F (after 33)*; *Theobald (after 34)*.

verse, and there is something curious
about the repetition in l. 25. If it were
set as prose there would be no need to
emend ll. 18 and 21, as is often done,
for metrical reasons. It reads like an
uneasy compromise.

21. This line is metrical if *you* is
almost elided before a heavily stressed
your.

27. *favour*] appearance, as in well-

favoured and ill-favoured. Cf. IV. iii.
86.

32. *desperate*] dangerous because
magical.

35. *toward*] impending.

37. *strange beasts*] Hanmer's reading 'unclean' depends on the fact that
Noah took in the clean beasts by
sevens and the unclean by pairs.

43-4. *put me to my purgation*] test the

lady, I have been politic with my friend, smooth   45
with mine enemy, I have undone three tailors, I
have had four quarrels, and like to have fought one.

Jaques. And how was that ta'en up?

Touch. Faith we met, and found the quarrel was upon
the seventh cause.   50

Jaques. How seventh cause? Good my lord, like this
fellow.

Duke Sen. I like him very well.

Touch. God 'ild you sir, I desire you of the like. I press in
here sir, amongst the rest of the country copula-   55
tives, to swear and to forswear, according as
marriage binds and blood breaks. A poor virgin sir,
an ill-favoured thing sir, but mine own; a poor
humour of mine sir, to take that that no man else
will. Rich honesty dwells like a miser sir, in a poor 60
house, as your pearl in your foul oyster.

Duke Sen. By my faith, he is very swift and sententious.

Touch. According to the fool's bolt sir, and such dulcet
diseases.

truth of my assertion. Since Touchstone is working up to his set piece on
duelling, he is probably glancing at
trial by battle, a form of purgation by
ordeal introduced by the Normans. It
was not one of the Anglo-Saxon
ordeals, referred to in the note at
i. iii. 49.

44. *a measure*] a stately, formal
dance, and by extension simply a
dance.

45. *politic*] underhand.

smooth] amiable and agreeable on
the surface only, with a false air of
friendship.

48. *ta'en up*] made up.

50. *the seventh cause*] which they were
careful to avoid. See ll. 84–6.

54. *God 'ild you*] As at iii. iii. 67.

desire you of the like] the equivalent
of a mechanical 'and the same to you'.

55–6. *copulatives*] those wishing to
marry; one of Touchstone's Latin-
isms, borrowed from a grammar book.

62. *swift and sententious*] 'ready'

and 'rich in judicious observations'
(Schmidt).

63. *fool's bolt*] 'A fool's bolt is soon
shot', i.e. a fool speaks before he
thinks, answering the Duke's *swift*.
See Tilley (F515).

63–4. *dulcet diseases*] often dismissed
as the gibberish of the allowed fool.
Touchstone is answering the Duke's
sententious with a show of polite
modesty similar to that which has
linked *swift* to *the fool's bolt*. Quintilian,
when he discusses Seneca's style,
praises it for 'many bright thoughts',
multae in eo claraeque sententiae, but
considers it a bad model 'for the very
reason that it abounds in pleasing
faults', *quod abundant dulcibus vitiis*
(*Institutes of Oratory*, X. 1. 129ff., trs.
Watson, Bohn's Classical Library).
See T. W. Baldwin, *Shakespere's Small
Latine*, II, chapter 27, for Shakespeare's familiarity with Quintilian.
Rann's gloss is 'witty phrases, the
disease of those times'.

Jaques. But for the seventh cause. How did you find the   65
    quarrel on the seventh cause?

Touch. Upon a lie seven times removed. (Bear your body
    more seeming, Audrey.) As thus sir. I did dislike
    the cut of a certain courtier's beard; he sent me
    word, if I said his beard was not well cut, he was in   70
    the mind it was; this is called the Retort Courteous.
    If I sent him word again, it was not well cut, he
    would send me word he cut it to please himself;
    this is called the Quip Modest. If again it was not
    well cut, he disabled my judgement; this is called   75
    the Reply Churlish. If again it was not well cut, he
    would answer I spake not true; this is called the
    Reproof Valiant. If again it was not well cut, he
    would say, I lie; this is called the Countercheck
    Quarrelsome. And so to the Lie Circumstantial and   80
    the Lie Direct.

Jaques. And how oft did you say his beard was not well
    cut?

Touch. I durst go no further than the Lie Circumstantial,
    nor he durst not give me the Lie Direct. And so we   85
    measured swords and parted.

Jaques. Can you nominate in order now the degrees of
    the lie?

Touch. O sir, we quarrel in print, by the book; as you

80. to the] *F2*; ro *F*; the *Rowe*; to *Grant White*[1].

68. *seeming*] generally glossed 'seemly', but Daniel quotes several instances of 'carry your body swimming' = with a fashionable gait. Cf. *MND*, II. i. 130: 'with pretty and with swimming gait'.

did dislike] expressed an aversion.

75. *disabled*] disparaged, as at IV. i. 32.

80. *Circumstantial*] generally known in the duelling books as 'conditional'.

86. *measured swords*] as a preliminary to fighting. Cf. *Ham.*, v. ii. 257: 'These foils have all a length?'

89. *in print*] (1) after consulting printed manuals; (2) with precision.

by the book] Various contemporary books dealt with the etiquette of duelling, e.g. Sir William Segar, *The Booke of Honor and Armes* (1590), which has a chapter on 'the nature and diversitie of lies'; Giacomo di Grassi, *His true Arte of Defence* (1594); Vincentio Saviolo, *His Practise of the Rapier and Dagger* (1594), including 'A Discourse . . . touching the giuing and receiuing of the Lie'; George Silver, *Paradoxes of Defence* (1599). Though it may seem ridiculous to teach people how to kill one another politely, the authors had a laudable aim, to turn a brutal custom into a

have books for good manners. I will name you the   90
degrees. The first, the Retort Courteous; the
second, the Quip Modest; the third, the Reply
Churlish; the fourth, the Reproof Valiant; the
fifth, the Countercheck Quarrelsome; the sixth,
the Lie with Circumstance; the seventh, the Lie   95
Direct. All these you may avoid but the Lie Direct;
and you may avoid that too, with an If. I knew
when seven justices could not take up a quarrel,
but when the parties were met themselves, one of
them thought but of an If, as, 'If you said so, then I   100
said so'. And they shook hands and swore brothers.
Your If is the only peacemaker: much virtue in If.

Jaques. Is not this a rare fellow my Lord? He's as good
at anything, and yet a fool.

Duke Sen. He uses his folly like a stalking-horse, and   105
under the presentation of that he shoots his wit.

100. as] *F; not in Rowe.*   106. SD *Rosalind and Celia] F; Rosalind and Celia, in their proper Dress; Ros. led by a Person presenting Hymen. Capell.*

gentlemanly sport. Touchstone is giving advice on how to avoid a duel. Jonson, in *Every Man in his Humour*, had already entertained audiences with the elaborate instructions which governed the fighting. Cf. also Kastril, in *The Alchemist*, and Mercutio's mockery of Tybalt's stylish fighting.

101. *swore brothers*] became sworn brothers.

105. *stalking-horse*] either a real horse or some kind of hide under cover of which a sportsman approached game. This is the highest compliment Touchstone receives. The Duke bestows it with the same kind of generosity towards inferiors that Theseus shows in defence of the rude mechanicals, *MND*, v. i. 81 ff.

106. *presentation*] semblance.

SD. *Hymen*] Jonson's masque, *Hymenaei*, describes 'HYMEN (the god of *marriage*) in a saffron-coloured robe, his vnder-vesture white, his socks yellow, a yellow veile of silke on

his left arme, his head crowned with *Roses* and *Marioram*, in his right hand a torch of *pine tree*' (ll. 48–52). It is left to the producer to decide whether the masque shall be plainly a charade got up by Rosalind, or whether it is pure magic, like the masque in *The Tempest*, in which the actors were 'all spirits'. The part is often given to Amiens, whose entrance is indicated in F but who has nothing to say. The two singing-boys of v. iii are also available, should a solo singer be required, but the only indubitable song is choral.

Still music] Soft music, with a suggestion of a supernatural and benign visitation. J. S. Manifold says it would be recorders. See *The Music in English Drama from Shakespeare to Purcell* (1956) chapter 9. This, unlike the direction at IV. ii. 10, requires a number of professional musicians, apparently off-stage. They are available to play for the dance at the end of the scene (see l. 177, 'Play music').

Enter HYMEN, ROSALIND *and* CELIA. *Still music.*

Hymen.   Then is there mirth in heaven,
            When earthly things made even
                Atone together.
            Good Duke receive thy daughter,   110
            Hymen from heaven brought her,
                Yea brought her hither,
            That thou mightst join her hand with his
            Whose heart within his bosom is.
Ros. [*To the Duke.*] To you I give myself, for I am yours.   115
        [*To Orl.*] To you I give myself, for I am yours.
Duke Sen. If there be truth in sight, you are my daughter.
Orl. If there be truth in sight, you are my Rosalind.
Phebe. If sight and shape be true,
            Why then my love adieu.   120
Ros. I'll have no father, if you be not he.
        I'll have no husband, if you be not he.
        Nor ne'er wed woman, if you be not she.
Hymen.   Peace ho! I bar confusion.
            'Tis I must make conclusion   125
                Of these most strange events.
            Here's eight that must take hands
            To join in Hymen's bands,
                If truth holds true contents.

113. her] *F3*; his *F.*   114. his] *F;* her *Malone.*   115-16. SD *Rowe;* not in *F.*
119-20. *As Pope; one line F.*

They may also accompany the wedding song at l. 138. Hymen's verses are in italic, but there is no direction 'song'. They were perhaps a kind of recitative.

109. *Atone*] agree, are reconciled. The use of the word here has the effect of a New Testament echo, though Wright says that neither *atone* nor *atonement* occurs in the Authorized Version, which uses 'to set at one', 'to be at one'. The feeling here is solemn. It marks the play's conclusion as grave and pleasing. Shakespeare's comedy shows 'things as they ought to be' in a more than trivial sense.

113-14. *her hand . . . his bosom*] The F reading *his*, in the first line of the couplet, is pretty clearly a misreading of *hir*. Malone's belief that a similar misreading has affected the second line of the couplet has additional support from the argument of euphony.

117-18. *If there be truth in sight*] If my eyes are to be trusted.

119. *If sight and shape be true*] If my eyes and your appearance are to be trusted.

124. *bar*] prohibit.

129. *If truth holds true contents*] If you are still contented with your marriage

You and you no cross shall part.   130
You and you are heart in heart.
You to his love must accord,
Or have a woman to your lord.
You and you are sure together,
As the winter to foul weather.   135
Whiles a wedlock hymn we sing,
Feed yourselves with questioning,
That reason wonder may diminish
How thus we met, and these things finish.

Song.

Wedding is great Juno's crown,   140
O blessed bond of board and bed.
'Tis Hymen peoples every town;
High wedlock then be honoured.
Honour, high honour and renown
To Hymen, god of every town.   145

Duke Sen. O my dear niece, welcome thou art to me,
    Even daughter welcome, in no less degree.
Phebe. [to Silvius.] I will not eat my word; now thou art mine,
    Thy faith my fancy to thee doth combine.

Enter JAQUES DE BOYS.

147. daughter welcome,] *F*; daughter, welcome, *F4*; daughter-welcome *Theobald.*   148. SD *to Silvius*] *Capell; not in F.*   149. SD *Enter Jaques de Boys*] *Rowe; Enter Second Brother. F.*

partners now that disguises are cast off and you know the truth about them. 'True delights', at l. 197, is used like 'true contents' here.

139. Song] The purpose of the song is to give the astonished company time to hear each other's stories without imposing them on the audience, to whom they are not news. The singers can only be the attendant lords, who have been called on to sing twice before, at II. v. and at IV. ii, reinforced perhaps by the two singing-boys, unless one of them played Hymen. There is no need, however,

for Hymen to be a singer at all.

140. great Juno's crown] Juno was the patroness of marriage and of married women. See Ovid, *Metam.*, VI, 428 and *Heroides*, II, 41; Virgil, *Aeneid* IV, 19; Jonson, *Hymenaei*, 232–3: 'IVNO, whose great name / Is VNIO, in the anagram'.

147. *daughter*] in apposition to *niece.* Rosalind has already been formally presented to her father at l. 115, and received by him at l. 117. Celia has so far had no welcome.

149. *fancy*] amorous desire.

Jaq. de Boys. Let me have audience for a word or two.   150
       I am the second son of old Sir Rowland
       That bring these tidings to this fair assembly.
       Duke Frederick hearing how that every day
       Men of great worth resorted to this forest,
       Address'd a mighty power, which were on foot   155
       In his own conduct, purposely to take
       His brother here, and put him to the sword.
       And to the skirts of this wild wood he came,
       Where, meeting with an old religious man,
       After some question with him, was converted   160
       Both from his enterprise and from the world,
       His crown bequeathing to his banish'd brother,
       And all their lands restor'd to them again
       That were with him exil'd. This to be true,
       I do engage my life.   .
Duke Sen.   Welcome young man.   165
       Thou offer'st fairly to thy brothers' wedding;
       To one his lands withheld, and to the other
       A land itself at large, a potent dukedom.
       First, in this forest, let us do those ends
       That here were well begun and well begot: 170
       And after, every of this happy number
       That have endur'd shrewd days and nights with us,
       Shall share the good of our returned fortune,
       According to the measure of their states.
       Meantime forget this new-fall'n dignity,   175
       And fall into our rustic revelry.
       Play music, and you brides and bridegrooms all,
       With measure heap'd in joy, to th' measures fall.
Jaques. Sir, by your patience. If I heard you rightly,
       The Duke hath put on a religious life,   180

150. *Jaq. de Boys.*] *Rowe;* 2. *Bro. F.*   163. them] *Rowe;* him *F.*   166.
brothers']￼ *F* (brothers) *Capell;* brother's *F4.*

156. *In his own conduct*] under his
personal leadership.
164. *This to be true*] Even the most
serious news in Elizabethan times
tended to arrive as rumour and hearsay, and it was second nature for the

recipients to want some guarantee.
166. *thou offer'st fairly*] you bring a
handsome wedding present.
171. *every*] every one.
172. *shrewd*] sharp.

And thrown into neglect the pompous court?
Jaq. de Boys. He hath.
Jaques. To him will I. Out of these convertites,
    There is much matter to be heard and learn'd.
[*To Duke Sen.*] You to your former honour I bequeath,   185
    Your patience and your virtue well deserve it.
[*To Orl.*] You to a love that your true faith doth merit:
[*To Oli.*] You to your land and love and great allies:
[*To Sil.*] You to a long and well-deserved bed:
[*To Touch.*] And you to wrangling, for thy loving voyage 190
    Is but for two months victuall'd. So to your pleasures.
    I am for other than for dancing measures.
Duke Sen. Stay, Jaques, stay.
Jaques. To see no pastime, I. What you would have
    I'll stay to know at your abandon'd cave.   *Exit.* 195
Duke Sen. Proceed, proceed. We will begin these rites,
    As we do trust they'll end, in true delights.

185. SD *Rowe (and at 187, 188, 189, 190); not in F.*   186. deserves] *F*; deserve
Pope.   196. We will] *F2*; wee'l *F.*   197. SD *A dance . . . Epilogue*]. *A
Dance.   Capell; Exit F; not in F2;* Epilogue. *Theobald².*

181. *pompous*] resplendent, in no disparaging sense.

183. *convertites*] 'One that hath abandoned a loose, to follow a godlie, a vicious to lead a virtuous life' (Cotgrave). *NCS* recalls the famous abdication of the Emperor Charles V, who in 1555 renounced his imperial title and retired to live near the monastery of San Geronimo de Yuste in Spain. The Duc de Joyeuse created a sensation when he entered the Capuchin order in 1587, and repeated the performance, after backsliding, in 1599. This nobleman had the temperamental trait which distinguishes Duke Frederick. John Chamberlain reported on 15 March 1599 that 'The Duke of Joyeuse is once more become humerous and surrendering all his state . . . is returned again to be a Capuchin' (*Letters*, ed. N. E. McClure, 1939).

188. *You to your land*] At v. ii. 9–12, Oliver gives his land to his brother, and is going to turn shepherd, but this is before he learns who Celia is. Lodge spends much time on the heart-searchings of the proud brother, entangled with a shepherdess. Shakespeare is not much interested, or has less time to spare.

197. SD. The dance is indicated at ll. 177–8 and rejected only by Jaques at l. 192. F reads *Exit* at the end of the Duke's speech but there is no reason why the Duke, who has said '*We* will begin' at l. 196, should not stay. This exit probably marks the departure of the dancers before Rosalind's epilogue. F2 improbably implies the presence of the rest of the cast while she speaks, by emending *Exit* to *Exeunt*. Commentators have missed old Adam from this gathering, a testimony to his charm. The player who took his part was probably doubling, perhaps Jaques de Boys.

*[A dance, after which Rosalind is left alone to speak the
Epilogue.]*

Ros. It is not the fashion to see the lady the epilogue;
but it is no more unhandsome than to see the lord
the prologue. If it be true that good wine needs no   200
bush, 'tis true that a good play needs no epilogue.
Yet to good wine they do use good bushes; and
good plays prove the better by the help of good
epilogues. What a case am I in then, that am
neither a good epilogue, nor cannot insinuate with   205
you in the behalf of a good play? I am not furnished like a beggar, therefore to beg will not become me. My way is to conjure you, and I'll begin
with the women. I charge you, O women, for the
love you bear to men, to like as much of this play   210
as please you. And I charge you, O men, for the
love you bear to women—as I perceive by your
simpering none of you hates them—that between
you and the women the play may please. If I were
a woman, I would kiss as many of you as had   215
beards that pleased me, complexions that liked
me, and breaths that I defied not. And I am sure,
as many as have good beards, or good faces, or
sweet breaths, will for my kind offer, when I make
curtsy, bid me farewell.   *Exit.*   220

211. please you] *F*; pleases you *F3*; pleases them *Hanmer*; please them *Steevens*³;
And I] *F*; and so I *Steevens*³, *conj. Farmer.*   220. SD *Exit.*] *F*; *Exeunt. F2.*

200-1. *good wine needs no bush*] a
proverbial reference to the green
branches which vintners hung out to
advertise their wares. See Tilley
(W462).

204-6. *that . . . play*] 'that have
neither presented you with a good
play, nor come prepared with a good
epilogue to prejudice you in favour of
a bad one' (Rann).

206-7. *furnished*] Rosalind, led in
by Hymen, is gorgeously dressed.

208. *conjure you*] maintaining her
pose as a magician.

214-15. *If I were a woman*] a boy-
player is speaking.

216-17. *liked me*] pleased me.

217. *defied not*] took no objection to
(Walter).

220. *bid me farewell*] take leave of
me with your good wishes=applaud
the play.

Appendix A

'A table set out'. II. v, vi and vii.

Since attendants are instructed to 'cover', at II. v. 28, some sort of meal must be laid, but not necessarily on a table. In George Turbervile's *Noble Arte of Venerie* (1575), Queen Elizabeth is shown seated in a stately manner, with a cloth spread at her feet, while at a little distance a party of her gentlemen loll on the ground around a similar picnic cloth. Dover Wilson's long stage direction here suggests that he visualizes the scene in this way, perhaps with Turbervile's woodcut in mind. Sir John Harington tells how he was once entertained in Ireland 'at a fern table and fern forms under the stately canopy of heaven' (*Nugae Antiquae*, (1804), I, p. 251). The tradition that Shakespeare played Adam includes a reference to people sitting at a table (see Intro., p. lxxiii), and the Duke welcomes Adam to his 'table', but this may refer to food rather than to furniture. Lodge describes a rather formal celebration in which 'Gerismond, the lawful king of France banished by Torismond, who with a lusty crew of outlaws lived in that forest, that day in honour of his birth made a feast to all his bold yeomen, and frolicked it with store of wine and venison, sitting all at a long table under the shadow of limon trees' (*Rosalynde*, p. 60).

The attendants might set up boards on trestles and carry them off at the end of scene v, were it not that nobody has yet sat down to the feast, which does not take place till scene vii. Meanwhile, in scene vi, Orlando must enter supporting Adam, at the end of his strength, and set out to find food for him. With a table already on the stage he will not have far to go. Supposing the table is left visible at the end of scene v it must be set very far upstage, and the scene between Orlando and Adam must be played very far down. Even so there will be an awkwardness about their entrance and exit. *NCS* suggests the use of an 'inner stage', but this theoretical concept is no longer accepted. The Globe had no permanent alcove located behind the back wall, large enough to set and play a scene in and revealed or concealed by

132

curtains.[1] It was possible to drape a tiring-house door to make something like a tent, but what sort of accommodation would this be for the Duke's 'banquet', however unpretentious? It could be concealed throughout scene vi only by being imperfectly visible in scenes v and vii. The simplest explanation is probably the right one, that the attendants unobtrusively remove the feast as part of their comings and goings in the background at the end of scene v, and bring it on again at the beginning of scene vii. There are almost 100 lines spoken before Orlando finds the company actually engaged in eating.

Why introduce the 'banquet' at all at scene v? The play appears to drift from one part of the forest to another part of the forest for no particular reason, but Shakespeare has in fact exerted himself to supply his characters with some occupation and purpose, rather than produce them arbitrarily on an empty stage. Their occupations are homely and natural. They may set a table, eat and drink, hear a song, fetch up goats, keep a prearranged appointment, deliver a letter, look for one another, marry or play at marrying. We watch a way of life. Moreover, whether or not we see the 'banquet' at scene vi, we have seen it at scene v, and can be reassured as to the fate of Orlando and Adam.

APPENDIX B

'I take thee Rosalind for wife', IV. i. 128
'Get you to church', III. iii. 75–6.

Harold Brooks has called my attention to the validity of the mock-marriage, which comes very near to being a real one, a fact of which Rosalind, Celia and the Elizabethan audience must all have been aware. Canon law accepted that any kind of marriage was better than no marriage. According to Pollock and Maitland, in the twelfth century

Espousals were of two kinds: *sponsalia per verba de futuro*, which takes place if man or woman promise each other that they will hereafter become husband and wife; *sponsalia per verba de praesenti*, which takes place if they declare that they take each other as husband and wife now, at this very moment. It is thenceforth the established doctrine that a transaction of the latter kind creates a bond which is hardly to be dissolved.

1 See R. Hosley, 'The playhouses and the stage', pp. 15–34, in *A New Companion to Shakespeare Studies*, ed. K. Muir and S. Schoenbaum (1971).

They go on to say

The scheme . . . was certainly no masterpiece of human wisdom. Of all people in the world lovers are the least likely to distinguish precisely between the present and the future tenses. In the middle ages marriages or what looked like marriages, were extremely insecure. The union which had existed for many years between man and woman might with fatal ease be proved adulterous, and there would be hard swearing on both sides about 'I will' and 'I do'.[1]

Marriage *per verba de praesenti* was still valid in the sixteenth century.[2] The church disapproved, unless its blessing was subsequently asked, especially if the marriage was consummated before the couple came to church. The fourth Lateran Council, in 1215, had directed the publication of banns. It was reported with concern, in a Diocesan Visitation of 1578, that seven couples had 'married without bannes askinge some [in] feilds, som in chappells and some in prophane places yea it is doubted whether they be marryed at all'.[3] This reads like a description of Touchstone's attempt to marry 'in the fields', which Martext does not balk at, until it appears that there is no one to give the woman. 'Truly she must be given, or the marriage is not lawful.' 'Giving in marriage' was not an article of canon law, but a custom going back to Saxon times and to a patriarchal system. Christian marriage required no more than the consent of the two persons most concerned. It is doubtful what we are to think of Martext's scrupulosity. That he was straining at a gnat after swallowing a camel? Jaques does not find the proceedings at all acceptable.

The civil law did not recognize a private espousal as conferring property rights, or identifying heirs, and insisted on the publicity of a declaration 'at the church door'. But nonetheless, the troth-plight marriage, provided the couple were careful about their tenses, was legally valid. They were not free thereafter to divorce or to marry again and the children were legitimate. In 1563 the Council of Trent required a priest and witnesses, but by then England was no longer under papal jurisdiction.[4] In 1843, it was

1 F. Pollock and F. W. Maitland, *The History of English Law before the Time of Edward I* (1898), II, pp. 364ff.
2 E. Schanzer recommends Henry Swinburne's *Treatise of Spousals* as evidence of the way the law was interpreted around 1600, when it was written. See 'The marriage-contracts in *Measure for Measure*', *Shakespeare Survey 13* (1960), pp. 81–9.
3 J. S. Purvis, *Tudor Parish Documents* (1948), p. 72.
4 W. S. Holdsworth, *A History of English Law* 4th ed., II, pp. 87–9.

declared in the High Court that the presence of a priest has always been necessary to a valid marriage. This stands as a legal decision, but it is not a historian's judgement.[1]

Orlando's troth-plight is to Rosalind, with Ganymede strictly as surrogate, and Rosalind is there in person to receive it and give her own. She is not trying to catch Orlando unawares and to commit him to more than he intends, but the whole scene lights up and its exchanges gain poignancy when the implications of the ceremony are known, beginning with Celia's otherwise inexplicable confusion when asked to play the priest: 'I cannot say the words.' That Rosalind knows precisely what she is doing is plain when she rejects the grammatically ambiguous 'I will' and insists upon the vital present tense. '*Ros.* Ay, but when? *Orl.* Why now, as fast as she can marry us. *Ros.* Then you must say, "I take thee Rosalind for wife".' 'I might ask you for your commission' is an acknowledgement that Orlando, on his side, does not know what he is doing. What authority has he to take a Rosalind whose consent he has never asked? He has put the question to a shepherd-boy called Ganymede. 'But I do take thee' is her admission that her answer is made in her own person and is in the fullest sense affirmative. 'There's a girl goes before the priest, but certainly a woman's thought runs before her actions' sums up, a trifle ruefully, what she has just done, and is followed by a tremendous outburst of high spirits, in which she pretends to be a capricious and demanding wife.

D. P. Harding's 'Elizabethan betrothals and *Measure for Measure*', in *The Journal of English and Germanic Philology*, XLIX (1950), pp. 139–58, investigates this subject thoroughly, discussing many troth-plights in Shakespeare's plays. *As You Like It* is not one of them, presumably because on the surface the mock-marriage is a game. The play makes no more use of its underlying seriousness than to supply the immediate tensions of the scene.

1 Pollock and Maitland, op. cit., p. 372.